RADICAL HISTORY *Review*

The Iranian Revolution Turns Thirty

Editors' Introduction   1
Behrooz Ghamari-Tabrizi, Mansour Bonakdarian, Nasrin Rahimieh,
Ahmad Sadri, Ervand Abrahamian

FEATURES

The Crowd in the Iranian Revolution   13
Ervand Abrahamian

Khomeini and the Iranian Revolution in the Egyptian Press:
From Fascination to Condemnation   39
Hanan Hammad

Iranian Anti-Zionism and the Holocaust: A Long Discourse Dismissed   58
Mahdi Ahouie

Revolution, Trauma, and Nostalgia in Diasporic Iranian
Women's Autobiographies   79
Nima Naghibi

CURATED SPACES

The Theory of Survival: An Interview with Taraneh Hemami   93
Behrooz Ghamari-Tabrizi

Memory, Mourning, Memorializing:
On the Victims of Iran-Iraq War, 1980–Present   106
Behrooz Ghamari-Tabrizi
Photography by Melissa Hibbard and Hamid Rahmanian

REFLECTIONS

The Revolution Will Not Be Fabricated   123
Minoo Moallem

Has Iran's Islamic Revolution Ended?   132
Saïd Amir Arjomand

The Revolution and the Rural Poor   139
Djavad Salehi-Isfahani

Postrevolutionary Persian Literature: Creativity and Resistance   145
Kamran Talattof

Reflections on Literature after the 1979 Revolution in Iran
and in the Diaspora   151
Persis M. Karim

Postrevolutionary Trends in Persian Fiction and Film   156
M. R. Ghanoonparvar

Islamic Revolution and the Circulation of Visual Culture   163
Mazyar Lotfalian

Intellectual Life after the 1979 Revolution:
Radical Hope and Nihilistic Dreams   168
Ali Mirsepassi

(RE)VIEWS

Contested Narratives of the Present:
Postrevolutionary Culture and Media in Iran
Review of Mehdi Semati, ed., *Media, Culture, and Society in Iran:
Living with Globalization and the Islamic State*; and Nasrin Alavi,
We Are Iran: The Persian Blogs
Niki Akhavan   177

Notes on Contributors   185

Editors' Introduction

This issue of *Radical History Review* marks the thirtieth anniversary of the Iranian revolution. The 1979 revolution brought about radical changes in the Iranian political, social, and cultural institutions, reverberated across the globe, and caused rifts and realignments in international relations. The complex and evolving nature of the postrevolutionary dynamics in Iran call for renewed reflections on the roots of the revolution, the processes leading to its victory, and its impact on the Muslim world and the global balance of power.

While this special issue was in production, the tenth presidential election in Iran and its aftermath caught the world's attention. In the following introduction, we speak about how the inherent contradiction in the postrevolutionary constitution became the point of reference on the one hand for the idea of republicanism and on the other for autocratic theocracy. The massive demonstrations against what the former president Mohammad Khatami called a "velvet coup against the people and the republic" has demonstrated that the Iranian revolution remains unfinished and its basic principles continue to be deeply contested.[1] The unanticipated response by hundreds of thousands of members of the electorate and by the allegedly defeated candidates, who refused to accept the fraudulent results, shook the country and generated an unprecedented crisis of legitimacy for the Supreme Leader Ayatollah Khamenei. It is unclear whether the current protest movement will redirect the revolution toward its original democratic ideals or if its suppression will strip the Islamic regime of its republican core.

The events that followed the establishment of the Islamic Republic—the American hostage crisis of 1979–81, the devastating eight-year war between Iran and Iraq (1980–88), Tehran's ideological and political leverage in Lebanon, recent diplomatic tensions surrounding Iran's development of nuclear energy, and various domestic miscarriages—can obscure the sense of empowerment and euphoria the

Radical History Review
Issue 105 (Fall 2009) DOI 10.1215/01636545-2009-001
© 2009 by MARHO: The Radical Historians' Organization, Inc.

great majority of Iranians experienced in the wake of the revolution. With a fleeting solidarity across class, gender, ideological, and religious lines, the overwhelming majority of Iranians (with the exception of small groups opposing the toppling of the monarchic regime or weary of the mass fervor for radical change) demanded freedom from the political repression that had tightened its grip on the nation since the CIA-sponsored 1953 coup that had overthrown the elected prime minister, Mohammad Mosaddeq, and inaugurated the reign of Mohammad Reza Shah Pahlavi.

By all accounts, the Iranian Revolution remains an unfinished project. Three decades after the revolution, it is fairly easy to underline the inherent contradictions between the revolutionary movement and its institutionalized manifestations. Whereas the discourse of the revolutionary movement was one of negation, liberty, and justice, the postrevolutionary state was established through the language of "blood and iron" and survival by any means possible. With the collapse of the monarchy in 1979, the coalition that made the revolution possible also vanished. The consolidation of power around a vision of Islamic government known as the *velāyat-e faqih* (guardianship of the [clerical] jurist) denied many participants in the revolutionary movement a share in the emerging postrevolutionary state.

The sudden disintegration of the old regime with its military might shocked both its Western supporters and the clerical leadership of the revolution. The clergy was neither ready to assume power nor able to conceive the organizational structure of the Islamic Republic. An amplified sense of a revolutionary *geist* led to an exaggerated sense of idealism and a determination to realize pure revolutionary objectives. This revolutionary confidence also augmented the resolve of the postrevolutionary state during its initial power struggle. Major competing factions in postrevolutionary politics operated from uncompromising platforms, leading to a state policy of the total annihilation of all ideological opponents and to the decade-long reign of terror. When millions of Iranians chanted in the streets of Tehran and other towns and provinces around the country "Esteqlāl, āzādi, jomhuri-ye Islami" ("Independence, liberty, Islamic Republic") and "Barābari, barādari, hokumat-e ʿadl-e Ali" ("Equality, brotherhood, Imam Ali's rule of justice"), they were plainly demonstrating their appreciation for an Islamic allegory of justice and equality. Islam was understood but not spoken of in practical and organizational terms. It was up to the new regime to render the symbolic language of slogans into tangible and immediate realities of state building. Although Ayatollah Ruhollah Khomeini had already outlined the meaning of an Islamic state in his 1971 manifesto *Islamic Rule*, the influence of that document on the formation of the postrevolutionary regime proved negligible.

The revolution created a "new Man [*sic*]," in the Fanonian sense, through a violent process by which people freed themselves from the yoke of a tyrannical regime. In the idiom of the 1968 Paris uprising, initially this had appeared even to many participants in the demonstrations as "demand[ing] the impossible." But the victory of the revolution unequivocally ended the period of symbolic appropriation of Islam by a diverse spectrum of political factions and social groups. As Michael Fischer observed, "political victory requires a spelling out in political and institutional terms of what previously could be left in vague philosophical and moral language."[2] Thirty years later, building a state that corresponds to the moral and philosophical language of the revolution remains a major point of contestation in Iranian politics.

The institutionalization of an Islamic Republic (Iran's very first experience of both a republican and a theocratic state apparatus) led to revamping the existing structures of governance and to an adoption of Islamic injunctions as the overarching source of political and legal authority. At the outset, the Islamization of the state adversely affected various religious and ethnic minorities, as well as secular political parties. It significantly curtailed existing women's rights in regard to family law and diminished the public mobility of many women by implementing a mandatory *hijab* (modest "unrevealing" dress and covering of hair). The process of change has not always been smooth and continues to expose differences in definitions and interpretations of political and religious doctrine. In the past thirty years, there have been vigorous debates and disagreements about the relationship between Islamic injunctions and the promulgated laws of a representative democracy. Even a number of prominent religious leaders questioned the legitimacy and feasibility of the Islamic state and warned against the determination of young Islamists to impose expansive Islamic values and mores onto society.

The contradiction between an Islamic ideal and popular sovereignty has been one of the main sources of conflict in the Islamic Republic—especially after Khomeini's death in June 1989. In addition to a host of opposition figures from outside the polity, numerous Shi'i clerics have been placed under house arrest, jailed, or even physically obliterated for their dissenting views. Despite the authority that the Islamic injunctions afford the supreme leader and the Guardian Council to exercise the ultimate veto power, elections are regularly held at local and national levels. The postrevolutionary constitution engendered unintended sociopolitical and ideological consequences through its ambiguous references to "Islamic criteria" in defining the limits of public freedom, civil rights, legislation, and economic planning. By locating Islam in the public sphere, not only did the new constitution alter the political apparatus, legal system, education, and gender relations in Iran but it also transformed Islam from an a priori source of legitimacy into a contested body of discourses. In effect, to Islamize the post-revolutionary society, the Islamizers had to struggle continuously over the meaning of Islam and its bearing on specific contemporary social, economic, and cultural issues.

Prior to the establishment of the Islamic Republic and the institutionalization of *velāyat-e faqih*, the Shi'a clergy operated independently from the state, both financially and in their internal organization. Shi'a clerical establishments lacked an ecclesiastical hierarchy through which a dominant interpretation of the Shari'a

(Islamic legal corpus) could be canonized. By extending the scope of traditional juristic authority to include previously unexamined matters of governance, Khomeini revolutionized the existing structures of clerical independence from the state. Far from enjoying consensus, Khomeini's political philosophy scandalized many influential Shi'a grand ayatollahs and the followers of other sources of emulation. They disagreed on legal grounds with Khomeini's formulation that empowered jurists, and they feared that this doctrine would undermine the traditionally pluralist core of Shi'a jurisprudence.

The imposition of religious codes since the outset of the revolution has generated many controversial results and contradictions both within the religious establishment and in civil society. In many respects, the eight-year war (following the Iraqi invasion of Iranian territories in 1980) delayed the manifestation of these contradictions. But they became prominent soon after the end of the war, when internal frictions of the ruling parties and the conflict between the state and a burgeoning civil society became increasingly visible. The deadly stalemate that led to Khomeini's abandonment of his "politics of ultimate ends" and to his reluctant capitulation to the United Nations Security Council Resolution 598 ending the war exposed the role of religious leadership to public scrutiny. It was at this juncture that a significant segment of the elite cadres of the revolution began a serious debate over the hitherto unassailable axioms of the Islamic Republic. With this emerging "reform movement," the unintended consequences of the Islamization policies became evident. The new movement began to question the obscurantist attempts to Islamize civil liberties and formal legal rights. In particular, gender relations, both in theory and as a result of women's real gains in economic and social spheres, have become a centerpiece of this movement.

Unprecedented debates on Islamic hermeneutics provided philosophical grounding for questioning the hegemonic role of religion in the public sphere. Many former advocates of *velāyat-e faqih* now questioned the necessity of the absolutist rule of the jurist in a Muslim polity. Remarkable theological innovations and unprecedented ideas regarding the role of jurisprudence in Muslim societies have resulted from these fertile discussions. As one of the main theoreticians of the reform movement in Iran, Said Hajjarian, aptly observes: "The doctrine of *velāyat-e faqih* transformed Shi'ism into a state ideology. However, in contrast to its ostensible appearance in merging religion and the state, and thereby *sacralizing* the political sphere, *velāyat-e faqih* played the role of a catalyst for the *secularization* of the Shi'a juridical establishment."[3] Paradoxically, the establishment of a theocracy seems to have facilitated the secularization of Shi'a jurisprudence. In the early 1990s, a social movement for democratic access to political power and for the right to live independently from unyielding state supervision overtook Iranian politics as a storm that swept Mohammad Khatami to power in 1997. It was then that members of the parliament, community activists, lawyers, and a wider community of religious intellectuals and journalists were able to openly voice their skepticism regarding the exclusive authority of religious leaders to interpret Islam and to control all aspects of public life.

The postrevolutionary state instituted severe limitations on the manner in which men and women can conduct their lives in public—and to some extent even in private. Yet the adoption of appropriate and religiously sanctioned modes of appearance and conduct provided new ladders of upward mobility for women, enabling them to enter professional niches and the higher ranks of educated groups. Although women's rights are still curtailed in conformity with Shari'a law and women's dress and conduct remain limited by Islamic strictures, their access to education has been steadily improving. As a result the percentage difference between female and male literacy rates has dropped from 23.4 percent in 1976 to 8.3 percent in 2006. In addition to receiving comprehensive primary education, women comprised close to 60 percent of the incoming university students in 2008. Although the state implemented aggressive education programs, particularly in rural areas, the remarkable rise in the number of women in education could also be attributed to the paradoxical effect of the construction of gender-segregated spaces. Religiously sanctioned modes of appearance encouraged parents who otherwise were skeptical of modern education to allow their daughters to attend school. Women have also gained unprecedented prominence on the cultural and literary scene. The cultural industries are domains in which women can be seen in greater numbers than ever before in the history of the country.

Another seemingly startling paradox is evident in the Islamic Republic's approach to gay, lesbian, bisexual, and transgender relations and rights. While homosexual relations, particularly among men, have come under rigorous assault from the authorities, with a number of male homosexuals executed, tortured, and jailed on charges of "immorality" or under alleged rape convictions, the state has been relatively tolerant toward transgendered individuals seeking sex-reassignment surgery, even providing funding for such surgeries. This "tolerance," however, should not be attributed to any underlying acceptance of transgender identities; rather, it is indicative of the state's desire to *normalize* gender relations, whereby heterosexual *males* and *females* are the only categories recognized by Iran's Islamic legal and constitutional codes.

Iranian art cinema has by far been the most internationally recognized cultural product of postrevolutionary Iran. Compared to only three international awards allotted to Iranian movies prior to the revolution, Iranian films have obtained more than three hundred international prizes since 1989. Many of the films that have received prizes at international festivals are not widely seen in Iran, but there is a flourishing market for commercial and popular films serving wide audiences in Iran.

Cultural policies of the revolution have also had their paradoxical implications. The revolutionary government started by setting draconian limits on cultural imports from the West, most important on movies and music. These curtailments spurred on indigenous productions that initially served the ideological needs of the state but later found their own directions. The censorship of music and entertainment (both domestic and foreign) has been difficult to sustain, particularly in light of the popularity of the Internet, satellite television, and new electronic media. The new channels of dissemination frequently help Iran's thriving underground music industry. Women's voices, their manner of appearance and depiction, and the nature of their interaction with their male counterparts, however, continue to be restricted by rigid limits of censorship. Another important legacy of the revolution and of the Iran-Iraq war is the mass migration of Iranians abroad. Iranian migrants have settled in countries across the globe, but the world's largest Iranian diaspora community is located in the United States. These patterns of migration and settlement have led to new literary and artistic phenomena attesting to emerging forms of Iranian transnationalism. These communities have generated cultural articulations that examine and reinterpret their relationship to their homeland in a mélange of nostalgia and radical critique.

No single issue of a journal can provide comprehensive coverage of the initial domestic and international reception of the 1979 Iranian Revolution or its subsequent manifold social, cultural, political, economic, religious, ideological, and foreign-policy consequences, which were also shaped by a host of other post-1979 domestic, regional, and global developments. The editors of this issue are pleased to be able to include a selection of essays by leading researchers in the field that examine select themes related to the outbreak of the revolution, its reception, and its consequences inside and outside Iran, offering new critical insight into various often neglected dimensions of the revolution and the postrevolutionary state and providing the latest scholarship on topics covered.

The feature articles section of the journal begins with Ervand Abrahamian's study of the social composition, characteristics, and tactics of the crowds participating in mass demonstrations in opposition to the autocratic state from 1978 to 1979 that culminated in the overthrow of the Pahlavi dynasty (r. 1925–79). Providing a detailed and extremely helpful chronology of the mass protests and the state's reaction to these protests, he demonstrates the dynamic nature of the revolutionary mass movement, which drew support from a broad socioeconomic spectrum of the primarily urban population, and the crowds' articulation of a range of grievances against the state that were eventually harnessed by Khomeini, who emerged as the unifying and charismatic symbolic leader of the revolutionary movement while still in exile. Above all, Abrahamian stresses the primarily urban composition of the revolutionary crowds (chiefly working and lower middle classes), their reliance on informal (neighborhood or university) networks, and the crowds' principal recourse to nonviolent tactics.

The Iranian Revolution and the subsequent establishment of the Islamic Republic resonated in different ways throughout the Middle East and beyond.

While most studies of Iran's international relations during this time have tended to focus on relations with the United States or Western European states, Hanan Hammad's essay makes a major contribution to our broader understanding of the coverage of the revolution in other parts of the Middle East by focusing on commentaries in the Egyptian press (with Egypt also serving as both the initial and final location of exile for the Shah [d. July 1980] after he left Iran in January 1979). She shows that the Iranian Revolution, coinciding with the relaxation of the Egyptian state's restrictions on the oppositional press (by Anwar el-Sadat), was covered by the Egyptian official, Islamist, Marxist, and liberal press, always with an eye to Egypt's own domestic political configurations, as well as in the framework of the contrasting political perspectives in Egypt concerning the 1979 peace treaty with Israel and Egypt's close alliance with Washington and the Shah (in the framework of the Cold War). The Marxist and the Islamist press appeared to welcome the revolutionary movement, while the liberal press adopted a more equivocal stance given the role of the clergy in the revolution, and the official press denounced the revolution as a machination of outside powers. Hammad further outlines how the establishment of the Islamic state in Iran and its execution of former officials, its suppression of other political factions, its persecution of the Bahā'īs, the clashes between the postrevolutionary state and Iran's Sunni religious-ethnic minorities, and the Islamic Republic's changed relations with the Palestinian Liberation Organization (PLO) led to an increasingly critical stance in the pages of the officially tolerated Egyptian Marxist and liberal press. These developments also initiated a more ambivalent stance in the Islamist press, with some Islamist commentators castigating the Iranian Shi'i state's treatment of minority Sunni groups, others considering the new Iranian state's policy of political executions and the persecution of the Bahā'īs contrary to Islamic principles of tolerance, and still other Islamists attempting to rationalize many of the policies of the Islamic Republic and placing greater emphasis on the state's attempts to introduce "Islamic economics" and so on.

Mahdi Ahouie's essay focuses on President Mahmoud Ahmadinejad's refutation of the Holocaust as a "myth" and his simultaneous statements that even if the Holocaust had occurred (though contesting the extent of the event) it was perpetuated by Europeans and was subsequently utilized by Zionists and their Western allies as a rationalization for the Zionist colonization of Palestinian territories. In regard to the denial of the Holocaust, Ahouie considers such statements as "quite unprecedented in Iran," while he sees the linkage between the Holocaust and the Israeli state as having had intellectual-political precedents in Iran (in both Islamic and secular-leftist discourses) dating back to 1948. He traces Ahmadinejad's anti-Zionist diatribes to earlier Iranian Shi'i commentaries on Israel and Zionism rooted in the religious conflict between Islam and Judaism, to the influence of Marxist antiimperialist thought after the 1960s in the context of the Israeli-Palestinian conflict, and to the influence of European anti-Semitism.

The final feature, by Nima Naghibi, examines the intersections of the revolution, memory, and trauma in autobiographical memoirs by Iranian women in the diaspora, which have enjoyed great popularity in the West in recent years, particularly in the United States, which she contributes in part to a "colonial desire to unveil the simultaneously eroticized and abject Muslim woman" and a "civilizational discourse" of universal human rights that has been manipulated by certain groups as a justification for U.S. neo-imperialism in the aftermath of 9/11. In the remainder of the essay, she examines the rapid proliferation of Iranian diasporic women's autobiographies as a new postrevolutionary transnational literary genre and elucidates the multiple ways in which these biographies negotiate the Iranian Revolution as a key moment of "trauma" in the lives of the authors, by variously portraying the revolution as an event of dispossession and exile from an original idyllic "national" and "childhood" home.

In the "Curated Spaces" section, Behrooz Ghamari-Tabrizi interviews Taraneh Hemami, who curated the 2008 multimedia installation exhibit Theory of Survival in San Francisco. Hemami describes the exhibit, the title of which was based on a 1969 pamphlet by the Iranian revolutionary-Marxist Amir Parviz Pouyan, as an attempt both to foreground the diversity of participants and aspirations during the Iranian Revolution and to capture the experience of defeat, disillusionment, demise, and exile of those revolutionary participants and ideologies that subsequently found themselves under attack by the postrevolutionary Islamic state. She stresses that many Marxist activists during the revolution and earlier followed Pouyan's refutation of survival under autocracy and were willing to give their lives for a just and egalitarian future society, commenting: "What I find interesting is theorizing the survival of an ideology which itself refuted the theory of survival." The next article in this section—by Ghamari-Tabrizi, with accompanying photographs by Melissa Hibbard and Hamid Rahmanian—examines the role of the volunteer militia (Basij) and the Revolutionary Guards veterans of the Iran-Iraq war in Iranian society and politics after 1988. Ghamari-Tabrizi points out that these veterans, many of them disabled or suffering from the continued effects of exposure to chemical weapons, had participated in the war not only to defend their country's territorial sovereignty but also to defend and solidify the postrevolutionary Shi'i state's espoused religiously sanctioned, antisecular, and anti-Western social and moral values. However, with the end of the war, these veterans would find the state, under the presidency of Akbar Hashemi Rafsanjani, gravitating toward a platform of free-market economy and the relaxation of certain restrictions on "morality" and modes of entertainment and public conduct. Ghamari-Tabrizi then traces the emergence of two distinct ideological-political camps in the ranks of the veterans in reaction to the new post-1988 social, political, and economic transformations: those veterans who "sought to advance their cause through theological interventions in promoting religious and political pluralism" and the "absolutists," who "raised the flag of Islam and designated themselves as the only true Muslims genuinely committed to revolutionary ideals," with the former group throwing their weight behind the reformist political camp that came to power during Khatami's presidency (1997–2005) and the latter group gaining their moment of victory with the election of Ahmadinejad as president in 2005.

In the "Reflections" section, a number of leading scholars in the field, from across disciplines and with a diverse range of ideological perspectives and methodological groundings, were invited to reflect on particular dimensions and consequences of the revolution in the past thirty years. Minoo Moallem challenges what she regards as the dominant Western historiographic model of, and epistemological approach to, gauging the success or failure of revolutions in accordance with particular definitions of modernity that narrowly define freedom according to Western standards and fail to appreciate the manifold nuances of social and political dynamism in postrevolutionary Iranian society and politics and its modes of self-empowerment grounded in religious concepts of rights and discursive paradigms. In the case of Iranian women, for example, she argues that while the Islamic Republic imposed certain restrictions, the conditions created by the revolution and the discourse of Islam itself at the same time "have effectively integrated women as citizen-subjects in the Islamic state, allowing political negotiations around gender and women's issues." This rejection of the prevalent Western historiographic and sociological recourse to opposing absolutes of secular/religious or modern/antimodern is taken up in a different context by Saïd Amir Arjomand in his essay on theoretical conceptualizations of revolutions and the dominant "anatomy of revolution" paradigm that sees revolutions as going through certain stages: "the typical cycle of the rule of the moderates (1979–80), taken over by the radicals (1981–88), and finally a 'Thermidorian' return to more moderate rule." According to such a narrative, Arjomand argues, the Iranian Revolution would have entered its final phase with the presidencies of the pragmatic moderates Hashemi Rafsanjani (1989–1997) and Khatami (1997–2005). Such a narrative paradigm can only regard the presidency of the hard-line Islamist Ahmadinejad (2005–) as a historical anomaly. In effect, according to the anatomy-of-revolutions model, this ostensibly anomalous development in Iranian revolution, in addition to the clerical leadership of the revolution itself, places the Iranian Revolution outside the boundaries of "modernity" and "modern" revolutions. Instead, Arjomand demonstrates that revolutions assume a dynamic developmental logic of their own, with accompanying and shifting matrices of power irreducible to a particular model.

Djavad Salehi-Isfahani also takes on essentializing and totalizing accounts of the revolution by turning our attention to the conditions of the rural poor in post-revolutionary society. Emphasizing that the 1978–79 revolutionary movement consisted primarily of urban participants, Salehi-Isfahani rejects totalizing accounts of the abject failure of the revolution to transform society for the better, underscoring the major improvements in the living standards and, particularly, in the self-image of the poor rural population. He highlights the policies of the state that have brought about major "improvements in basic health, education, and infrastructure" and, once again, shows that the seemingly antimodern religious character of the Islamic Republic has actually served as a harbinger of modernization policies in the social realm. For example, "Another aspect of Iran's revolution, its Islamic ideology, . . . made it easier for religiously conservative families to send their girls to school."

The remaining "Reflections" essays focus on literary, artistic, cultural, and intellectual currents in postrevolutionary Iran. Kamran Talattof discusses not only the proliferation of literary output after the initial lull following the revolution, despite the persistence of censorship, but also new creative literary styles and the existence of widespread criticism of postrevolutionary state and society by many authors and poets in allegoric styles, as in the case of magic realism. Moreover, he highlights the emergence of new literary genres, such as the poetry and literature of war following the outbreak of the Iran-Iraq war, and above all the dominance of women as both producers and consumers of literary works due to the rapid increase in literacy rates and the burgeoning women's rights movement, whose social concerns have found resonance in many works of literature. In addition, Talattof discusses the growth of satirical as well as children's literature, the spectacular expansion of journalistic activities, the notable increase in translations of Western books, and the increase in the number of literary awards and book fairs after the revolution, without discounting the many hurdles and travails experienced by authors, poets, and journalists, such as the "chain murders" of many writers and intellectuals in 1998, in addition to censorship. The highly dynamic and vibrant nature of Iranian postrevolutionary literature is also examined by Persis Karim, who devotes particular attention to works by authors in diaspora communities, including works in both Persian and other languages. She, too, stresses the much greater visibility of women writers and the "increase in female readership" both in Iran and in Iranian diaspora communities, while simultaneously pointing to the greater availability to a non-Iranian readership of works by Iranian-born authors writing in the diaspora. Karim shows that, in addition to emergent literary themes such as exile and hyphenated Iranian identities, the freedom of expression afforded diasporic women writers has resulted in new styles of "self-disclosure," particularly in the case of autobiographical memoirs also discussed earlier by Naghibi.

M. R. Ghanoonparvar reflects on both [Iranian] Persian fiction and cinema, more specifically on the "intellectual" and "socially engaged" trends. He outlines the highly overt political nature of literary works in the initial postrevolutionary period, which saw a brief opening in the freedom of expression, followed by the postrevolutionary state's imposition of renewed censorship, which resulted in a return to allegoric forms of social and political criticism in literary and cinematic works, albeit with new stylistic adoptions. Tracing the origins of certain trends to prerevolutionary styles, Ghanoonparvar contrasts the magic realist style of sociopolitical criticism with the "escapist" trend in postrevolutionary literature that seeks instead to provide readers with a release from the realities of daily life. He, too, discusses the rapid proliferation of autobiographical works and their wide appeal to readers after the revolution, as well as the emergence of war literature and film, the increase in stories and films focusing on the lives of children, and the new genre of diasporic literature, often overladen with "themes of nostalgia, cultural assimilation, and split identity." Ghanoonparvar further examines the increase in the number of women film directors and films addressing women's lives in society, again underscoring the highly dynamic, prolific, and complex nature of the postrevolutionary cultural scene. Mazyar Lotfalian also reflects on the vibrant developments in Iranian visual culture after the revolution, focusing specifically on painting, cinema, TV, and the annual Shi'i rituals of commemorating the battle of Karbala and the martyrdom of the third Shi'i imam in 680 AD. Among other key themes, he draws attention to the role of technology, the market, and the domestic and international dissemination of Iranian visual culture, produced both inside Iran and in the diaspora. Lotfalian also highlights the centrality of Islam as a motif in the production and exhibition of Iran-related visual culture by Iranian-born artists and by museums outside Iran (either in an affirmative explanatory fashion or in the form of critiques of Islam), particularly after 9/11. Above all, he argues that Iranian artistic productions have, as never before, attained contemporary international recognition since the revolution.

The final essay in this section, by Ali Mirsepassi, investigates Iranian intellectual-philosophical trends since the revolution. Stating that the Iranian Revolution "called into question the precept that modernization brings secularization," Mirsepassi examines the impact of the revolution on Iranian intellectual currents. The unified revolutionary mass movement against the autocracy soon gave way to the consolidation of power by the Islamic faction and the clampdown on other political groups and ideological orientations, as well as the postrevolutionary state's violent imposition of certain moral values, and emerging rifts within the Islamic ranks. These developments, Mirsepassi maintains, undermined many former certainties and "spread a mood of nihilism[;] it also engendered an ongoing endeavor among Iranian intellectuals and the general population to reevaluate old beliefs and certainties while imagining new ones in light of all that has taken place."

The one common thread in postrevolutionary intellectual currents, according to Mirsepassi, has been the centrality of divergent categories of "the West" as a referential framework, with some intellectuals calling for a complete overhaul of Iranian society and culture through the complete adoption of Western Enlightenment values of rationality and subjectivity, other intellectuals calling for a mediated adoption of Western rationality and values to complement Islamic rational philosophy and values (as in the case of some reformists who supported the presidency of Khatami), and still another group, affiliated with Ahmadinejad, calling for a further distancing of Iranian society from Western values—the latter relying heavily on Western antimodernist intellectual currents articulated by Friedrich Nietzsche, Martin Heidegger, and Michel Foucault, which are redolent of the "decline of the West" paradigm. Mirsepassi concludes that both the strictly pro-Western and the anti-Western intellectuals advance nihilistic worldviews marked by a "disconnection from the existing world of practical reality," as reflected in the economic, social, and political concerns of the populace at large.

Finally, in her review essay, Niki Akhavan compares two recent books on postrevolutionary culture and media. Aptly calling her essay "contested narratives of the present," Akhavan illustrates how Mehdi Semati's edited volume, *Media, Culture, and Society in Iran: Living with Globalization and the Islamic State* (2007), offers a nuanced analysis of the subject by highlighting the contradictions and interconnectivities of the Iranian state and society. By contrast, Akhavan argues, Nasrin Alavi's *We Are Iran: The Persian Blogs* (2005) establishes a rigid binary between an Iranian society and an Iranian blogosphere that is almost entirely opposed to the monolithic, theocratic state.

Our special thanks to Tom Harbison and Atiba Pertilla of the *RHR* and the anonymous reviewers of the submissions received for this issue.

—Behrooz Ghamari-Tabrizi, Mansour Bonakdarian, Nasrin Rahimieh, Ahmad Sadri, and Ervand Abrahamian

Notes

1. Official Web site of former president Khatami, www.khatami.ir/fa/news/910 (accessed July 14, 2009).
2. Michael Fischer, *From Religious Dispute to Revolution* (Cambridge, MA: Harvard University Press, 1982), 184.
3. Said Hajjarian, *Az shāhed-e qodsi tā shāhed-e bāzāri: ʿUrfi-shodan-e din dar sepehr-e siyāsat (From the Divine to the Bazaari Witness: The Secularization of Religion in the Sphere of Politics)* (Tehran: Tarh-e No, 2001), 83.

The Crowd in the Iranian Revolution

Ervand Abrahamian

There had been no indiscriminate looting. The work was not that of "mobs."
It was an amazing feat of organization, timing, and discipline . . . I have never
admired the Iranian people as much as in the past few months. Their courage,
discipline, and devotion to the cause of overthrowing the monarchy has been
amazing.
—Anthony Parson, British Ambassador to Iran during the revolution

Crowds have traditionally been stereotyped as irrational, fickle, swinish, and
bloodthirsty "mobs" easily manipulated by some foreign "hidden" hand. Yet George
Rude persuasively challenged this conventional view in the 1960s — at least for
Europe — in his pathbreaking *The Crowd in History* and *The Crowd in the French
Revolution*.[1] Rude showed crowds to be rational, predictable, and, on the whole,
peaceful. Crowds consisted of demonstrators rather than rioters; collective bargain-
ers and social protesters rather than erratic desperadoes; and integral members of
the community rather than dregs of society. On the whole, they showed respect for
life, targeting specific forms of property rather than indulging in gratuitous acts of
violence against human beings. Rude's view was later reinforced by Emmanuel Le
Roy Ladurie, whose classic *Carnival in Romans: A People's Uprising at Romans,
1579 – 1580* found crowds to be not only rational but also masters of satire and mock
humor that deflated the pomposity of those on high.[2]

    Although the stereotypical view has been widely discarded for European
crowds, it continues to be alive and well in Western perceptions of the Middle East.

Radical History Review
Issue 105 (Fall 2009)   DOI 10.1215/01636545-2009-002
© 2009 by MARHO: The Radical Historians' Organization, Inc.

Thus Elizabeth Monroe, a leading British historian of the modern Middle East, pontificated in a much cited *New York Times* article published in 1953 and entitled "Key Force in the Middle East: The Mob":

Provide Tehran with a political stir and out pours the mob from its slums and shanty towns no matter what the pretext for a demonstration. . . . Identical crowds can be drawn into the street by very different slogans. . . . The recipe for making a mob is always the same: Take a cluster of mean streets: fill with idle or semi-employed people, sprinkle with raw notions of social betterment; top with hunger or despair at rising prices, stir and bring to boil. Of these ingredients, the most important are the unemployed and the cramped quarters, for they insure that the rumor which sets men moving reaches the maximum of ears in the minimum of time. . . . In a few seconds men that were separate beings have become a solid united mass, yelling, throwing missiles, running twenty and thirty abreast and flecked with saliva, toward fresh targets, capable of any violence and recklessness. They can be whipped in a moment into a frenzy of rage and despair. The Middle Eastern mob of today is so full of dumb resentment that it can change from a collection of separate human beings into a mad thing. . . . "Mob" is short for *mobile vulgus*—a people on the move.[3]

This stereotypical picture has been reinforced by the recent resurgence of Islam as a political force in the Middle East.[4] Orientalists—especially those in distant places—invariably depict Middle Eastern crowds as warlike jihadists, frenzied zealots, atavistic crazies, paranoid xenophobes, and enraged fundamentalists driven by homicidal if not suicidal martyrdom complexes. They are said to be symptomatic of the "Arab street" and the "Muslim mind." Despite Edward Said, Orientalism is alive and well.

The main aim of this article is to show that the crowd—which played a more central role in the Iranian Revolution of 1977–79 than in any other major revolution—behaved less like an irrational mob than as the rational entity described by Rude and Ladurie, perhaps even more so. Revolutions have been described as people's grand festivals and even as their rude intervention into high politics. This holds especially true for the Iranian Revolution.

The Iranian drama began with demonstrations at Tehran University in October 1977. It continued with seminary protests in Qom in January 1978. It accelerated in the course of the year with five cycles of forty-day mourning commemorations for those killed in the disturbances, followed by mass rallies—especially for 'Aid-e Fetr (Day of Sacrifice) in September and for Muharram in December. The latter drew as many as 2 million demonstrators in Tehran alone (with a population of nearly 4.5 million at the time). The whole drama climaxed in February 1979 when vast numbers—responding to Ayatollah Khomeini's call—poured into the streets to immobilize military contingents suspected of planning a coup d'état.

Wars, famines, financial meltdowns, and peasant jacqueries are often considered the midwives of revolution. None of these phenomena was present in Iran. Instead, the crowd appeared omnipresent. As the British MI-6 man in Tehran noted in his diary on the revolution: "Never before had the common people and the mob been such a catalyst of history." He added, "The triumph of the revolution was brought about by a mass popular movement with its force and fury, language and imagery."[5] Michel Foucault, writing from a very different perspective, came to a very similar conclusion. "The bare-headed crowd," he declared, acted like a "human tidal wave," expressing "authenticity," "awareness," and "political spirituality in a spiritless world."[6] The *New York Times* credited "the wave of rioting" for "sweeping from the throne one of the world's most durable-looking rulers."[7] Likewise, an American sociologist has argued that the Iranian Revolution contained far more popular participation—especially in the form of street protests—than any other political upheaval, including the French and Russian Revolutions.[8]

In analyzing the behavior of the crowd in the Iranian Revolution, this article hopes to throw light on a number of closely related questions: Who were the faces in the crowd, in particular, what social groups played important roles? What slogans did they use and what did their words reveal about public mentalities? How much did this discourse express religious or socioeconomic grievances? How were the demonstrations organized—by "conspiracies" from above or by ad hoc groups from below? How could unarmed civilians bring down one of the world's largest military juggernauts? And, most important of all, why did the public, which had no theoretical grounding in the Gandhian theory of nonviolent civil disobedience, readily resort to such a tactic? Except in its final stages, the revolution can be seen as a remarkable example of nonviolent civil disobedience.

Revolutionary Beginnings (October 1977)

Chronology can be as controversial in Iran as elsewhere. According to conventional wisdom—accepted by the present and previous regimes, as well as by most foreign commentators—the bombshell that ignited the revolution was a newspaper attack on Grand Ayatollah Khomeini published in January 1978. In fact, this article, published in a semiofficial daily, had been preceded by months of intermittent student protest in Tehran, which themselves followed months of international pressure on the Shah to relax police controls and respect basic human rights. Amnesty International, the International Commission of Jurists, the Jean Paul Sartre Committee, mainstream papers such as the *Sunday Times*, and Jimmy Carter in his presidential campaign had drawn attention to the dire lack of political liberties in Iran. Amnesty International had even described Iran as "having the highest rate of death penalties in the world, no valid system of civilian courts, and a history of torture beyond belief."[9] Responding to bad publicity, the Shah in May 1977 privately assured the International Commission of Jurists that in future the secret police SAVAK (Sazeman-e Ettela'at va Amniyat-e Keshvar, or National Intelligence and Security Organization) would not resort to torture.[10] He also promised that political dissidents would be tried in civilian rather than military courts, that they would have court hearings within twenty-four hours, and that they could choose their own defense attorney, who would in turn be protected from state prosecution. For the very first time since the 1953 coup that had given the Shah dictatorial powers, political dissenters obtained a semblance of legal protection.

This slight relaxation had far-reaching and unintended consequences. Old organizations—notably the secular National Front, the more religiously inclined Liberation Movement, the communist Tudeh Party, the Writers' Association, the Association of Teachers, and the Society of Bazaar Merchants and Guilds—regrouped after decades of inactivity. And new organizations—such as the Association of Militant Clergy, the Committee for the Defense of Political Prisoners, the Group for Free Books and Free Thought, the Association of Iranian Jurists, and the National Organization of University Professors—appeared for the first time. They all began to publish their own broadsheets, petitions, and newsletters.

In mid-October 1977, the Writers' Association—formed of leftist intellectuals—took the groundbreaking step of holding ten poetry-reading nights at the Goethe House.[11] This center of the German-Iranian Cultural Society was located in northern Tehran near the country's two main campuses: Tehran and Arya Mehr (later renamed Industrial) Universities. The speakers were prominent black-listed writers. They began with veiled attacks on censorship—and continued with not so veiled ones on the regime, equating the Pahlavis with the Nazis and the Romanovs. Eventually the podium allowed other participants—fifty-seven men and three women—who took the opportunity to read their own politically charged poetry. Despite a news blackout, information spread by word of mouth; by the tenth night, thousands—including high school teachers and students—were making their way from all parts of the city to the Goethe House. This led the police to close down the sessions and arrest some fifty people who had congregated outside the auditorium. Meetings, however, continued inside Arya Mehr University, where five thousand people soon staged a sit-in demanding the prompt release of the arrested fifty individuals. This sparked the first street clashes. On November 14, protesters marched from the two campuses to central Tehran via Eisenhower Avenue, chanting "Death to the Shah," "Brotherhood of Workers, Peasants, and Students," and "Unity, Struggle, Victory"—the main slogan of the Student Association. The police attacked with batons, injuring dozens and arresting another forty. Nineteenth-century European revolutions often started in opera houses; the Iranian Revolution can be said to have begun in poetry-reading sessions.

These clashes were soon compounded by others—in the Tehran slums and in far away Washington, D.C. That autumn, Tehran municipality launched an "urban renewal" program in the city's southern slums, bulldozing shantytowns known as *halab abad* (literally, tin districts). Such activities inevitably prompted protesters to stage a street sit-in and throw bricks at the bulldozers. The police retaliated by charging into the protesters. The situation became particularly tense on November 6, when squatters refused to take their protests to the government-sponsored Resurgence Party and instead insisted on marching to the Shah's Niavaran Palace in the far northern suburb of Tehran. One old man insisted on "visiting the Shah at his own house." The police fired. Although the press did not cover these events, rumors claimed that one person was killed and forty were injured.[12]

The scenes in Washington were better publicized. On November 15, the Shah with much fanfare visited the White House. It was customary for the Shah to pay an annual visit to the United States. It was also customary for the Iranian Student Confederation in Exile to greet these royal visits with vociferous protests. This time they turned even more clamorous because SAVAK officials in the Iranian embassy tried to counter the protesters by flying in from Texas and California their own supporters, many of them military cadets studying in the United States. The secret police thought it could beat the protesters at their own game, but a fiasco resulted. The two sides clashed outside the White House, prompting the Washington police to use tear gas. The wind, however, blew the gas onto the White House lawn, where the Shah and President Carter were in the midst of praising each other. Television cameras projected into the international arena the mind-boggling picture of His Imperial Highness wiping tears from his eyes. This promptly fed the wild rumor in Iran that the "most powerful empire in the world would not have permitted such an embarrassment unless it had lost confidence in its own puppet."[13] This new rumor reinforced an already prevalent one that the new U.S. president had raised the issue of human rights simply to undermine the Shah. Rumors were to play an important role throughout the next eighteen months. Rumors—known also as urban legends—are often dismissed as quaint and bizarre delusions. But as Marc Bloch learnt from personal experience in the trenches of World War I, rumors, however "fantastic," should be taken seriously, for they reveal much about collective mentalities, especially "preconceived notions" embedded in popular culture.[14]

The scene in Washington fueled more protests in Tehran, leading to a university-wide strike on December 7, the unofficial Iranian student day. On that day in 1953, a few months after the CIA coup, three students—two Tudeh activists and one from the National Front—had been killed in Tehran University while protesting the state visit of Vice President Richard Nixon. By the end of 1977, the *Washington Post* reported that after years of relative quiet, the streets of Tehran now witnessed scenes of almost daily protests.[15] According to the Liberation Movement, sixteen students lost their lives in these clashes.[16] More protests erupted during the year's last week, when Carter tried to repair the earlier damage by paying a return visit to the Shah and congratulating his host for having "created an island of stability in a sea of instability." Carter was now seen as propping up the regime. Significantly, students who took to the streets and were promptly arrested were sent not to military tribunals as in past decades, but to civilian courts, which released them or gave them light sentences. Their trials — covered extensively by the official media — sent a clear and loud message to the world that the regime had "opened up." It also inadvertently sent the message that the cost of protesting was no longer exorbitantly high. Despite their importance, these early clashes did not appear in the chronology of the revolution later drawn up by the *New York Times*;[17] according to the newspaper, the revolution did not begin until January 1979.

Forty-Day Cycles (January–August 1978)

On January 7, 1978, *Ettela'at* (*Information*), the semiofficial daily, attacked the exiled Grand Ayatollah Khomeini in a scurrilous article entitled "Iran and the Black and Red Imperialism."[18] Timed to mark the anniversary of the 1963 protests against the Shah's so-called White Revolution, the article denounced Khomeini as a "black reactionary" (clerics dressed in black, and *sayyeds*, the male descendents of the Prophet, wore black turbans). It insinuated that Khomeini was a foreigner — his grandfather had lived in Kashmir and some relatives used the family name Hendi ("Indian"); that he was funded by unnamed Arab countries; that he was a tool of landowners expropriated by the White Revolution; that he was in cahoots with British and Russian imperialism — both of which supposedly felt threatened by the White Revolution; and, to top it all, that he had led a licentious youth, drinking wine and dabbling in Sufi love poetry. Although conventional narratives invariably describe the article as the bombshell that ignited the revolution, the regime, including the Shah, had been making similar accusations since 1963. *Ettela'at* editors remembered this precedent when they showed some hesitation about running the article.

The day after the article appeared, theology students in Qom stayed away from classes and instead went in groups to the homes of the grand ayatollahs, beseeching them to speak out against this libelous attack.[19] They were warmly welcomed not only by Kazem Shariatmadari, a grand ayatollah with a liberal reputation, but also by his more conservative colleagues Moussavi-Golpayegani and Shahabaldin Marashi-Najafi. They lobbied even Sadeq Rouhani, the local senior cleric most closely identified with the regime. The day ended with the seminary students calling for a mass meeting to be held the next day at the city's main mosque.

The call was well received, especially by high school students and bazaar shop assistants. Some ten thousand people gathered at the mosque, and after listening to sermons criticizing the regime, they marched to the police station throwing stones at the Resurgence Party building and shouting "Death to the Shah," "Long Live Khomeini," "Long Live the Unity of Seminaries and Universities," and "Down with the Yazid Regime" (Yazid was the Sunni caliph held responsible by the Shi'is for the martyrdom of Imam Hussein at the historic battle of Karbala in 680 AD).

As they converged on the police station, regular army contingents rushed in shooting. Unsurprisingly, the first casualty in Qom was a seminary student. The authorities placed the total number of dead at two; the opposition claimed over seventy.[20] Shariatmadari publicly complained about the government preventing his students from visiting hospitals and morgues to cover up the full extent of the "massacre." Throughout the next twelve months, the regime and the opposition gave out drastically different casualty figures. The public without fail accepted the opposition figures. In Iran, as elsewhere, public perceptions proved far more potent than the real facts.

In conformity with a tradition common to most Middle Eastern religions, Shariatmadari called on the nation to show respect for the dead by attending forty-day memorial services at the local mosques of the deceased (the Shi'i term for these forty-day services is *Arbe'in*). His call was quickly taken up by all opposition groups. It was also circulated widely through word of mouth, through underground publications and tape cassettes, and, most important, through foreign broadcasts, especially the British Broadcasting Company (BBC) — so much so that royalists to this day place blame for the revolution squarely on the shoulders of the BBC. According to them, this was the sinister "foreign hand" that pulled down the Shah. Thus began five cycles of forty-day clashes.

The first cycle began on February 18–19, when clashes erupted in a number of cities. The most serious ones occurred in Shariatmadari's hometown, Tabriz, where a crowd of twenty thousand marched from the central mosque to the modern business quarter chanting antiregime slogans. They brought with them twenty scruffy street dogs with signs bearing the names of the royal family;[21] Shi'ism deems dogs unclean. The police chased the dogs in and out of the crowds, trying their best to catch them. (The scene would have appealed to Borat, as well as to his main inspiration, Mikhail Bakhtin, who in his Kazakhstan exile had written much on the carnival-like aspects of popular protests.) As they made their way into downtown Tabriz, the demonstrators ransacked over seventy buildings: the offices of the Resurgence Party, of SAVAK, and of the Iran-American Cultural Society, as well as luxury hotels, fancy boutiques, liquor stores, and cinemas specializing in Hollywood films. They also ransacked the premises of the Pepsi-Cola Company in Iran and of the Saderat Bank, leaving untouched its cash.[22] These establishments were reputed to be owned by Baha'is, a religious offshoot of Shi'ism deemed heretical by mainstream Shi'is and in recent times accused of close association with Israel. The *Times* of London noticed that the "rioters had chosen their targets carefully."[23] The *New York Times* added that the "huge mob controlled all the 12 kilometers from the university to the railroad station" and was not dislodged until army reinforcements arrived on the scene.[24] The government numbered the dead at six; the opposition spoke of "hundreds."[25] The Shah placed Tabriz under martial law and denounced the protesters as "Islamic Marxists." Over 650 demonstrators were soon brought to trial; they were mostly college and high school students, shop assistants, and work-ers from local factories.[26] This early upheaval does not conform to the conventional notion that the protests became more radical over the course of time. Immediately after the Tabriz upheaval, opposition groups called for another round of forty-day commemorations—this time for the Tabriz dead. They also asked the public to honor the dead by not celebrating the forthcoming Iranian New Year known as Nowruz. The regime promptly accused them of lacking respect for national traditions.

The second cycle fell on March 30. This time the worst clashes erupted in Yazd, Ahwaz, and Dezful. In Yazd, twenty thousand people marched from the main mosque to the center of the city, where they confronted the military. The opposi-tion claimed that the death toll topped one hundred.[27] The third cycle began on May 8, when strikes closed down most bazaars and educational establishments in many cities. The Shah reacted by canceling a long-standing trip to Eastern Europe. The fourth cycle fell on June 18, marked by street incidents in a large number of cities. Forty days later, on July 28, more clashes erupted, the worst one occurring in Mashed, where tanks were used. According to the opposition, more than 250 people perished.[28] To break this spiral of violence, opposition groups—led by Shariatmadari—called for peaceful rallies to celebrate the forthcoming 'Aid-e Fetr, the festival that ends the annual Ramadan fast. That year the Day of Sacrifice fell on September 4.

An unexpected calamity, however, intervened. On August 19, the anniver-sary of the 1953 coup, unknown arsonists in Abadan burnt down Cinema Rex, which specialized in family films. Some 430 people—including entire families with grandparents and children—were incinerated. Rumors spread that the theater doors had been locked shut. The regime blamed unnamed "Islamic Marxists." The opposition blamed the regime, arguing that the fire department's response had been intentionally slow, that the same police chief had ordered the January shootings in Qom, and that SAVAK had recently firebombed a number of homes and offices belonging to dissidents.[29] The public readily believed the opposition. After a mass burial, ten thousand relatives of the dead marched through Abadan shouting "Burn the Shah. End the Pahlavis. Soldiers You Are Guiltless. The Shah Is the Guilty One." The *Washington Post* reported that the demonstrators conveyed one clear and simple message: "The Shah must go. . . . Seemingly to a man, residents of this hot, humid town at the head of the Persian Gulf accuse the local police and the fire departments of responsibility."[30] The *Financial Times* expressed astonishment that so many, even those with vested interests in the regime, pointed fingers at SAVAK. "At the heart of the problem," it concluded, "was the lack of public trust. The public is unwilling to give the Shah the benefit of the doubt."[31] The gutted cinema became known as the Royal Kebab House.

Rallies and General Strikes (September–December 1978)

'Aid-e Fetr was celebrated with nationwide mass rallies. In Tehran, separate processions started at dawn from four locations and made their way by mid-afternoon to
the vast Shahyad Square (to the Memorial to the Monarchy) on the western road
leading out of the city.[32] They started from the university campuses; from middle-
class residential areas in the northeast; from Jaleh Square near the central bazaar;
and from the railway station in the southern working-class district. The first procession was marshaled by college students; the second by neighborhood youths; the
third by bazaar shop assistants; and the fourth by local high school students.

Emad Baqi, a high school student who later became a gadfly journalist, remi-
nisces that the task of grassroots organizing in the southern slums was left to high
school students like himself and his classmates.[33] In making a pitch for "history
from below," Baqi challenges conventional notions that the revolution was made
from above. According to him, the real activists were not local clerics, many of whom
shied away from politics, but youngsters like his classmates, many of whom were
influenced by the works of Ali Shariati, a Fanonist who had died in England on the
eve of the revolution. Baqi's local cleric deemed Shariati a Marxist *kafer* (unbeliever)
masquerading as a radical Muslim. Baqi mentions that some of his schoolteachers
turned out to be secret Marxists. For Baqi, the revolution was a spontaneous out-
burst. A similar picture is drawn by Mahmud Golabdarahi, then a forty-year-old
freelance writer and former Tudeh Party member. In his intermittent diary of the
revolution entitled *Lahzah-ha* (*Snapshots*), he narrates how he frequently com-
muted the twenty-five miles from his home in Karaj to central Tehran to take part in
unorganized street protests.[34] According to him, the procession from northeastern
Tehran on 'Aid-e Fetr was coordinated mostly by neighborhood *bacheh-ha* (lads)
without any central organization.

The four processions together stretched twenty kilometers and eventually
filled the expansive Shahyad Square. Although newspaper editors and anchormen
in distant capitals continued to generalize about atavistic and frenzied mobs, reporters on the actual scene were impressed by the discipline and size of the crowd. The
Financial Times estimated the crowd to comprise "tens of thousands" and described
it as the largest in twenty-five years.[35] The *Guardian* placed the figure at two hundred thousand.[36] *Time* magazine vividly described the scene:

They marched, tens of thousands strong, defiant chanting demonstrators
surging through the streets of Tehran, a capital unaccustomed to the shouts
and echoes of dissent. The subject of their protests was the politics of
Iran's supreme leader, Shah Muhammad Reza Pahlavi. Some carried signs
demanding his ouster. Others called for a return of long denied civil and
political liberties. . . . The crowd, at times numbering more than 100,000, was
a colorful, sometimes incongruous cross section of Iranian society: dissident

students in jeans, women shrouded in black chadors, the traditional head-
to-foot veil, peasants and merchants, and most important, the bearded black
robed Muslim mullahs.[37]

One of the four processions passed the U.S. embassy to send a clear message to
its occupants. William Sullivan, the American ambassador, writes that he placed
observers on the embassy roof to get a "better assessment of just what this phenomenon was":[38]

As a demonstration, it was unique in the experience of modern Iran. At least
a hundred thousand Iranians participated in the march — well organized
and marshaled in their parade with almost military efficiency. The marshals
themselves were young men, often moving on Honda motorcycles, ahead of the
march, organizing traffic, blocking cross streets, and preparing the right of way.
There were walkie-talkie radios, first-aid groups, water and refreshment units,
as well as cheerleaders. . . . It was an awesome display of political power . . . I
could only marvel at the organization and the preparations that must have gone
into the demonstration.

The protesters' chants — often rhythmic and involving plays on Persian words —
lose much of their bite in translation. The favorite ones were: "Independence, Freedom, Islamic Government"; "Iran Is Our Country, Imam Hussein Is Our Leader";
"Iran Is Our Country, Khomeini Is Our Leader"; "America Out of Iran"; "We Want
the Return of Khomeini"; "Free Political Prisoners"; "Free Ayatollah Taleqani" (a
left-leaning popular cleric in Tehran); "Fifty Years of the Pahlavis, Fifty Years of
Treachery"; "Silence Betrays Islam" (a dig at apolitical clerics); "Long Live Pales-
tine"; "Soldiers — You Belong to Us"; "Brother Soldiers, Why Do You Shoot [Your]
Brothers?"; "Shah Supports Treason. Carter Supports the Shah"; "Who Takes Our
Oil? The Americans. Who Takes Our Gas? The Soviets. Who Is Their Puppet? The
Shah"; "The Resurgence Party Is a Money-Grabbing Party"; "We Are Not against
Women. We are against Corruption"; "The Shah Is a Pimp"; "Farah, You Are a Slut"
(a reference to the empress); "We Have One Dog Named Farah Diba. We Have
Another Named Reza Pahlavi." A statistical study of these chants shows that a high
percentage was mocking or satirical.[39] Desmond Harney, the British MI-6 man in
Tehran, commented: "The truth of twenty-five years is coming out — and the people
(all of us) are fascinated. The Persian democratic tradition has been preserved and
is alive and well *alhamdolellah* (Thanks be to God). And we are hearing real Persian
spoken again, not the pompous, stuffy rubbish of the old order, but free, humorous,
satirical, anecdotal, and fierce."[40]

As the demonstrators made their way through Tehran they threw stones
at bank windows but lowered their voices near hospitals so as not to disturb the
patients. Some wore jogging shoes and American-style T-Shirts. When some flashed

Churchillian V-signs, Golabdarahi tried to tell them that the clenched fist was more appropriate. Others carried effigies of "Satan Carter" dressed as a young boy—in Persian the term *shaytan* (satan) means both "devil" and describes an unruly child. Shopkeepers distributed sweets and water. Florists gave out carnations so that demonstrators could hand them to the soldiers. Some office workers, including civil servants, threw pictures of the Shah out of buildings, so that the crowds could tear them apart. As the processions wound through the city, the crowds renamed major landmarks: Pahlavi Avenue became Mossadeq Avenue (renamed after the nationalist premier overthrown in the 1953 CIA-backed coup); Old Shemran became Shariati Avenue; Eisenhower became Freedom Avenue; and Shahyad became Freedom Square. Similar rallies were staged in most provincial capitals. A National Front spokesman told French reporters that the world should take these rallies as a de facto referendum ending the monarchy.[41]

Although 'Aid-e Fetr passed without major bloodshed, intermittent clashes erupted on the following days and weeks. Groups of fifty to sixty youngsters would gather in city squares, often on bicycles and motorbikes, brazenly mocking the authorities and sometimes ransacking cinemas, cabarets, banks, and liquor stores. Golabdarahi writes that the youngsters tended to be good humored and made sure that the premises they attacked were empty so that no one would suffer any bodily harm. He also writes that these youngsters knew each other only by their first names and in due course got to know him by face. It was clear that in the weeks after 'Aid-e Fetr the regime was losing control of the streets.

The Shah tried to reestablish order by declaring martial law in twelve cities—Tehran, Karaj, Qom, Tabriz, Isfahan, Shiraz, Mashed, Abadan, Ahwaz, Qazvin, Kazerun, and Johram. In the early hours of September 8, he appointed General Gholam Ali Oveissi, notorious as the "Butcher of Tehran" because of his role in suppressing pro-Khomeini demonstrations in 1963, as the capital's new military governor. Oveissi promptly moved tanks into downtown Tehran and ordered troops to fire into a crowd that had gathered in Jaleh Square. A European journalist wrote that the subsequent "carnage" resembled a "firing squad."[42] September 8 has gone down in Iranian history as Black or Bloody Friday—reminiscent of Bloody Sunday in Russia in 1905. The government put the dead at eighty-seven, the opposition at over four thousand.[43] One exiled paper claimed that over three thousand graves had been dug hastily for the victims.[44] Although the public readily accepted the higher estimate, trials held immediately after the revolution show the true figure to have been closer to the lower one.[45]

Rumors spread that the soldiers who had fired into the crowd at Jaleh Square must have been Israelis since Iranians would not have carried out such a horrendous deed. Some claimed to have seen mysterious foreign planes land at the airport that very same morning. An American anthropologist was told by one of her local informants that "her cousin had seen Israeli troops shooting into the crowd."[46]

Harney wrote that many readily accepted such "absurd rumours." He added that Black Friday, coming so close to the Abadan "holocaust," created an unbridgeable gap between "rulers and ruled."[47] He further added: "The hatred and passion and discontent in the people is terrifying—not just the typically radical student. It is easy to forget, of course, that most of the middle or junior officials one meets were students abroad themselves a few years back where they were radicalized for a time. That process has gone on for twenty years or more—and they are to be found at every level."[48]

If the iron fist was designed to intimidate the public, it failed abysmally. Demonstrators continued to gather in city squares mocking the authorities. Protesters continued to plaster walls with such slogans as "Down with the Hangman Shah"; "If I Sit, If You Sit, Who Will Stand Up?"; "Blind Obedience in the Military Helps Imperialism"; "Marx, If Only You Were Alive, You Would See That Religion Is Not the Opium of the People"; and, in English, "Yonkee [*sic*] Go Away." A collection of such graffiti carries the apt title *The Walls Speak*.[49] Moreover, protesters continued to meet inside the university as well in the cemetery of Behesht-e Zahra (Zahra's Paradise) in southern Tehran. Baqi narrates that both places were transformed into large sanctuaries where political groups held impromptu daily meetings and openly sold newsletters, books, cassettes, posters, and cartoons. Furthermore, strikes began to spread from colleges, high schools, and bazaars to government offices, private companies, telecommunications, newspapers, railways, ports, airlines, factories, mines, and, most serious of all, to the petroleum industry—in the words of one American newspaper, "turning off the oil tap was the opposition's trump card."[50] Oil workers demanded an immediate lifting of martial law and threatened not to produce petroleum for the outside world until they had "exported Ali Baba and his Forty Thieves." By the fortieth day after Black Friday, nationwide general strikes had brought the whole economy to a grinding halt. The *Financial Times* aptly declared that "the dam had burst."[51] Sullivan, the American ambassador, was "astounded" to hear the Shah claim that the "planning was so sophisticated" that it must have been done by the CIA and the British MI-6 since it was way beyond the capabilities of the Soviet KGB and their Iranian clients.[52]

Black Friday not only polarized the situation but also shifted the balance of power within the opposition. It shifted the center of gravity away from Shariatmadari and the more moderate opposition, who favored the 1906 constitution, toward Khomeini and the more radical groups, both secular and religious, who called for the overthrow of the monarchy and the establishment of a republic. In the words of the *Guardian*: "The opposition now cuts across all sectors of society, embracing Westernized intellectuals, religious bazaaris, unhappy housewives, and lower middle-class students. Whoever raises a banner against the Shah—whether Communist, Right-wing nationalist or a Mullah—is virtually guaranteed an instant following."[53] Grand Ayatollah Hassan Tabatabai-Qomi, the most conservative cleric in

Mashed, tried to stem the tide by announcing that Imam Reza (the eighth imam of the so-called Twelver Shi'i, killed in the ninth century and buried in Mashed) had visited him in a dream and inquired why malcontents were undermining the world's sole Shi'i monarch. In Shi'ism, as in most traditional cultures, dreams are seen as containing supernatural messages. Of course, the beauty of dreams is that others cannot question their veracity. In this case, however, Khomeini remarked that his old colleague Qomi must have eaten too much rice before going to sleep.

In the months following Black Friday the regime suffered three additional blows. First, an earthquake devastated the region of Tabas in southern Khurasan. Whereas the government was slow in responding, the Imam Reza Foundation in Mashed was highly effective in dispatching seminary students with large amounts of emergency aid. When Empress Farah visited the region, the local population coolly received her, blaming her for having rebuilt the area after a previous earthquake with "authentic mud houses" instead of with modern concrete structures as they had requested.[54] In this case, the regime was traditional, the public modern. It was also rumored that the earthquake had been triggered by secret underground American nuclear tests.

Second, a group of employees in the Central Bank published a list of 177 millionaires who had supposedly transferred billions of dollars abroad.[55] Harney writes that this was "highly effective" in giving the "upper class jitters."[56] Even though the list was probably embellished, it appeared highly believable. It named the obvious suspects—courtiers, generals, ministers, and entrepreneurs linked to the regime. Such people were reputed to be not just rich but filthy rich. And such rich people were expected to be scurrying off with their ill-begotten wealth to greener lands before the deluge hit. In fact, many on the list beat the Shah in fleeing. The perception of unbridled corruption in high places was so prevalent that even American journalists who in the past had been sympathetic to the regime now published articles on how the Shah and his immediate family had amassed a "staggering fortune" worth billions rather than millions.[57] "Bankers," reported the *New York Times*, "say that a substantial part of the $2 billion to $4 billion transferred from Iran to the United States in the last two years belongs to the royal family."[58]

Third, on November 4, army officers shot a conscript who had thrown down his rifle and rushed to join campus protesters inside Tehran University. This sparked what became known as the Day Tehran Burned. Angry students poured from the campus, lining the streets with burning tires to prevent the movement of army vehicles and ransacking not only the usual buildings around Ferdowsi Square but also the nearby British embassy. They targeted the latter because a few days earlier the British foreign minister, in an attempt to mollify the Shah's complaints about the BBC, had denounced the opposition as "fanatical reactionaries." The *Christian Science Monitor* reported that the campus shooting—rumored to have taken thirty lives—led "rampaging mobs to set ablaze Tehran": "I have never seen anything like it. Block after block of burned out shells. It looked like a war had been and gone."[59] The "apocalyptic scene" also reminded Harney of the London blitz. He added that the intruders into the British embassy were "boyish, prankish, rather than terrifying, and uninterested in either looting or harming embassy officials."[60] The British ambassador elaborated:

> It was evident as we toured the city on November 6 that their discipline and selectivity had been remarkable. The damage, once the burnt out carcasses of vehicles and litter had been cleared away, was much less than had appeared the night before. There had been no loss of life, something unbelievable to witnesses of the scenes of the previous day. The attacks on property had been carefully timed to coincide with the late lunch break when office buildings, etc, were empty. Banks which stood alone had been gutted. Banks with domestic apartments above them had not been torched. There had been no indiscriminate looting. . . . The Jewish carpet shops on Ferdowsi Square were untouched whereas adjacent banks and liquor shops had been razed.[61]

Golabdarahi depicts a very similar picture. He writes that protesters eagerly ransacked the British embassy and the banks on Ferdowsi Square but left untouched jewelry stands, Armenian-owned liquor stores, and, most surprising of all, expensive radio shops. Golabdarahi explains that people had high regard for radios in general and for the BBC in particular. "Everyone," he writes, "tuned every day into the BBC. They looked up to it as if it was the sun."[62]

Confronted by persistent opposition, the Shah was forced into an about-face. He dismissed Oveissi; replaced the prime minister with a mild-mannered general; arrested sixty senior officials including his prime minister of twelve years and the director of SAVAK; lifted censorship; promised free elections; released more political prisoners, including Ayatollah Taleqani; and, most surprising of all, went on national television to tell the country that he had heard their "revolutionary message." The American ambassador, Sullivan, writes that military "morale" had deteriorated to such a point that officers could no longer rely on their troops: "Many of the demonstrators in the streets confronting the troops were the sons and brothers of the men who held the rifles. Although military units were regularly being rotated from one city to another, in order to avoid the problems inherent in such confrontations, the troop commanders' estimates and the opinions of our military advisers stationed with the Iranian forces suggest that the situation was very spongy indeed."[63]

Faced with such a dire situation, the Shah instructed his new premier to arrange with Taleqani orderly processions to commemorate Muharram—especially the two high holy days of Tasu'a and 'Ashura that mark the martyrdom of Imam Hussein and his family. The government agreed to permit processions on these two days so long as demonstrators did not mock the royal family and did not trespass into the northeastern residential districts where the Shah and the top elite lived.

The Tasu'a and 'Ashura rallies, held on December 10–11, were coordinated from Taleqani's home where his extended family had links not only with university students and the Liberation Movement but also with the National Front, the Writers' Association, and the Society of Bazaar Merchants and Guilds. One daughter was affiliated with the Islamic-leftist guerrilla organization, the Mojahedin, and a son with one of the Marxist guerrilla organizations. The *Los Angeles Times* described the Tasu'a rally as an "impressive and highly disciplined show of strength" whose "main message was that the present regime is isolated from the people. . . . This message will get to the U.S. if not to the Shah."[64] It noted that the processions were accompanied by clerics atop minibuses who discouraged the use of "provocative slogans" via loudspeakers. The day passed without bloodshed.

The 'Ashura rally was even larger, drawing in those who had been apprehensive the previous day. One young participant told a foreign journalist: "On Tasu'a, I was the only member of my family who participated. On 'Ashura, the whole family participated."[65] The *Financial Times* wrote that the rally totaled over 1 million and brought in "all social classes."[66] Others, including General Abbas Qarabaghi, the chairman of the Joint Chiefs of Staff, estimated it over 2 million.[67] Like those on Tasu'a and the Day of Sacrifice, the rallies began from four different parts of the city and converged on Shahyad Square, now renamed Freedom Square. Harney observed that troops had evacuated much of the city and instead formed "a temporary Maginot Line shielding the homes of the rich."[68] As before, the demonstrators changed place names: Jaleh became Martyr's Square, Shahnaz became Imam Hussein Square, and Reza Shah became Revolution Avenue. They chanted the stock slogans, adding such new ones as "Every Day Ashura; Every Month Muharram, Every Place Karbala"; "Imam Khomeini Is Our Idol Breaker"; "We Are Not the Shah's Nation; We Are the Iranian Nation"; "Neither East Nor West, but Islam." The *Los Angeles Times* reported that the 'Ashura rally was not only larger than the Tasu'a one but that its tone was also much more aggressive both against the Shah and the United States.[69] Ignoring pleas for restraint, the crowds openly shouted "Death to the Shah," "Yankees Go Home," and the "Shah Is a Dog Chained to the Americans." The same reporter added that the whole day was "a tremendous victory for the opposition" and that the mood was "militant" but nevertheless "happy." The day ended with a rally ratifying a sixteen-point proclamation demanding the establishment of an Islamic Republic, the return of Khomeini from exile, "social justice" for the "deprived masses," and the expulsion of the "imperial powers." It also held out a hand of friendship to the armed forces.[70] Khomeini, now in exile in Paris, proclaimed the rally a referendum ending the monarchy. Similar peaceful rallies were held in other cities. In Isfahan, however, the gathering turned violent when the authorities tried to organize a counterdemonstration by trucking in some one hundred peasants. Angry crowds retaliated by attacking a luxury hotel.[71] Even though Muharram passed without bloodshed in Tehran, Golabdarahi writes that it was widely rumored that as many as four hundred to five hundred people had been killed in scattered parts of the city.[72]

The *Washington Post* concluded that the "disciplined and well organized march [in Tehran] lent considerable weight to the opposition's claim of being an alternative government."[73] The *New York Times* reported that "not a single violent incident disrupted the procession" and that "most of the marchers exhibited little religious or political frenzy. The mood was serious, determined, and utterly calm."[74] The message was obvious: "The government was powerless to preserve law and order on its own. It could do so only by standing aside and allowing the religious leaders to take charge. In a way, the opposition has demonstrated that there already is an alternative government."[75] Similarly, the *Christian Science Monitor* reported that a "giant wave of humanity swept through the capital declaring louder than any bullet or bomb could the clear message: 'The shah must go.' "[76] "The sheer weight of the procession," wrote the same reporter, "took all seasoned observers by surprise. More than a quarter of Tehran's population had turned out to register their protest." It was rumored that the Shah had stopped reading Iranian newspapers because they now referred to him as simply "the shah" without all his honorific titles. It was also rumored that people could see the face of Khomeini reflected on the moon. This was probably an unconscious inversion of the ancient claim that the shah was the shadow of God on earth. These rumors became so widespread that Khomeini's advisers in Paris held a press conference to deny them. They accused the regime of spreading absurd stories so as to discredit the whole opposition. Golabdarahi, however, admits that one night, when he got home, his family was on the roof claiming they could see Khomeini's face on the moon. He laughed, but when he looked up, he, too, saw the face.[77]

Final Debacle (January–February 1979)

The Shah left Iran on January 16, five weeks after 'Ashura. Just before leaving, he named Shahpour Bakhtiyar, a National Front leader, as the new prime minister. Bakhtiyar was promptly disowned by his own organization on the grounds that the monarch did not have the constitutional authority to make such appointments. Mass celebrations greeted the Shah's departure. According to the *New York Times*, "a million jubilant citizens formed a great river of humanity flowing down Tehran's streets."[78] Crowds displayed the blunt headline in *Ettela'at*: "Shah Gone." Some exclaimed, "Shah Went, Shah Went Under." The *Christian Science Monitor* correspondent admitted that she "had never seen such a vast gathering."[79] Despite the festive atmosphere, some walls were plastered with the ominous warning: "Don't be fooled. He also departed just before the 1953 coup."

Khomeini returned to Iran two weeks later, on February 1, after two and a half decades of exile. The headline in *Ettela'at* announced that "Imam Has Come." The BBC reported that "pandemonium" broke out as "three million" greeted the "father of the revolution" returning to reclaim his revolution.[80] The size of this crowd far exceeded that of previous ones, mostly because thousands were bussed in from the provinces. Golabdarahi noticed that a few coming from Mashed had handguns and boasted that they were ready to revenge dead relatives. The army again cordoned off the northern part of the city with a two-mile-long convoy formed of seventy-eight Jeeps and fifty-four trucks full of machine guns and heavily armed soldiers. Foreign journalists noted that some soldiers displayed Khomeini's picture and placed carnations in their gun muzzles. The journalists added that officers feared defections in the ranks and thus shied away from outright confrontation with the millions of well-wishers.[81] One foreign correspondent wrote that "for several millions" this was a "day of catharsis." Some handed out carnations to American journalists and thanked them for making it possible for Khomeini to return.[82] As Khomeini made his way from the airport into central Tehran, the crowds in the southern slum districts became so large that they created a "monumental traffic jam," forcing him to take a helicopter to his first destination, Behesht-e Zahra cemetery. The *New York Times* correspondent, in a flush of old-fashioned Orientalism, reported that the "capital was in a mood of rapture":

> There was nothing formal, nothing Occidental, about the triumphal procession.
> It was gaudy, excessive, thoroughly Oriental in its excitement. The Ayatollah
> had asked for restraint and his agents urged that chants be limited to "God is
> Great!" People screamed themselves hoarse and trotted alongside the Moslem
> leader until they were exhausted. Street vendors sold Khomeini badges,
> Khomeini pennants, Khomeini portraits. If the Ayatollah had hoped to avoid a
> new cult of personality like the one that had surrounded the Shah, he failed.[83]

Khomeini was helicoptered onto Lot 17 in Behesht-e Zahra where the martyrs of Jaleh Square were buried. He paid his respects to the dead and, then, in sharp contrast to the hesitant and vacillating Shah of the previous months, outright pronounced the premier Bakhtiyar's government illegitimate, the monarchy terminated, and himself the true voice of the people with the right to appoint a new prime minister. Vox populi—if not *vox dei*—had spoken. Khomeini also added that "final victory will not come until all foreign influence is terminated." Four days later, he appointed Mehdi Bazargan, the head of the Liberation Movement, as premier, thus forcing the country to choose between Bazargan and Bakhtiyar, between his and the Shah's prime ministers.

Crowds continued to play decisive roles until the very end of the revolution. For example, they barred Bakhtiyar's ministers from entering their offices. In the words of the *New York Times*, tens of thousands, including civil servants, immobilized the whole machinery of government.[84] They assaulted police stations and took over provincial cities—especially Isfahan, Qom, Amol, and Shiraz. They plastered Khomeini's pictures on royal statues and, having pulled down the largest of the statues in Tehran, gave it a mock funeral at Behesht-e Zahra cemetery. They placed human shields on highways to prevent army reinforcements from moving into Tehran. They surrounded the Parliament building, pressuring the deputies to resign en masse. These actions undermined any constitutional legitimacy Bakhtiyar may have had. The crowds continued forming in the streets in large numbers to show solidarity with Bazargan and opposition to Bakhtiyar. The latter brushed off the revolutionary crowds, claiming that "people had nothing better to do since cinemas and schools were closed."[85] This merely gave the demonstrators additional reason to mock him.

Crowds, moreover, gathered on a daily basis around the main barracks and tried to win over rank-and-file soldiers. Wild rumors had spread that officers had executed hundreds of disloyal cadets and soldiers. The *New York Times* reported that "many officers in the 487,000-man American-equipped army have been impressed by the number of people the Ayatollah and other religious leaders have been able to turn out into the street demonstrations, undeterred by automatic weapons and fire."[86] Furthermore, on the final days of the revolution on February 10–11, huge crowds readily responded to Khomeini's call to fill the streets to immobilize the elite Imperial Guards thought to be plotting a coup. Many even slept in the streets. Khomeini was fully aware of the experience of the CIA-organized coup of August 1953 when the then premier Mohammad Mossadeq had blundered into asking his supporters to stay home and thus had given the military its golden opportunity to seize power. The ghosts of 1953 continued to haunt Iran. Golabdarahi stresses that the memory of August 1953 weighed heavy in February 1979. Large groups—including recently released supporters of the main guerrilla organizations, the Marxist Fedayin and the Islamic Mojahedin—broke into armories, distributed weapons, especially AK-45s, transported some to the university, and, most dramatic of all, helped cadets fight pitched battles with Imperial Guards trying to gain control of the air force base near Jaleh Square. Most adult males knew how to use weapons since they had served in the military as conscripts. The Imperial Guards resorted to helicopter gunships, the cadets to anti-aircraft weapons. According to Western eyewitnesses, February 10 marked by far the deadliest day of confrontations in the entire revolution. It is thought that over 175 people died that day.[87] One of the casualties was the correspondent of the *Los Angeles Times*; he was one of the very few foreigners killed in the revolution.

The final climax came on February 11, when Qarabaghi announced that the armed forces would remain strictly "neutral" in the political struggle between the two rival prime ministers. According to Qarabaghi, the armed forces had lost all semblance of cohesion, with many officers sympathizing with the opposition, disliking hotheads such as Oveissi, and even withholding live ammunition from tanks, fearful that they could fall into the wrong hands.[88] For Qarabaghi the final straw came when Bakhtiyar ordered him to bombard the crowds breaking into the armories. He concluded that Bakhtiyar had lost all touch with reality. With the armed forces out of the scene, Bakhtiyar's fate was sealed. In the morning of February 11, Tehran radio declared the triumph of the Islamic Revolution. The BBC announced that "in one fell swoop Iran had become an Islamic Republic."[89] The *New York Times* added: "Millions of jubilant people poured into the streets to witness the climax of the year-old ordeal."[90] *Le monde* remarked that the scene, especially the barricades, was reminiscent of the Paris Commune of 1871.[91] The *Financial Times* speculated that these final two days were by far the "bloodiest" in the previous thirteen months.[92]

Conclusion

On the whole, the crowd in the Iranian Revolution tended to be peaceful. When, on occasion, it indulged in violence, it targeted not human beings but specific forms of property. The thirteen months of this revolution produced only four reported incidents in which opposition crowds willfully shed blood. In Shiraz, a Shi'i crowd raided the Baha'i neighborhood, killing at least two unarmed men. In Paveh, communal violence broke out between Kurds and Azeris. In Khuzestan, mobs lynched three Afghan workers—Afghan migrants, who formed an underclass, were often unjustly blamed for rapes, muggings, and break-ins. And in Tehran, at the height of the November disturbances, students almost stabbed to death a general who had inadvertently ventured near the university campus. Other incidents of physical violence against persons by the crowds were mostly instigated by SAVAK, which organized counterdemonstrations and relied on armed hooligans to intimidate the opposition.[93] The assaults on the armories carried out on the final days of the revolution were organized not so much by crowds as by guerrilla bands led by the Fedayin and the Mojahedin.

Three other conclusions can also be drawn from the whole drama. First, the revolution was made through peaceful protests, even though concepts of civil disobedience, such as the one developed by Mahatma Gandhi, remained relatively unknown in Iran. Iranians resorted to street politics not due to Gandhian influence, but because of their own historical experiences. In 1891–92, protests had compelled Nasser al-Din Shah to cancel a tobacco monopoly sold to a British entrepreneur. In 1905–9, demonstrations and sit-ins had brought about the Constitutional Revolution. In 1919, public outrage had led to the cancellation of the Anglo-Persian Agreement that intended to incorporate Iran into the British sphere of influence if not the actual British Empire. In 1941–46, street rallies, especially May Day meetings, had given the labor movement considerable political clout. In 1951–53, mass demonstrations had been instrumental in premier Mossadeq's nationalization of the British-owned oil company. Those familiar with the writings of Ahmad Kasravi, and most educated Iranians had been brought up with his histories, knew that mass interventions had played key roles in the country's recent past. One can say that demonstrations were to Iranians what apple pie is to Americans. It was mainly because of this national tradition that Khomeini and the main opposition leaders, who did not necessarily disapprove of violence, never adopted the strategy of armed struggle. In fact, they categorically rejected pleas to declare an armed jihad, contrary to widespread Western perceptions.

Second, most of the crowds, especially in the first half of 1978, were products of ad hoc groups in colleges, high schools, and the bazaars. They were not orchestrated by mysterious central conspirators or by some hidden foreign hand. They relied mostly on informal networks and, where possible, grouped around local mosques. The main impetus came from below, not from above. Well-known clerics such as Taleqani did not play important roles in organizing demonstrations until the final three months. The clergy, especially those around Khomeini, did not establish central bodies such as the Revolutionary Council and the Pasdaran (Revolutionary Guards) until the very last weeks of the upheaval. For much of the crisis, grassroots groups acted autonomously and had contact with prominent figures only through proclamations, cassettes, and broadcasts—especially the BBC, to whose Persian-service broadcasts many Iranians listened daily.

Finally, the total number killed in the demonstrations was far less than conventional wisdom would have us believe. Immediately after the fall of the Shah, one of Khomeini's close associates claimed that the "blood of 67,311 martyrs had nourished the Iranian Revolution."[94] Even though this tally has attained official status, the real figure was far more modest. Two social scientists in United States, working with data collected by a sociologist at Tehran University, estimate the total to be near three thousand—all but five hundred killed in the final two months.[95] Similarly, Baqi, who, immediately after the revolution worked in the Martyr's Foundation, estimates the total to be near twenty-eight hundred, and this probably includes those incinerated in the Abadan cinema fire.[96] These estimates do not provide much in the form of specifics.

But information provided by the Bazargan government leads one to the conclusion that the real number was even more modest. Immediately after the revolution, the new government came out with an illustrated "book of martyrs" entitled *Lalehha-ye Enqelab: Yadnameh-e Shaheda (Tulips of Revolution: Memorial for the Martyrs)*—in Iranian iconography tulips represent spring, rebirth, and life-sustaining blood.[97] Totaling 830 illustrated pages, the book gave as much information as was then available. Even though it cast a wide net including demonstrators killed in 1951–53, the book identified only 578 as having been shot in the streets during the turbulent months of 1977–79. Unsurprisingly, the book was soon taken out of circulation. Of the 578 total, the book identified 12 as killed in late 1977; 314 in 1978; 52 in January 1979; and 160 in February 1979. Most had been young: 28 had been in their early teens, 114 in their late teens, 212 in their early twenties, 76 in their late twenties, 44 in their early thirties, 26 in their late thirties, 24 in their early forties, 20 in their late forties, and 19 in their fifties. They also included 7 children and 5 individuals over 60 years. By occupation, the dead included 50 high school students, 44 professionals and white collar employees, 37 manual workers, 28 college students, 19 bazaar employees, 14 military conscripts, 6 clerics, and 5 seminary students. This clearly did not tally with the official line that the revolution was led and made by the clergy. Many of the others were probably recent high school graduates with no fixed occupations. None were described as peasants or farmers. All but 31 were identified as being killed in urban centers—147 in Tehran, 36 in Qom, 20 in Dezful, 19 in Mashed, 17 in Tabriz, 15 in Ahwaz, 13 in Isfahan, 10 in Kermanshah, 10 in Shiraz, 7 in Abadan, 7 in Hamadan, 4 in Yazd, and 4 in Qazvin. Even though women had been conspicuous in the large rallies, they accounted for no more than 10 among the identified dead. In short, the typical victim of street shootings during the revolution was a young urban man. Most sectors of Iranian society opposed the old regime. But the battering ram that brought down that regime was formed mostly of young urban men from working- and lower-middle-class families. They, more than anyone else, formed what Khomeini heralded as Iran's *mostazafen*: the dispossessed, the downtrodden, and the wretched of the earth.

Table 1. Chronology

1977	
October 11–19	Poetry-reading sessions in Tehran
October–November	Bulldozing of Tehran shantytowns
November 15	Protest outside White House
November 16–22	Demonstrations at Industrial University
December 7	University strikes
December 31	Carter congratulates Shah on creating an "island of stability"
1978	
January 7	Editorial attack on Khomeini
January 8–9	Qom demonstrations
February 18–19	Forty-day mourning for Qom dead; casualties in Tabriz
March 30	Forty-day mourning for Tabriz dead; casualties in Yazd and Ahwaz
April 25	Demonstration at Tehran University
May 8	Forty-day mourning for Yazd dead; casualties in Kazerun
May 11	Major demonstration; Shah cancels foreign trip
May 15	Military occupies Tehran University
June 18	Forty-day mourning for Kazerun dead; clashes in many cities
July 28	Forty-day mourning for dead of June 18; casualties in Mashed
August 11	Martial law in Isfahan; mass demonstrations in many cities
August 19	Abadan cinema fire
August 26	Amuzegar replaced by Sharif-Emami as prime minister
September 4	'Aid-e Fetr mass demonstrations in major cities
September 8	Black Friday; martial law declared in Tehran and eleven other cities
September 14	Khomeini and Shariatmadari call for peaceful resistance
September 18	Earthquake in Tabas

(continued)

Table 1. Chronology *(continued)*

1978 *(continued)*	
September 24	Oil workers strike
September 30	Telecommunication workers join general strike
October 5	Khomeini leaves Najaf
October 3–8	General strike including civil servants
October 6	Khomeini arrives in Paris
October 11	Press strikes against censorship
October 13	Censorship lifted
October 16	Forty-day mourning for Black Friday; street clashes
November 1	Huge crowd celebrates release of Taleqani and some one thousand political prisoners
November 4	Students shot toppling Shah's statues in Tehran
November 5	Tehran burns; British embassy ransacked
November 6	Azhari replaces Sharef-Emami as prime minister
	Shah on TV says he has heard the "voice of the people"
	Khomeini calls for an Islamic Republic
November 27	Bank list of millionaires
December 1	First day of Muharram; people on rooftops at night shouting "God is great"
December 2	Troops fire on Tehran crowd
December 3	Khomeini urges soldiers to desert if ordered to fire on crowds
December 10–11	Million-person march in Tehran to Shahyad Square
December 13	Clashes in Isfahan
December 18	General strike (including oil workers)
December 26–28	Clashes in Qazvin and Tehran; university professor killed
December 29	Bakhtiyar appointed prime minister
	Khomeini appoints Bazargan to settle oil strike
December 29–30	Clashes in Mashed; tanks used
1979	
January 5	Khomeini asks oil workers to produce for home consumption
January 13	Shah appoints Regency Council
	Khomeini appoints Revolutionary Council
January 16	Shah leaves
January 19	Shah's statues toppled in Tehran
January 26	Large demonstrations against Bakhtiyar
January 28	Bloody Sunday in Tehran
February 1	Khomeini returns to Tehran; vast crowd greets him
February 5	Khomeini appoints Bazargan as prime minister
February 9	Fighting in Tehran airbase
February 10	Military declares neutrality between Bazargan and Bakhtiyar
February 11	Triumph of the Iranian Revolution

Notes

This article was prepared for the Annual Endowment Lecture at Portland State University in April 2008. I would like to thank Misagh Parsa for commenting on an earlier version.

1. George Rude, *The Crowd in History, 1730–1848* (New York: John Wiley, 1964); *The Crowd in the French Revolution* (New York: Oxford University Press, 1959). See also George Rude, *Ideology and Popular Protest* (New York: Pantheon, 1980).

2. Emanuel Le Roy Ladurie, *Carnival in Romans: A People's Uprising at Romans, 1579–1580*, trans. Mary Feeney (New York: Penguin, 1979).

3. Elizabeth Monroe, "Key Force in the Middle East: The Mob," *New York Times*, August 30, 1953.

4. Edward Said, *Covering Islam: How the Media and the Experts Determine How We See the Rest of the World* (New York: Pantheon, 1981).

5. D. Harney, *The King and the Priest: An Eyewitness Account of the Iranian Revolution* (London: Tauris, 1991), 1, 51.

6. G. Stauth, "Revolution in Spiritless Times: An Essay on Michel Foucault's Enquiries into the Iranian Revolution," *International Sociology* 6 (1991): 159–80. See also Janet Afary and Kevin Anderson, *Foucault and the Iranian Revolution* (Chicago: University of Chicago Press, 2005).

7. Eric Pace, "Shah, Seeking Modern Society, Built Police State and Offended Moslem Faithful," *New York Times,* July 28, 1980.

8. Charles Kurzman, *The Unthinkable Revolution in Iran* (Cambridge, MA: Harvard University Press, 2004), 121.

9. Amnesty International, *Annual Report for 1974* (London: Amnesty International, 1975).

10. International Commission of Jurists, *Human Rights and the Legal System in Iran: Two Reports by W. Bulter and G. Levasseur* (Geneva: International Commission of Jurists, 1976).

11. Writers' Association, *Dah shab (Ten Nights)* (Tehran: Amir Kaber Publication, 1978); N. Pakdaman, "Ten Poetry-Nights," *Kankash*, no. 12 (1995): 125–70.

12. Revolutionary Tudeh Organization, *Zendebad-e jonbesh-e tudeh-ye aban va azar '56 (Long Live the Mass Movement of October-December 1977)* (Rome: Revolutionary Tudeh Publication, 1977), 1–21.

13. "Mr. 'Human Rights' Meets King Torture," *Resistance* 5 (1977).

14. Marc Bloch, *Réflexions d'une historien sur les fausses nouvelles de la guerre (Reflections of a Historian on False News of the War)* (Paris: Editions Allia, 1999).

15. William Branigin, "Iranian Riot Police Clash with Student Protest March," *Washington Post*, November 18, 1977.

16. "Attack on the Industrial University," *Payam-e mojahed*, no. 52 (1977).

17. "A Chronology of Major Events in Iranian Turmoil," *New York Times*, February 12, 1979.

18. "Iran and the Black and Red Imperialism," *Ettela'at*, January 7, 1978.

19. Liberation Movement, *Qiyam-e hamaseh-e Qom va Tabriz (The Epic Uprising of Qom and Tabriz)* (Belleville, IL: Liberation Movement Press, 1978), 1–139.

20. Liberation Movement, "Report on the Qom Massacre," *Payam-e mojahed*, no. 53 (1978).

21. "Report on the Tabriz Demonstration," *Payam-e mojahed*, no. 54 (1978).

22. Revolutionary Tudeh Organization, *Jaydanbad khaterat-e qiyam-e kunen-e Tabriz (Long Live the Memory of the Bloody Uprising of Tabriz)* (Rome: Tudeh Revolutionary Organization, 1978), 1–40; see also Mojahedin Organization, *Qiyam-e khunen-e Tabriz (The Bloody Uprising of Tabriz)* (Aden: Iranian Student Confederation, 1978), 1–16.

23. *Times*, May 11, 1978.

24. Paul Hofmann, "Behind Iranian Riots," *New York Times*, March 5, 1978.

25. "Tabriz on Fire," *Payam-e mojahed*, no. 53 (1978).

26. "Six Hundred and Fifty Arrested in Tabriz," *Iran Times*, March 3, 1978.

27. "The Yazd Massacre," *Payam-e mojahed*, no. 57 (1978).

28. Soroush Research Group, *Taqvem-e tarekh-e enqelab-e islam-ye Iran* (*Calendar of the Islamic Revolution in Iran*) (Tehran: Soroush Press, 1989), 108.

29. S. Nabavi, "Abadan, 19th August, Cinema Rex," *Cheshmandaz* no. 20 (1999): 105–27. After the revolution, an official investigation, set up because of pressure from the relatives of victims, discovered that the arsonists were a handful of religious fanatics from Isfahan working on their own. In a blatant non sequitur, the clerical judge concluded that since the deed was so diabolical the perpetuators could not possibly be Muslims; he pronounced them secret Marxists.

30. William Branigin, "Abadan Mood Turns Sharply against the Shah," *Washington Post*, August 26, 1978.

31. Anthony McDermott, "Peacock Throne under Pressure," *Financial Times*, September 12, 1978.

32. "Huge Processions from Four Corners of Tehran," *Kayhan*, September 5, 1978.

33. E. Baqi, *Tarekh-e shafah-ye enqelab* (*Oral History of the Revolution*) (Tehran: National Library, 1982), 1–145.

34. M. Golabdarahi, *Lahzah-ha* (*Snapshots*) (Tehran: Kayhan Publishing, 1979), 1–347.

35. A. Whitley, "Tehran Demonstration," *Financial Times*, September 8, 1978.

36. L. Thurgood, "Why the Shah Must 'Liberalise,'" *Guardian*, October 1, 1978.

37. "The Shah's Land," *Time*, September 18, 1978.

38. William Sullivan, *Mission to Iran* (New York: Norton, 1981), 159–60.

39. M. Mokhtari, "Investigation into Slogans during the Uprising," *Aghaz-e now*, nos. 3–4 (1986–87): 40–52. See also M. H. Panahi, *Jami'ah shinasi-i shi arha-yi inqilab-i Islami-i Iran* (*An Introduction to the Islamic Revolution in Iran and its Slogans*) (Tehran: Al-Hoda Publications, 2000).

40. Harney, *Priest and the King*, 22–23.

41. *Kayhan*, September 5, 1978.

42. J. Gueyras, "Iran's Black Friday," *Le monde*, September 11, 1978.

43. Foreign Broadcasting Information Services, September 11, 1978; and Soroush Research Group, *Calendar*, 137.

44. "Calendar of Events," *Khabarnameh*, no. 56 (1979).

45. "Confidential Report on September 8th Massacre," *Ettela'at*, April 9, 1979.

46. Janet Bauer, "Poor Women and Social Consciousness in Revolutionary Iran," in *Women and Revolution in Iran*, ed. G. Nashat (Boulder, CO: Westview, 1983), 158.

47. Harney, *Priest and the King*, 19, 25.

48. Ibid., 76.

49. Sa'ed, *Divarha sukhan meguyand* (*The Walls Speak*) (Tehran: Movement for Freedom Press, 1979).

50. Tony Allaway, "Shah's Foes Strike by Cutting Oil Exports," *Christian Science Monitor*, November 5, 1978.

51. Andrew Whitley, "The Struggle to Retain His Grip," *Financial Times*, October 13, 1978.

52. Sullivan, *Mission to Iran*, 156.

53. Liz Thurgood, "Why the Shah Must 'Liberalise,'" *Guardian*, October 1, 1978.

54. Andrew Whitley, personal communication. At the time Whitley served as the main correspondent in Tehran of both the BBC and the *Financial Times*.

55. Society of Employees of the Central Bank, "Thievery Statistics," *Khabarnameh*, no. 56 (1979).
56. Harney, *Priest and the King*, 92–93.
57. William Branigin, "Shah and Family Have Amassed One of World's Biggest Fortunes," *Washington Post*, January 17, 1979.
58. Ann Crittenden, "Bankers Say Shah's Fortune Is Well above a Billion," *New York Times*, January 10, 1979.
59. Tony Allaway, "Uprising in Tehran," *Christian Science Monitor,* November 6, 1978.
60. Harney, *Priest and the King*, 59, 63.
61. Anthony Parsons, *The Pride and the Fall* (London: Jonathan Cape, 1974), 93–126.
62. Golabdarahi, *Lahzah-ha*, 187.
63. Sullivan, *Mission to Iran*, 215.
64. J. Morris, "Thousands Acclaim Iran Exiled Religious Leader," *Los Angeles Times*, December 11, 1978.
65. J. Morris, "Iran Demonstrators Openly Urge Death to the Shah," *Los Angeles Times*, December 12, 1978.
66. A. Whitley and S. Henderson, "Million in Peaceful March against the Shah," *Financial Times*, December 11, 1978.
67. A. Qarabaghi, *Haqayeq darbareh behran-e Iran (The Truth about the Iranian Crisis)* (Paris: Sahil Publications, 1983), 87.
68. Harney, *Priest and the King*, 116.
69. Morris, "Iran Demonstrators Openly Urge Death to the Shah."
70. "Resolution Passed at the 'Ashura Rally," *Khabarnameh*, no. 26 (1978).
71. William Branigin, "Bloody Isfahan: Rumor Gone Wild," *Washington Post*, December 13, 1978.
72. Golabdarahi, *Lahzah-ha*, 44.
73. Jonathan C. Randal, "In Iran, a Throng Votes No," *Washington Post*, December 12, 1978; R. W. Apple, "Big Tehran Crowd Marches Peaceably," *New York Times*, December 11, 1978; and Apple, "Reading Iran's Next Chapter," *New York Times*, December 13, 1978.
74. Apple, "Big Tehran Crowd Marches Peaceably."
75. Apple, "Reading Iran's Next Chapter."
76. Tony Allaway, "Iran Demonstrates," *Christian Science Monitor*, December 12, 1978.
77. Golabdarahi, *Lahzah-ha*, 178.
78. R. W. Apple, "A Million Marchers Rally," *New York Times*, January 18, 1979.
79. G. Godsell, "Tehran's Joy—and Grim Resolve," *Christian Science Monitor*, January 22, 1979.
80. BBC, February 1, 1979.
81. R. W. Apple, "Khomeini Arrives in Tehran," *New York Times*, February 1, 1979.
82. J. Markham, "Joy Explodes in Tehran Streets," *New York Times*, February 2, 1979.
83. R. W. Apple, "Khomeini Threatens to Arrest Bakhtiar," *New York Times*, February 2, 1979.
84. Nicholas Gage, "Surge of Support for Islamic Rule," *New York Times*, February 8, 1979.
85. Nicholas Gage, "Over a Million March in Tehran," *New York Times*, February 9, 1979.
86. J. Markham, "Ayatollah Steps up Pressure," *New York Times*, February 4, 1979.
87. Y. Ibrahim, "Scores Dead in Iran," *New York Times*, February 11, 1979.
88. Qarabaghi, *Truth about the Iranian Crisis*, 55–65.
89. BBC, February 11, 1979.
90. Y. Ibrahim, "Jubilation, Anxiety, and Sadness Mix as Tehran Erupts in Frenzy," *New York Times*, February 12, 1979.

91. P. Balta and D. Pouchin, "La victoire de la revolution en Iran" ("The Victory of Revolution in Iran"), *Le monde*, February 13, 1979.

92. A. Whitley, "Iran Slides towards Anarchy," *Financial Times*, February 13, 1979.

93. For such incidents, see M. Parsa, *Social Origins of the Iranian Revolution* (New Brunswick, NJ: Rutgers University Press, 1989), 229–37.

94. Ayatollah Lahuti, "The Iranian Revolution Was Nourished by the Blood of 67,311 Martyrs," *Ettela'at*, May 21, 1979.

95. A. Ashraf and A. Banuazizi, "The State, Classes, and Modes of Mobilization in the Iranian Revolution," *State, Culture, and Society*, 1 (1985): 3–40.

96. E. Baqi, "Statistics on Those Sacrifices in the Revolution," *Iran emruz*, July 30, 2003. See also C. Kadivar, "Deaths in Revolutionary Iran," *Ruzegar-e now*, August 8, 2003.

97. Society for Islamic Charity, *Lalehha-ye enqelab: Yadnameh-e shaheda* (*Tulips of Revolution: Memorial for the Martyrs*) (Tehran: Society of Islamic Charity Publication, 1979), 1–830. The statistics that follow do not include those who were not individually identified.

Khomeini and the Iranian Revolution

in the Egyptian Press

From Fascination to Condemnation

Hanan Hammad

In March 1980, while the former shah of Iran was undergoing surgery at the Military Hospital in Cairo, protests broke out on several university campuses across the country. Protestors were outraged because the Egyptian president, Anwar Sadat, had invited the deposed Shah to spend his final days in Egypt. One student lost his life and dozens were arrested when demonstrators against both the Shah and Sadat were confronted by riot police. News of the protests did not appear in the official daily press, which instead carried news of the Shah's health and Sadat's hospitality. The newly established opposition press not only publicized what the official organs ignored, or tried to hide, but also refuted Sadat's claims about the "moral superiority" behind housing the terminally ill Shah. The socialist paper *al-Sha'b* believed that granting the Shah refuge countered the Egyptian national interest because it would burden Egypt with protecting the Shah and worsen relations between the peoples of Egypt and Iran. The Islamist publications *al-Da'wa* and *al-I'tisām* added that housing the Shah contradicted Islam. The three publications had found their way to the newsstand with Sadat's blessing late in the 1970s when he had plans to transform the one-party system into a multiparty system. While he had expected these publications to work in his favor, they ultimately lent voice to his secular and religious opposition. The public disagreement between Sadat and the press opens

Radical History Review
Issue 105 (Fall 2009)   DOI 10.1215/01636545-2009-003
© 2009 by MARHO: The Radical Historians' Organization, Inc.

questions about how Sadat's view of the Iranian Revolution and the former Pahlavi regime differed from those of various political factions, how the regime and the opposition utilized the press to gain popular support, and to what extent the Egyptian press was able to reflect dissenting views under authoritarian rule.

This article analyzes how the Egyptian press covered the Iranian Revolution and the Khomeini regime between 1978 and 1981. It discusses which issues related to the revolution and the revolutionary regime the press discussed, as well as the attitudes of different groups of Egyptian politicians and intellectuals toward the revolution as these attitudes found expression in the press. Coverage of the Iranian Revolution and the resulting Islamic regime provides an excellent opportunity to study the complex relationship between the Egyptian press and the state under Sadat (r. 1970–81). In addition to having significance across the globe and in the Muslim Middle East, the revolution became a controversial domestic issue in Egyptian politics for several reasons. Prior to the Iranian Revolution, Sadat had stood as a staunch ally and supporter of Muhammad Reza Shah Pahlavi and saw him as a model third world ruler able to survive by allying himself with the West rather than confronting it. Iran under the Shah was the only Middle Eastern state at the time that maintained cordial relations with Israel. Sadat believed the Shah would be helpful in his plans for rapprochement with the West and peace negotiations with Israel. Therefore Sadat's enmity toward the regime of Ayatollah Ruhollah Khomeini, once the latter cut off relations with Cairo in late April 1979, was equally unflinching. Khomeini challenged Sadat's efforts to generate legitimacy from religion by claiming that the Egyptian-Israeli agreement contradicted Islam. The Iranian boycott of Cairo strengthened the regional isolation imposed on Egypt by the Arab countries that had rejected the peace treaty between Egypt and Israel. The Islamic Revolution coincided with many changes in Egypt, including the country's transition to a multiparty system, the end of the state monopoly over the press, and the growing influence of Egyptian Islamist groups in both the political and the sociocultural spheres. Despite sectarian differences, Egyptian Sunni Islamists celebrated the success of the Iranian Revolution as if it were their own. They not only supported the Shi'i Iranians against the secular Sunni Iraqi regime, but they also condemned the Sunni Iranian separatists, even when the latter were Arabs or Kurds.

This study argues that domestic politics and the regional consequences of Sadat's visit to Jerusalem in 1977 shaped the coverage of the Iranian Revolution in the Egyptian press and determined which issues related to the revolution would be covered and which ones would not. Despite official state control, the Egyptian press was able to represent diverse Egyptian attitudes toward the Pahlavi regime and the revolutionary Islamic Republic. This spectrum of opinion ranged from extreme pro-revolutionaries to those who followed the official Egyptian line. Based on a comprehensive and systematic survey of both official and opposition newspapers, this study argues that Egyptian intellectuals with different positions on the political spectrum showed ambivalence toward the Islamic Republic and the revolution that spawned it. The nearly universal enthusiasm of secular leftists, Sadat loyalists, and Islamists immediately following the revolution eventually gave way to skepticism and even condemnation of the Islamic regime.[1] Yet the government's view on Iran was only reflected in the writings of the top editors of the official press and did not color the entire coverage either in the official or the opposition publications. This argument contradicts the views of Fahmi Houwaidi who maintains that the Egyptian press and Arab media have reflected the government position toward Iran since the revolution.[2]

The Egyptian press was slow in recognizing the Iranian Revolution. Only the leftist newspaper *al-Ahālī* properly interpreted the mass demonstrations in Iran in early 1978 as a mass revolution led by clergymen. Contrary to Rudi Matthee's claim that the Egyptian secular left did not give due credit to the religious elements of the revolution, this study proves that *al-Ahālī* preceded all other publications, including those of the Islamists, in realizing the nature of the religious leadership of the revolution.[3] It was the first newspaper in Egypt to publish an interview with Khomeini and to introduce him to readers as the leader of the revolutionary movement in Iran. Egyptian Islamists proved as slow as many others in understanding the developments in Iran throughout 1978. In the fall of 1978, the Islamist press hailed steps taken by the last government of the Shah to appease the discontented masses on the assumption that Pahlavi Iran was heading toward a more Islamic system.[4] From late 1978 on, the Iranian Revolution became an important event worthy of coverage, yet issues and attitudes toward the revolution differed before and after Khomeini consolidated his power. The attitude writers held toward domestic Egyptian issues served as a good prediction of how they would view the Iranian Revolution.

Egyptian Issues in an Iranian Revolution

In general, the Egyptian press focused on the root causes of the Islamic Revolution. There was a relative consensus among leftists, liberals, secularists, and religious writers in both the official and the opposition press that the main causes of the Shah's downfall were his proclivity for dictatorship and corruption, along with a failed economy and alliances with Israel and the United States. Yet we can trace differences as well. Egyptian leftists accused Sadat's policies of favoring the rich, ignoring the interests of the poor masses, and increasing dependency on the West, namely, the United States. Unsurprisingly, therefore, the leftist opposition in *al-Ahālī* and the "leftist" state-owned magazine *Rūz al-Yūsuf* also criticized the Shah's social and economic policies. The leftist press saw the revolution as arising from the Shah's autocratic policies, combined with economic mismanagement and corruption. They held the imprisonment of thousands of political activists, an inflation rate of 40 percent, and a wide gap between a small, wealthy elite and the poor masses to be some of the primary reasons behind the Revolution.[5] The leftist publications argued that the Shah wasted the country's resources on huge and unnecessary military expenditures. They criticized economic changes that favored foreign companies and that inevitably led to the collapse of indigenous industries.[6] Both Islamic and secular writers cited the abandonment of Islamic traditions, the imitation of the West, and the Shah's alliance with the United States and Israel as issues.[7] Yet Islamist coverage also attacked Iranian Bahāʾīs and Jews, something that did not exist in the rest of the Egyptian press. Although Khomeini received the head of the Iranian Jewish community and made assurances concerning Jewish rights, the Egyptian Islamist press considered Bahāʾīs and Jews partners of the Shah in stealing the fortunes of Muslim Iran and oppressing Muslim Iranians.[8] It saw them as tools of foreign enemies rather than as part of the Iranian ethnic and religious mosaic.[9] It conveyed the vision of the Muslim Brotherhood, along with that of other political Islamists, that Muslims were facing a religious war waged by non-Muslims, namely Jews, Christians, and Bahāʾīs. The Islamist press focused on the adoption of what it considered Westernization. It criticized the regime for opening dance and cinema academies, which it saw as cutting off the connection with the Iranian Islamic past, thus imprisoning Islam inside mosques and turning men of religion into state employees.[10] It accused the Shah of dragging women and Iranian society into moral decay, while failing to achieve technological progress.

Liberals focused on the lack of democracy and on the human rights violations by the Shah's notorious internal security force, SAVAK. Nine out of ten causes for the revolution given by Mustafā Amīn were related to the absence of liberties.[11] While liberals and leftists were concerned with the lack of liberties for all the Iranian opposition groups, the Islamist press restricted the discussion to brutality against Iranian Islamists. In their view, Navvāb Safavī, the leader of the militant Fedaʾiyan-e Islam group executed in 1955, was the greatest martyr in the cause of freedom in modern Iranian history and Safavī, not Muhammad Musaddiq, was the national hero of Iran during the fifties.[12] Overall, the Egyptian press thought the Shah's policies responsible for the massive discontent that led to the revolution. The *al-Musawar* magazine and the *al-Ahrār* newspaper were the only exceptions in this respect. *Al-Musawar* was a state-owned magazine that always closely followed the official line. *Al-Ahrār*, meaning "the Liberals," was the newspaper of the right-wing al-Ahrār Party. Although al-Ahrār was formally an opposition party, it supported Sadat's free-market policies, advocated a more aggressively capitalist economy, and supported a rapid rapprochement with the West. Both *al-Musawar* and *al-Ahrār* focused on the "foreign factor" and accused external forces such as France, the United States, and the Soviet Union of promulgating the revolution. They adopted the Shah's claim that the revolutionaries are "a coalition of Muslim extremists and liberals whose aim is the destruction of everything achieved by the Shah."[13] An obsessive fear of communism caused them to agree in their assessment of an impending communist threat and to ignore the domestic grief caused by the Shah's policy. The two publications did not change their position after the success of the Iranian Revolution and the declaration of the Islamic Republic.[14]

The religious leadership and the Islamic slogans of the Iranian Revolution gained importance in the Egyptian press because they coincided with the return of Egyptian political Islam after two decades of suppression. Sadat had meant to mobilize Islamists against leftists and Nasserists; Sadat himself employed Islam as a source of legitimacy after his popularity had been damaged by the Food Riot of January 1977. He called himself "the believer president" and was keen to be photographed during Friday prayers and other religious rituals. He used the slogan, "building the state of faith and science." In 1979, he amended the constitution, making Shari'a, Islamic law, the main source of legislation and adding religion as a mandatory subject to the education curriculum. The official media served as Sadat's channel to deliver his image as a pious president. The media also carried his speeches, which were antagonistic to the Egyptian left and the Soviet Union. As I mentioned above, *al-Ahālī* preceded all other publications in underlining the religious leadership of the revolution. After *al-Ahālī* was shut down, the Marxist Philip Gallāb of *Rūz al-Yūsuf* continued its mission and explained how Shi'ism facilitated the emergence of the ayatollahs' religious leadership and how the brutality of the Shah's regime and of his American-equipped forces made mosques and Shi'i clergy the opposition's refuge.[15]

The Islamist press was as slow as most of the official publications in recognizing the Islamic leadership. Only in January 1979 did the ayatollahs Khomeini, Hosayn-'Ali Muntazarī, and Mahmud Talqānī emerge indisputably as religious leaders of the movement. The Muslim Brotherhood and its press organs saw in the Iranian Revolution new proof that Islam, not Western ideologies, could infuse Muslims with enough power and enthusiasm to overthrow a repressive regime supported by a superpower. They found in the revolution inspiration and hope that they could defeat secular ideologies and achieve Islamic progress.[16] Such organizations considered God's support the real cause of the revolution's success.[17] This view also ultimately found its way into the official press. The Sufi Ahmad Bahjat of *al-Ahrām* called it "a gift from God to Muslims on the fourteen hundredth anniversary of the revelation of the Qu'ran."[18] The Egyptian diplomat Mustafā al-Fiqī, who embraced Arab nationalism, wrote about the new example of popular revolution under Islamic leadership, which proved that Islam could play a role in politics much more substantial than simply applying *al-hudūd al-shar'īah* (Islamic punishment code).[19]

From Celebration to Ambivalence

That celebratory view of the Islamic leadership faded away a few months after Khomeini's return to Tehran. After the triumph of the revolution, revolutionary groups and parties divided, and Khomeini's powerful followers worked to eliminate liberals and leftists. Although there were brief periods of free press and assembly, Revolutionary Committees and Hezbollah, the Party of God, increasingly cracked down on individual and political freedoms. Both groups constituted extremist "bands of thugs" that emerged among Khomeini's followers on his return to Tehran in February 1979.[20] Egyptian intellectuals grew skeptical over these developments. Revolutionary Committees comprising mostly unemployed and uneducated fanatical young men gave themselves the liberty to break into private homes to arrest whoever might have possessed alcoholic beverages. Their interference in people's daily lives was condemned even by the Egyptian author Houwaidi, who was a staunch proponent of the Revolution.[21]

Ambivalence and skepticism about the revolution started with the revolutionary violence and the execution campaigns against officials of the previous regime and against revolutionaries opposing Khomeini. The end of diplomatic relations between Cairo and Tehran due to Sadat's agreement with Israel aggravated the situation. Even those who shared Khomeini's negative view of the Egyptian-Israeli peace agreement and had shown a great support for the revolution now found themselves at odds with the new regime in Tehran.[22] As early as March 1979, the Sufi Mustafā Mahmūd urged the new regime in Iran to give up fanaticism and adopt a political system compatible with the spirit of tolerance and modernity in Islam, instead of what he called an "iron, merciless dictatorship."[23] Mahmūd protested the employment of the Qur'an to serve the interests of those who loved power and argued that the Islamic system did not contradict Western democracy. The liberal Wafd activist Wahīd Ra'fat called the ongoing executions "a human rights ordeal" and "assassinations and murders" because defendants lacked judicial rights. He concluded that the revolutionary regime contravened Islamic law and was only "the reign of black terrorism and the law of savagery."[24] Anīs Mansūr, who previously considered the revolution a victory of humane and truly Islamic values over corruption,[25] expressed bitter frustration with the revolution a few months later. Khomeini had become, according to Mansūr, "a voice of torture or a torturing whip,"[26] "thirsty for blood and revenge."[27] Echoing the writings of the liberal secular lawyer Ra'fat, the Marxist Salāh Hāfiz, the Sadat loyalist Mansūr, and the Sufi Mahmūd called the Revolutionary Committees "committees of torture" because they broke into private homes, arresting and then executing people after only superficial investigations. These writers were in agreement about criticizing Khomeini's revolutionary regime, although they differed on everything else. Hāfiz wrote that "the Ayatollahs did not hesitate to interpret Islam as if it was a religion of equality in slaughtering; slaughtering Arabs and Kurds, slaughtering Muslims and non-Muslims, and slaughtering enemies and partners of the Revolution. They have slaughtered the traditions and instructions of Islam."[28] That commentary came after Hezbollah had carried out a major attack against the Iranian left in September 1979, followed by the government's military attacks on Kurdish autonomists.

The executions and violence did not, however, lack advocates in both the official and opposition press. Bahjat excused the "revolutionary executions" and employed Qura'nic symbols claiming that "if the Revolution of Iran is compared with the French or the Russian Revolutions, it will seem to be benevolent and absent of bloodshed."[29] He justified the execution of sixty-four people during the first month after Khomeini's return, saying they were responsible for killing thousands. The Islamist press made use of these same arguments.[30] It quoted Ayatollah Sādiq Khalkhālī, who gave the execution verdicts and was known as the new regime's "hanging judge," saying, "I followed the judgments of Islam in my verdicts," and accusing his critics of being "Zionist imperialists."[31]

The Iranian Revolution triggered interest among Egyptian Sunnis about Shiʿism. The Egyptian press tried to educate readers and to explain how Shiʿism facilitated the emergence of popular leadership among the ulama, the Muslim clergy.[32] Despite its good intentions, the Egyptian press relied on Sunni sources to explain Shiʿi theology and beliefs. It was doubtless more convenient to interview Egyptian Sunni ulama and quote works by Egyptian Sunni authors.[33] This resulted in a misrepresentation of some Shiʿi views.[34] To prove good will, corrections and explanations by Arab Shiʿi scholars were welcomed and published.[35] When Iranian students took the staffers of the American embassy in Tehran hostage, the official press became Shiʿi bashers. Shiʿism was held responsible for the perceived mistakes of the revolutionary regime.[36] The official press employed sectarian differences to deny the compatibility of Khomeinism with Islam. To achieve this, some writers used the beliefs of some Ghulāt Shiʿis, who represent a small fragment of Shiʿis, as if they were shared by the Twelver Shiʿis, who form the vast majority of Iranians and world Shiʿis. *Ghulāt Shiʿi*, in Arabic, literally means "the extremist Shiʿi," a descriptor derived from their extreme religious, rather than political, views. Attributing the beliefs of some Ghulāt Shiʿis to the Twelver Shiʿis aimed to distort Shiʿism and widened the gap between Sunnis and Shiʿis as a whole. For example, Abd al-'Azīz Khamīs, the editor handpicked by Sadat for *Rūz al-Yūsuf*, wrote on November 19, 1979: "Sunnis, the *Madhhab* [Islamic school of law] of the majority, condemned Shiʿis for believing that Gabriel committed a mistake in delivering the message of God and delivered it to Muhammad instead of 'Ali Ibn Abī Tālib, the cousin of the prophet. This is what makes many Sunnis consider all different Shiʿi sects deviants and apostates."[37]

Interestingly, the rapprochement between revolutionary Iran and the Syrian regime, which was at odds with Cairo, was laid to Shiʿism having brought the 'Alawi Shiʿi Hāfiz al-Assad in line with Shiʿi Iran.[38] This made for an unreasonable claim because the Syrian regime was secular, and a wide gap exists between the beliefs and dogma of the 'Alawi sect and the Imami sect, to which Iranian Shiʿis belong; the former are widely considered heretical by the latter. The official press used *'Alawi* as a derogatory term for the Syrian Ba'th regime. Two motives precipitated raised sectarian division decades after al-Azhar in Cairo, which is regarded by many as the most prestigious Sunni institute in the world, gave a fatwa legitimizing the worship of Islam according to both the Shi'i Imami and Shi'i Zaydi schools of law. First, there was the defense of Islam and the attempt to avoid the embarrassment caused by the hostage crisis. The Egyptian press felt a duty to reverse the campaign in the Western media against Islam and all Muslims by singling out Shi'is as "bad Muslims" or merely heretics. Second, the official press explained the rift between Sadat and the Islamic regime in Tehran by emphasizing sectarian differences, claiming that Khomeini had violated Islam and even portraying him as a *Jahili*, or someone completely ignorant of Islam.[39] Most items dealing with this issue were written by the top editors in the official press. They aimed to delegitimize Khomeini's regime and to brand it as harmful to Islam. These writers did not oppose political uses of Islam; indeed, they tried to prove that it was Sadat's regime that truly represented Islam.

A New Regime in Tehran and Old Issues in Cairo

After two decades of severe repression under Gamal Abdel Nasser, political Islamists were allowed and encouraged to return to the political arena in Egypt under Sadat in the mid-1970s. While they were rebuilding their institutions, reissuing their publications, and reorganizing themselves on the grassroots level, the Iranian Revolution surprised them as much as it surprised the world. For the Egyptian Islamists, the revolution served as a great source of inspiration, and it emboldened them to try to repeat its success in Sunni Egypt. They identified with the revolutionary forces and dismissed any sectarian differences between their Sunni *madhhab* and Iranian Shi'ism. Their unconditional endorsement continued regardless of any potentially problematic developments inside Iran. Despite attacks on Sunni Arabs and Kurds, the rapprochement between Iran and a Syrian regime that had massacred the Syrian Muslim Brothers in the summer of 1979, and even the outbreak of war between Iran and Iraq, the Egyptian Islamists continued to support the revolution. The Egyptian Islamists considered the success of the Iranian Revolution their own. They did not differentiate between the Sunni and Shi'i *madhhabs* and believed "Shi'ism in Iran means Islam."[40] The Islamist press celebrated the Islamic Constitution in Iran and emphasized that it was completely compatible with Islamic law. *Al-Da'wa* shifted attention away from articles characterizing Iran as a Shi'i state to show how the constitution granted Sunnis rights to follow their family laws and to study their *madhhab* where they constituted a majority.[41] It underlined the entirely theoretical possibility of a Sunni becoming president of the Islamic Republic.[42] Meanwhile, it ignored references to the Hidden Imam and *Marja'-i Taqlīd*, two doctrines recognized only by Shi'i that fundamentally differentiate Shi'i and Sunni *madhhabs*. The Hidden Imam for Twelver Shi'is is the last of the twelve legitimate successors of the Prophet Muhammad. *Marja'-i Taqlīd*, literally, "a reference point for emulation," is a religious authority who through his learning and probity is qualified to be followed in all points of religious practice and law by the generality of Shi'is. For the Islamist press, the recognition of non-Muslim minorities, except the "heretical" Bahā'īs, in the constitution gave proof of its democratic nature. The press also hailed the Iranian experience in "Islamic economics" and dismissed doubts among the Western media and Iranian opposition about the capacities of the clergy to solve socioeconomic problems. The main argument of the Islamists was "faith alone is able to achieve miracles."[43] Here, the Muslim Brotherhood applied its slogan, "al-Islam huwa al-hall [Islam is the solution]." It maintained that an Islamic regime could solve all problems of any Muslim society. The Islamist press did not critically examine the application of the constitution, offered its full endorsement, and emphasized that 98.2 percent of Iranians had chosen to become an Islamic Republic.[44] It intentionally omitted that "the Islamic Republic" had been the only alternative offered on the ballot and that the religious leadership had refused to give the choice of a democratic republic or a constitutional monarchy.

The application of the Islamic legal code was found problematic and controversial in the Egyptian press. While the Islamist press enthusiastically welcomed it, the official press did not pay adequate attention to the issue. The daily press covered Iranian women's protests against the imposition of the Islamic veil, hijab, which requires women to cover head to toe except for their faces and hands. Yet only very few commentaries dealt with the issue. *Al-Ahrām* ran two cartoons in favor of anti-hijab Iranian women by the leftist poet and cartoonist Salāh Jāhīn.[45] Interestingly, the first person who dared clearly and openly write against Khomeini's Islamic dress code was the Sufi Mahmūd. In mid-March 1979, Mahmūd criticized the imposition of the hijab and the banning of song and other fine arts such as painting and sculpture.[46] Although he supported building an Islamic political system, he defended arts as a means of educating humanity and considered forcing women to wear Islamic garb and to withdraw from the workplace as "iron, merciless dictatorship." Hāfiz of *Rūz al-Yūsuf* took the argument one step further and criticized both the Iranian ayatollahs and the official Egyptian sheikhs for their stand against women's rights. Hāfiz wrote that government sheikhs in Egypt advocated considering women as nothing more than genitals, while the country needed women to work in fields, hospitals, and elsewhere. He drew a parallel between what the Egyptian official clergy advocated and policies adopted by the Iranian ayatollahs. "She [Egypt] is a state where half of the economy depends on women's work and half of the culture seeks to isolate women. . . . In Iran the Revolution has chosen the reign of ayatollahs. . . . They have slaughtered the traditions and instructions of Islam."[47] Hāfiz's and Mahmūd's articles were courageous, because a large segment of Egyptian society was getting more Islamized due to the intensive propaganda of both political Islamists and the Egyptian regime itself. The veil was gaining in popularity, and calls for eliminating women from the workplace and for the implementation of

Hudūd, the Islamic punishments, emerged in parliament, on public television, and in schools.[48] Mahmūd's courage, in particular, is remarkable when compared to the stance of other authors who declined to deal openly and directly with the issue. Usāmah Mansī of *Rūz al-Yūsuf*, for example, neutrally offered the views of different Islamic schools of thought concerning music, without expressing a preference.[49] Mansī's neutrality appears rather odd given that he covered cinema and music for a secular magazine.[50] His reputation as a Sufi provided Mahmūd an opportunity to criticize the Iranian imposition of the Islamic codes without fearing the accusation of being "an anti-Islam secularist" or a "pro-communism infidel."

Decades of Western imperialism and the Cold War had made the Egyptian press suspicious of the policies of the two superpowers in the Middle East. Leftists, conservatives, secularists, and Islamists all equally blamed the U.S. for supporting the tyrannical Shah.[51] The official press, Islamists, and the right-wing opposition also worried that the Soviet Union might take advantage of the revolution to increase its influence in Iran and the rest of the Middle East. They considered Soviet support of the revolution a cover for a plan to control Iran through the communist Tudeh Party.[52] The active participation of the party in the revolution and the increasing Soviet penetration of Afghanistan preceding the Soviet invasion augmented these fears. However, the Tudeh Party was at no time allowed to play a role in the new government.[53] Sadat's regime shared the Islamists' antipathy toward the Soviets. Sadat was seeking to build an alliance with the United States while fighting communism. The hostage crisis at the American embassy in Tehran became a turning point for how the Egyptian press looked at U.S.-Iranian relations. The previous consensus about the "negative" role of the United States in Iran disappeared and the issue turned into a heated controversy. The crisis broke out when a group of Iranian students occupied the American embassy in Tehran and took its staffers hostage on November 4, 1979, to force the United States to surrender the Shah, who had just arrived in New York for medical treatment. The Palestinian Liberation Organization's (PLO) mediation to end the crisis peacefully failed, as did an American attempt to free the hostages by military force. The crisis continued for more than a year, and the hostages were released on Ronald Reagan's inauguration day, January 20, 1981. The official press in Egypt took the American side, while the opposition press took the Iranian side. Anti-Khomeini writers believed that taking the Americans hostage was a great favor to the United States and to President Jimmy Carter, who was campaigning for the presidential election.[54] Khamīs of *Rūz al-Yūsuf* considered the crisis to have helped the Americans overcome the "Vietnam complex" and to have encouraged them to attack whoever threatened their interests.[55] Sabrī Abū al-Majd of *al-Musawar* concluded: "By keeping the hostages, Khomeini succeeded in promoting the American presence in the Middle East."[56]

The official press commonly called the American staffers "a group of innocents" and demonized the Iranian students and Khomeini.[57] Diverging from the dominant line that saw religious fanaticism, even terrorism, behind breaking into the U.S. embassy, Gallāb considered the reception of the Shah in the United States the direct reason for the crisis. He held the former secretary of state Henry Kissinger and the businessman David Rockefeller responsible for fueling the anti-American sentiments among Iranians by putting pressure on the Carter administration to permit the Shah entry into the United States, despite reliable official reports warning it might provoke a crisis.[58] Gallāb, who opposed Sadat's regime, did not justify the occupation of the embassy or the taking of hostages. On the other hand, Fathī Radwān, one of the most prominent independent intellectuals of the past century, hailed the Iranian students for challenging the superpower.[59] Radwān's stand resembled that of the leftist opposition paper *al-Sha'b*, which justified the Iranian step as necessary to force the United States to surrender the Shah so that he could be tried for crimes of mass murder and theft.[60]

In addition to backing the surrender of the Shah, the Islamist press completely adopted the Iranian contention that the American staffers were spies and consequently did not have diplomatic immunity.[61] Although both Islamists and secular activists hoped to see the hostages freed, they opposed the American attempts to do so by force or by imposing an economic embargo on Iran.[62] The chairman of the Socialist Labor Party (SLP), Ibrāhīm Shukrī, harshly criticized Sadat's offer to facilitate any American effort to release the hostages. Shukrī warned that such an offer hurt the Egyptian interests.[63] This open confrontation with Sadat thwarted Sadat's original purpose for establishing the SLP as a small loyalist opposition party in 1978.[64] Although the party faithfully fulfilled that role for a short time, it felt its ambition to practice real opposition politics encouraged when several Wafd activists joined the party after the Wafd Party dissolved under pressure from Sadat. The disappearance of the Wafd Party and the continuing suppression of the al-Tajammu' Progressive Party provided the SLP with a chance to lead the opposition if it distanced itself from Sadat's policies.[65]

Fears of destabilizing the already unstable Middle East overshadowed the coverage of the Iranian Revolution in the Egyptian press. Two views coexisted over how an unstable Iran would affect the Arab-Israeli conflict. The first view held that the overthrow of the Shah had increased the importance of Egypt as an American ally in its anticommunist efforts and in maintaining stability in the Middle East. Consequently, the Egyptian position in the tough peace negotiations with Israel should improve. Others expected Israel to take advantage of the situation and to claim that it was the only secure ally of the United States in the region, putting the country in a stronger position vis-à-vis the Arabs. Alongside these two views, the Egyptian press expressed a euphoric wave of hope that the new regime in Tehran would add strength to Arab power in confrontations with Israel. This short-lived hope was generated by anti-Israel statements from the revolutionary leaders, their boycott of Israel, and because they housed representatives of the PLO in the former

Israeli embassy in Tehran in February 1979. Pro-Sadat editors urged Khomeini not to ally himself with the Arab regimes, such as Iraq and Libya, which had rejected the Egyptian peace agreement with Israel. They tried to remind him that those who were fighting Egypt in Baghdad were the same ones who had ejected him for the Shah's sake and that Mu'ammar Gadhafi of Libya was responsible for the mysterious disappearance of the Shi'i Lebanese Imam Sadr.[66]

Disappointment replaced hope for an Iranian role in favor of Egypt because of the Iranian rhetoric of exporting the revolution to other Muslim countries and the fast deterioration of Iranian relations with several Arab countries, including Egypt and Iraq. Exporting the revolution to the Gulf states with their large Shi'i communities increased ambivalence among Egyptian writers. Persian imperialism and Persian aggression against the Arabs thus became a theme in the official press.[67] The isolation of Egypt in the region by both Arab states and Iran due to the peace treaty with Israel provoked pro-Sadat commentators to launch a prolonged war of words against Iran and the rejectionist Arab states. The alliance of each of these states—namely, Syria, Iraq, and Libya, as well as the PLO—with Iran was always explained in a way that made them into Machiavellian losers, while Egypt was portrayed as the only winner and Sadat as the man of principles.[68] The failure of Palestinian mediation efforts to free the American hostages was repeatedly used to prove that Khomeini was hypocritical in dealing with the Palestinians and that they had wasted their great chance to improve their image in the West and the United States.[69] Khomeini's regime was also accused of hypocrisy in dealing with all Arabs. For example, rumors about sending Iranian volunteers to southern Lebanon provoked Fumīl Labīb of *al-Musawar* to ask: "If Iran is serious about liberating Arab land, why does it not give up threatening the Iraqi borders and threatening to annex Bahrain and give up attacking the Gulf and arranging coups and exporting revolutions?"[70] The Iraqi-Iranian conflict over Shatt al-Arab was another example of how the official press used Arab-Iranian relations to condemn Sadat's regional rivals in Iran and the Arab states. The Iraqi regime was accused of betrayal by accepting, in accordance with the Algeria Accord, the splitting of Shatt al-Arab with the Iranians, while Sadat was said to have restored occupied land to the Arabs.[71] The Islamist press took a similarly hostile stand against the Ba'thist regimes, despite the fact that they shared the Ba'thists' opposition to the peace treaty between Egypt and Israel. The Islamists of Egypt were outraged by the suppression Islamists faced in Syria and Iraq and by Iraqi and Syrian statements accusing Khomeini of Nazism when he consolidated his power at the expense of his secular allies in the summer of 1979.[72] The Islamic press accused both regimes of being dictatorships and of serving as agents of Moscow and the West.[73]

The Egyptian press selectively used the struggle over power inside Iran to idealize the Islamic Republic, as in the case of the Islamist press, or to demonize that regime, as in the case of the secular intellectuals and Sadat loyalists. The coverage in the official press differentiated between Khomeini and Grand Ayatollah Muhammad Kāzim Shariʿatmadārī. The former was depicted as a radical extremist, while the latter was considered a moderate and human rights advocate. While bloody confrontations between the regime and ethnic groups—most of them Sunnis such as the Arabs, the Kurds, Turkmens, and the Baluchis—attracted intensive news coverage, the struggle between the central government and ethnic and religious minorities was among the issues least dealt with by the Egyptian commentators. Non-Muslim minorities such as Bahāʾīs did not attract any news coverage at all. Media usually ignored quiet, persecuted minorities and paid more attention to groups that chose to rebel such as Arabs and Kurds. Jews were covered on several occasions, reflecting a trend in the international media since the Second World War;[74] since the Holocaust, international opinion has been more sensitive to any loss of life or prosecution faced by Jews than by any other community. For this reason the international media, which constituted the main source for foreign news coverage in the Egyptian press, paid attention to the case of the Jewish businessman Habibullah Ghanyan, executed in Iran in May 1979 for his alleged relations with Israel. The U.S. Congress declared that the United States would not remain passive if the Jewish community in Iran suffered any suppression, a stand well covered in the news.[75] Khomeini's reception of representatives of the Iranian Jewish community and his assurances to them of equal rights attracted deserved news coverage in the Egyptian press.

Meanwhile, the Egyptian press ignored the violence Bahāʾīs faced in Iran. The press took little notice that the Iranian constitution did not recognize Bahāʾīs as a legitimate religious minority. The Egyptian press may have wished to avoid controversy over religious freedom for individuals and groups who chose to leave the Islamic faith. The legal status of the Bahāʾīs in Egypt was no better than in the Islamic Republic. Since the 1940s they had been considered an outlawed, heretical group. The relatively rare comments on the issue of Iranian minorities in both the official and the Islamist press looked at minority groups, both Muslim and non-Muslim, with suspicion.[76] Bahjat warned Khomeini that minorities inside Iran such as Turkmen and Kurds would cause problems for the Islamic Revolution.[77] The Islamist press went further and considered the uprising of Sunnis Arabs and Kurds disloyalty to Islam, because they "follow national slogans under the banner of autonomy."[78] We can only understand the position of the Islamist press in light of the ideological rhetoric of the Muslim Brotherhood, which opposed nationalism in favor of the Muslim unity of the *Ummah* (community of believers) under an Islamic government. The Islamist press that had always advocated the rights of Muslim minorities living in non-Muslim countries chose to condemn Sunni Kurds for striving for ethnic and religious rights.[79] The absence of Iranian minorities' issues and even hostility toward them reflects the struggle of Egyptian intellectuals with such sensitive issues and their failure to reconcile conflicts between nationalism, religion, and ethnicity. The failure of postcolonial Middle Eastern states to forge equality among all their citizens must have affected the way the issue was handled.

Conclusion

Popular discontent and frustration with the ruling elites and their policies marked the commonalities between Egypt and Iran in the late 1970s. The anger of Egypt's populace delivered a violent shock to Sadat's legitimacy in the January 1977 riots. Yet lacking leadership and a defined agenda, the abrupt protest movement was quickly contained. It was subsequently denigrated by Sadat as "the Thieves' Riot." When their Iranian counterparts succeeded in toppling the regime of the Shah two years later, the discontented Egyptians saw their aspirations for change as attainable. The toppling of the Shah made Egyptian leftists celebrate the defeat of social injustice, while Egyptian Islamists rejoiced at the defeat of "Western moral decay" and Egyptian liberals cheered the end of an abusive and authoritarian regime. Although these political and intellectual opinions diverged on many issues within Egypt, they were united by their fascination with the success of the Iranian Revolution and its leadership. Despite state control over the press, Egyptian politicians and intellectuals succeeded in expressing their support for the revolution, which directly contradicted Sadat's support of the Shah against the newly established Islamic Republic. The revolutionary Iran was, in fact, so antipathetic to Sadat that it celebrated his assassination in October 1981 and named a street in Tehran after his assassin, Kalid al-Islambouli, even issuing a stamp in his honor.

The Iranian Revolution had direct relevance for Egypt. Sadat's decision to host the Shah in Cairo and grant his family Egyptian citizenship and Khomeini's subsequent decision to cut diplomatic relations with Egypt triggered a long-lasting hostility between Cairo and Tehran. Domestically, the issue triggered a second confrontation between Sadat and his domestic opposition. In addition to arguments over state policy toward the revolution, the revolutionary policies in Iran, perhaps more significantly, brought a whole set of sociocultural issues to the fore of the intellectual debate in Egypt.

With the success of the religiously led revolution and the establishment of the Islamic Republic, the value of secularism, the role of religion in politics, and women's participation in the workforce were no longer issues merely for the recently returned Muslim Brotherhood or isolated political groups such as the Islamist Takfir wal-Hijra. They now formed a substantial component of an ongoing debate among all Egyptian political and intellectual trends. These debates revealed that the decades of Westernization and secularism before 1952 and the subsequent development of Arab socialism under Nasser and its reinterpretation by Sadat had failed to establish in Egypt such openly declared principles as respect for human rights, equal citizenship, personal liberties and free expression.

Egyptian Islamists used the Iranian Revolution to reignite the debate with secularists over issues such as the equality of women and the rights of minorities, although the debate over women's rights was thought to have been decided decades earlier. The rights of minorities proved more problematic for Egyptian intellectuals. Islamists had a clear stand against non-Muslim minorities and even denied the rights of Sunni minorities whenever these rights contradicted what Islamists believed to be the needs of the Muslim *Ummah*. While the stand of Islamists is consistent with their agenda, the Egyptian secularists stood silent about the rights of Iranian Baha'īs, and remained so as well about the rights of this community in Egypt.

Notes

This essay is based on my MA thesis at the University of Texas, Austin. I thank my advisors, Kamran Aghaie and Abraham Marcus, for their guidance and help.

1. The surveyed opposition publications are *al-Ahālī* of al-Tajammu' Progressive Party, *al-Sha'b* of the Socialist Labor Party, *al-Ahrār* of the Liberal Party, *al-Da'wa* of the Muslim Brotherhood, and *al-I'tisām* of al-Jam'iyya al-Islāmiyya al-Shar'iyya. The surveyed official publications are the *al-Ahrām* and *Akhbār al-Yūm* newspapers and the *Ākhir Sā'a, Rūz al-Yūsuf*, and *al-Musawar* magazines.

2. Fahmi Houwaidi, "The Media and Arab-Iranian Relations," in *Arab-Iranian Relations*, ed. Khair el-Din Haseeb (Beirut: Centre for Arab Unity Studies, 1998), 121–135. Houwaidi's argument is consistent with the traditional approach of studying the media in less-developed countries. That approach assumes that the media does not have an independent or different ideology from the ideology of the ruling regimes, which are often dictatorial. See also 'Awātif 'Abd al-Rahman, *Dirāsāt fī al-sahāfa al-misriyya wa al-'arabiyyaa: Qadāyā mu'āsira (Studies in the Egyptian and Arab Press: Contemporary Issues)* (Cairo: al-'Arabī lilnashr wa al-tawzī', 1989).

3. Rudi Matthee, "The Egyptian Opposition on the Iranian Revolution," in *Shi'ism and Social Protest*, ed. Juan Cole and Nikki Keddie (New Haven, CT: Yale University Press, 1986), 248.

4. "Iran tatajihu nahwa al-Islam" ("Iran is Heading towards Islam"), *al-Da'wa*, October 1978, 11.

5. "Al-Muqāwama tatasā'd did shah Iran" ("Resistance Is Rising against the Shah of Iran"), *al-Ahālī*, April 12, 1978.

6. Philip Gallāb, "Iran ilā ayn?" ("Where Is Iran Heading?"), *Rūz al-Yūsuf*, November 27, 1978, 16–18.

7. "Al-ta'āmur al-yahūdī wa al-bahā'ī sabab al-thawra fī Iran" ("The Jewish Baha'i Conspiracy Is the Reason of the Revolution in Iran"), *al-Da'wa*, October 1978, 18.

8. Ibid. See also Abd al-Mun'im Salīm Jabbāra, "al-Khomeini bayna amāl al-muslimīn wal mu'amrat al-salibiyya wa al-shuyu'iyya!" ("Khomeini between Hopes of Muslims and Conspiracies of the Christians and Communists!"), *al-Da'wa*, March 1979, 8–9.

9. In his book on Iran after the revolution, the Islamist Houwaidi continues to describe Iranian Jews as Israeli agents. See Fahmi Houwaidi, *Iran Min al-Dakhil (Iran from Inside)* (Cairo: Markaz al-Ahram lil-Tarjama wal-nashr, 1987).

10. Jabbāra, "al-Khomeini bayna amāl al-muslimīn," *al-Da'wa*, March 1979, 8–9.

11. Mustafā Amīn, "Akhtā' ash-shah al-'ashrah" ("The Ten Mistakes of the Shah"), *Akhbār al-Yūm*, January 6, 1979. See also Hassan Rajab, "'Arsh al-tāwws ilāayn?" ("What is the Future of the Peacock Throne?"), *Ākhir Sā'ah*, January 10, 1979, 20–21.

12. For example, see Jābir Rizq, "Wa intasar al-shaʿbu al-Irānī" ("And the Iranian People Prevailed"), *al-Daʿwa*, March 1979, 59.

13. "Shah Iran ywājih matāʾib jadīda" ("Shah of Iran is Facing New Troubles"), *al-Ahrār*, August 14, 1978.

14. On May 4, 1979, the coeditor of al-Musawar, Sabrī Abū al-Majd, wrote that what had taken place in Iran had happened only with the help of the United States, which had forced the Shah to leave Iran and made the Iranian army change its position in the last moment and abandon Shahpur Bakhtiyār, the last prime minister under the Shah.

15. Philip Gallāb, "Al-Shah wa al-Shīʿa wa al-Shuyūʿyyūn" ("The Shah, the Shiʿa, and the Communists"), *Rūz al-Yūsuf*, January 8, 1979, 16–17.

16. Jabbāra, "al-Khomeini bayna amāl al-muslimīn," 8.

17. See Jābir Rizq, "Ruʾya Islāmiyya," ("An Islamic Vision") *al-Daʿwa*, April 1979, 13. See also Salīm Jabbāra, "Thawrat Iran bayna duʿāt al-ilhād wa duʿāt al-infisāl" ("The Iranian Revolution between Advocates of Atheism and Advocates of Separatism"), *al-Daʿwa*, November 1979, 9.

18. Ahmad Bahjat, "al-Hadiyya" ("The Gift"), *al-Ahrām*, February 21, 1979. See also Anīs Masūr, "Mawāqif," *al-Ahrām*, March 9, 1979.

19. Mustafā al-Fiqī, "Iran wa Kharītat al-Sharq al-Awsat" ("Iran and the Map of the Middle East"), *al-Ahrām*, February 3, 1979.

20. Nikki R. Keddie, *Roots of Revolution: An Interpretive History of Modern Iran* (New Haven, CT: Yale University Press, 1981), 259–60.

21. Houwaidi, *Iran min al-dakhil*, 254–56.

22. Husayn ʿAbd al-Rāziq of the al-Tajammuʿ Progressive Party claimed that his party opposed the revolutionary regime, despite the early full support it gave, because of the executions, the persecution of the Iranian left, and the imposition of the hijab. Husayn ʿAbd al-Rāziq, interview with the author, Cairo, June 2002.

23. Mustafā Mahmūd, "Tilka Hiya al-Mushkila yā Khomeini" ("This Is the Problem, Khomeini"), *al-Ahrām*, March 14, 1979.

24. Wahīd Raʾfat, "Mihnat huqūq al-insān wa ahdāth Iran" ("The Human Rights Ordeal and Iranian Events"), *al-Ahrām*, April 14, 1979.

25. Anīs Masūr, "Mawāqif" ("Stands"), *al-Ahrām*, March 9, 1979.

26. Anīs Mansūr, "Mawāqif," *al-Ahrām*, August 1, 1979.

27. Ibid. and his "Mawāqif," *al-Ahrām*, March 25, 1980.

28. Salāh Hāfiz, "Bayna mashāyikh Misr wa āyāt Iran" ("Between the Egyptian Sheikhs and the Iranian Ayatollahs"), *Rūz al-Yūsuf*, November 19, 1979, 15.

29. Ahmad Bahjat, "Huduʾ" ("Quiet"), *al-Ahrām*, March 19, 1979.

30. Jābir Rizq of *al-Daʿwa* wrote in July 1979, "Before our visit (to Iran) we wished the (Iranian) revolution had been merciful and had forgiven those (who were executed), but when we saw families of martyrs and saw wailing women and crying children who lost their fathers, we told ourselves if the revolution executed a hundred criminals of the SAVAK every day, it would not be effective enough to appease those suffering widows and orphans." Rizq, "Min al-Mansura bi-Pakistan ila Qom bi-Iran," *al-Daʿwa*, July 1979, 15.

31. "Raʾīs al-mahkama al-Thawriyya al-Irāniyya yatahdath" ("The President of the Revolutionary Iranian Court Speaks"), *al-Daʿwa*, September 1979, 16–17.

32. Among many examples, see: Ahmad Bahjat, "Milad thawra" ("Birth of a Revolution"), *al-Ahram*, February 20, 1979, and Gallāb, "Al-Shah wa al-Shīʿa wa al-Shuyūʿyyūn."

33. See a series of weekly articles by ʿAbd al-Hamīd al-Kātib in *Akhbār al-Yūm* between January

27 and March 3, 1979, entitled "Qisat al-harakāt wa al-Za'amāt al-Dīniyya fī Iran." ("The Story of the Religious Movements and Leaderships in Iran").

34. 'Abd al-Hamīd al-Kātib quoted the Egyptian author Ahmad Amīn whose book had provoked lots of criticism among Iraqi Shiʻi ʻulama when it was published in the 1940s. Al-Kātib, "Qisat al-harakāt wa al-zaʼamat al-dīniyya fī Iran (3): al-Madhhan al-shiʻi: sirr quwwat ayatollah?" ("The Story of the Religious Movements and Leaderships in Iran (3): Is the Shiʻi *Madhhab* the Secret of Ayatollah's Power?") *Akhbār al-Yūm*, February 10, 1979. See also: Aḥmad Amīn, *Ḍuḥā al-Islām* (*Forenoon of Islam*) (Cairo: Maktabat al-nahḍah al-miṣrīyah, 1961–1962).

35. *Akbār al-Yūm* ran a full-page correction article by the Lebanese Shiʻi author Mohammad Bāqir Shirī. See Mohammad Bāqir Shirī, "Hirsan . . . indama naktub ʻann al-madhahib al-diniyya" ("Careful When We Write About Religious Schools of Law"), *Akbār al-Yūm*, March 2, 1979.

36. For example, Anīs Mansūr wrote: "The Shiʻi *Madhhab* thinks the Imam Marjiʻ Islam Ayatollah Khomeini is infallible and nobody can review [his decisions]. Mistakes have accumulated and Khomeini himself became the biggest mistake." Anīs Mansūr, "Mawaqif," *al-Ahrām*, November 26, 1979.

37. On November 19, 1979, *Rūz al-Yūsuf*'s editor, 'Abd al- 'Azīz Khamīs, wrote: "Sunnis, the *Madhhab* of the majority, condemned Shiʻis for believing that Gabriel committed a mistake in delivering the message of God and delivered it to Muhammad instead of 'Ali Ibn Abī Tālib, the cousin of the Prophet. This is what makes many Sunnis consider all different Shiʻi sects deviants and apostates." See 'Azīz Khamīs, "Rajulun yuharibu nafsahu" ("A Man Fights Himself"), *Rūz al-Yūsuf*, November 19, 1979, 11.

38. Jamāl Salīm, "Mādhā warāʼ al-inqilāb al 'Irāqī?" ("What Is Behind the Iraqi Coup?"), *Rūz al-Yūsuf*, July 23, 1979, 4.

39. *Rūz al-Yūsuf*, February 4, 1980, caricature on front page.

40. Jabbāra, "al-Khomeini bayna," 8–9.

41. "Dustūr Islāmī fī Iran" ("An Islamic Constitution in Iran"), *al-Daʻwa*, December 1979, 54.

42. Ibid. Matthee makes the same observation. See Matthee, "Egyptian Opposition," 260.

43. "Al-Tajruba al-Irāniyya fī al-iqtisād al-Islāmī" ("The Iranian experience in the Islamic economy"), *al-Daʻwa*, May 1980, 19.

44. Ibid.

45. Salah Jahin, caricatures, *al-Ahrām*, March 16, 1979.

46. Mahmūd, "Tilka hiya al-mushkila."

47. Hāfiz, "Bayna mashāyikh Misr," 15.

48. Among many examples for writings that publicized these calls, see Salah Abu Ismaʼil, *Shahadatu Haqq fī Qadiyyati al-ʼAsr* (*A Truthful Testimony in the Contemporary Issue*), 2nd ed. (Cairo: Dar al-Iʻtisam, 1984). Abu Ismaʼil himself adopted the call while he was a parliament member in 1978.

49. Usāma Mansī, "Limādhā manaʼa al-Khomeini al-mūsīqā" ("Why Khomeini Banned Music"), *Rūz al-Yūsuf*, August 6, 1979, 52.

50. Salāh Muntasir of *al-Ahrām* provides another example of how the issue of women in Iran was dealt with vaguely. He admired the Iranian women for forcing Khomeini to show more flexibility.

51. 'Abd al-'Azīm Ramadān and Philip Gallāb are examples for how the leftist press dealt with the American policy in Iran. Mustafā Amīn is an example for how liberals dealt with the same issue.

52. Among numerous examples, see Zakariā Nīl, "al-Khomeiniūn wa al-muʿādalāt al-saʿba" ("The Khomeiniists and the Difficult Formulas"), *al-Ahrām*, February 15, 1979; Muhammad Ismāʿīl ʿAli, "Hawla ahdāth Iran wa amn al-Sharq al-Awsat" ("On Iranian Events and Security of the Middle East"), *al-Ahrām*, March 12, 1979; "Luʾbat al-Rūs fī Iran" ("The Russian Game in Iran"), *al-Musawar*, January 11, 1980, 14.

53. Keddie, *Roots*, 259. For more details on the elimination of the Tudeh Party from politics under Khomeini, see Said Amir Arjomand, *The Turban for the Crown: The Islamic Revolution in Iran* (New York: Oxford University Press, 1988), 154–63.

54. Yusuf Ṣabry, "Shiʿaru al-intikhabat haybatu Amrika" ("The Slogan of the Election Is the Dignity of America"), *Rūz al-Yūsuf*, March 3, 1980, 22.

55. ʿAbd al-ʾAzīz Khamīs, "Shukran lil-Khomeini" ("Thanks, Khomeini"), *Rūz al-Yūsuf*, December 10, 1979, 9.

56. Sabrī Abū al-Majd, "Matā tantahī luʾbat al-Khomeini?" ("When Is Khomeini's Game Over?"), *al-Musawar*, December 21, 1979, 4.

57. See Tharwat Abāza, "Yaʾbā Allahu hadhā wa al-muʾminūn" ("God and Believers Reject That"), *al-Ahrām*, November 12, 1979; Salāh Muntasir, "Qāla al-Hakīm" ("The Wise Man Said"), and "al-Islam barīʾ" ("Islam Is Innocent"), *al-Ahrām*, November 5 and 8, 1979.

58. Philip Gallāb, "Aghrab asrār al-azma al-Iraniyya al-Amrīkiyya" ("The Strangest Secrets of the Iranian-American Crisis"), *Rūz al-Yūsuf*, December 10, 1979, 14–15.

59. Fathī Radwān, "Suqūt Amrīkā" ("The Fall of the United States of America"), *al-Shaʿb*, December 4, 1979.

60. ʿAbd al-Rahman al-Jābrī, "al-Khomeini wa al-Shah wa Israel wa Amrīkā" ("Khomeini, the Shah, Israel, and the U.S.A."), *al-Shaʿb*, December 4, 1979.

61. ʿAbd al-Mutʿāl al-Jābrī, "Abʿād fial-nizāʾal-Irānī al-Amrīkī" ("Dimensions of the Iranian-American Conflict"), *al-Iʿtisām*, December 1979, 21–22.

62. Ibrāhīm Shukrī, "Dawr Israel al-mashbūh wa al-mudammir wa isāʾat ʿalāqatinā biʾl-diwal al-ʾArabiyya wa al-islāmiyya" ("The Suspicious Destructive Role of Israel and the Deterioration of Our Relations with Arab and Muslim Countries"), *al-Shaʿb*, April 29, 1980. See also Radwān, "*Suqūt Amrīkā*"; "al-Bayānu al-khitāmī liʾl-muʾtamar al-Islāmī al-ʿālamī yudīnu muhāwalāt al-wilāyāt al-mutahida li-fard hisār iqtisādī ʿalā Iran" ("The Final Declaration of the International Muslim Conference Condemns Imposing American Economic Boycott on Iran"), *al-Daʿwa*, June 1980, 10.

63. Shukrī, "Dawr Israel al-mashbūh."

64. For contemporary Egyptian parties, see Raymond A. Hinnebusch, *Egyptian Politics under Sadat: The Post-populist Development of an Authoritarian-Modernizing State* (Boulder, CO: Lynne Rienner, 1988). See also Hāla Mustafā, *al-Nizāmu al-siyyāssī wa qādayā al-tahawwul al-dīmuqratī fī Misr* (*The Political System and the Democratic Transformation in Egypt*) (Cairo: Merit liʾl-Nashr, 1999).

65. For details on the situation of the Wafd and al-Tajammuʿ Progressive Parties under Sadat, see Husayn ʿAbd al-Raziq, al-Ahālī *Sahīfa tahta al-Hīsār* (al-Ahali *Is a Newspaper Under Siege*) (Cairo: Dār al-ʾĐlam al-Thālith, 1994).

66. Sabrī Abū al-Majd, "al-Ladhīn Taradūka min al-Najaf wa Karbala yatamassahūn bika al-yawma!" ("Those Who Evicted You from Najaf and Karbala Today Are Pretending to Be Your Friends Today"), *al-Musawar*, March 9, 1979, 4–5.

67. Sabrī Abū al-Majd, "Tehran wa Baghdad tatanāfasān ʿala imtlāk al-khalīj wa tuʾaridānih liʾamaliyyāt ibtizāz rahība" ("Tehran and Baghdad Are Competing to Control the Gulf and Imposing on It Terrible Blackmail"), *al-Musawar*, December 14, 1979, 6–7.

68. Mursī al-Shāf'ī, "Thawrat Iran wa sunnā'ihā al-'Arab!" ("The Iranian Revolution and Its Arab Makers!"), *Rūz al-Yūsuf*, March 5, 1979, 3.

69. 'Abd al-Sattar al-Tawīla, "Tufūlat al-rāfidīn wa Hamāqat al-Thawra al-Irāniyya" ("The Childish Rejectionists and Stupidity of the Iranian Revolution"), *Rūz al-Yūsuf*, November 19, 1979, 10.

70. Fumīl Labīb, "Sawā'a al-sabīl 'inda al-Munazama wa fī Israel" ("The Straight Path for the PLO and in Israel"), *al-Musawar*, December 28, 1979, 12–13; and "Matā tatakhallasu al-Munazama min al-Falastīnī al-qabīh?" ("When Does the PLO Get Rid of the Ugly Palestinian?"), *al-Musawar*, January 18, 1980, 10–11.

71. Jamāl Salīm, "Yaqdhifūn misr bi'l-hijāra wa buyūtahum min zujāj" ("They Are Stoning Egypt and Their Houses Are Made of Glass") and "Dimuqārtiyyat al-takārita fī Baghdad" ("The Democracy of Tikrits in Baghdad"), *Rūz al-Yūsuf*, April 30, 1979, 14, and May 14, 1979, 8.

72. In the summer of 1979, the Syrian regime brutally crushed the Muslim Brotherhood. In 1980, the Iraqi regime executed the Islamist Shi'i leader Muhammad Bāqir al-Sadr.

73. 'Abd al-Mun'im Salīm, "Ru'ya Islāmiyya" ("An Islamic Vision"), *al-Da'wa*, August 1979, 63.

74. For coverage of Jewish migration from Iran, see *al-Ahrām* throughout 1979 and 1980.

75. "al-Hukūma al-Iraniyya tantazi' aslihat al-aqaliyya al-'Arabiyya" ("The Iranian Government Abolishes the Rights of the Arab Minority"), *al-Ahrām*, May 16, 1979.

76. One of the few exceptions was Hāfiz, who expressed concern about violence against minorities.

77. Ahamd Bahjat, "Mabrūk" ("Congratulations"), *al-Ahrām*, April 4, 1979.

78. Jabbāra, "al-Khomeini bayna," 8–9.

79. See Muhammad Mansūr Haība, *al-Sahāfa al-Islamiyya fī Misr Bayna 'Abd al-Nāsir wa al-Sadat 1952–1981 (The Islamic Press in Egypt between Nasser and Sadat 1952–1981)* (al-Mansūra: Dār al-Wafā li'l-Tibā'ah wa al-Tawzī', 1990).

Iranian Anti-Zionism and the Holocaust

A Long Discourse Dismissed

Mahdi Ahouie

For the first time since the 1979 revolution, a Holocaust revisionist discourse has started at the official level in Iran. The great leader of the revolution, Ayatollah Ruhollah Khomeini, never questioned the Holocaust, nor did he ever try to link the creation of the state of Israel in the Middle East to that tragedy. Reading through Khomeini's extensive discourse on Israel and Zionism during two and a half decades of his political activity (1963–89), one cannot find a single comment in rejection of the Holocaust. Other top leaders of the Islamic Republic, such as the current supreme leader Ayatollah Ali Khamenei and the former president Akbar Hashemi Rafsanjani, although they occasionally questioned the extent of the Holocaust, have not adopted Holocaust revisionism as a "strategy" for conducting rhetorical war against Israel.

Ayatollah Khamenei has rarely made public comments on the Holocaust. He made his most critical comment on the Holocaust while addressing the Second International Conference for the Support of the Palestinian Intifada in 2001. In that speech, he asserted that "the Zionists" had made up exaggerated numbers about the Jewish victims of the Nazis to prepare the ground for the occupation of Palestine.[1] Since then, however, he has not further brought up the issue in his various utterances on the Palestinian question. The former president Rafsanjani also questioned the extent of the Holocaust in his 1963 Persian translation of Akram Zu'aytir's *al-qadiya al-filastiniya* (*The Palestine Question*). But he also later refrained from making public comments against the Holocaust during his time in office.[2]

Radical History Review

Issue 105 (Fall 2009)   DOI 10.1215/01636545-2009-004

© 2009 by MARHO: The Radical Historians' Organization, Inc.

President Mahmoud Ahmadinejad's comments on the Holocaust shocked the world. Many figures in the West, from politicians to scholars, reacted to these comments, denouncing them as outrageous. In the Muslim world, however, the general impression is that Ahmadinejad's harsh tone against Israel has brought him more popularity among the masses, and some analysts have even argued that Ahmadinejad has thus managed to expand Iran's influence among Muslim and Arab people. At the domestic level, however, the Iranian president's controversial discourse on the Holocaust has been criticized as highly harmful to Iran's national interests.[3] Ahmadinejad's comments on the Holocaust should be divided into two categories: (1) calling the Holocaust a "myth" — a made-up story, with no roots in reality; and (2) linking the "alleged" Holocaust with the creation of the state of Israel in Palestine, suggesting that Israel should be relocated to Europe, where that tragedy "supposedly" happened.

The denial of the Holocaust as a total myth is quite unprecedented in Iran, even in the religious anti-Israeli discourse. Some revolutionary speakers have at times questioned the extent of the Holocaust, but nobody in the Islamic Republic before Ahmadinejad had officially called the Holocaust a myth in its entirety. A discussion of how the Iranian president learned about such extreme Holocaust revisionism goes beyond the scope of this essay. Rather, I want to focus on Ahmadinejad's linking Israel with the Holocaust here. My research aims to explore whether this approach has any precedents in Iranian prerevolutionary discourse, and my main hypothesis here is that the line of reasoning about the link between Israel and the Holocaust, and about a fruitful relocation of Israel to the West, shows continuity with an older discourse, extant in Iranian society since the creation of the Jewish state in 1948. Thus far, most existing analyses have largely dismissed this background, attributing Ahmadinejad's words simply to his dogma.

The Holocaust-based approach to the Palestinian question constitutes a complex discourse in need of careful analysis. Indeed, this perspective has a long history in Iranian society: it was imported into the Iranian religious discourse, partly from Arab anti-Zionism during the late 1940s and the 1950s, and partly from leftism during the 1960s.

The Emergence of Iranian Religious Discourse on Israel: A Brief History

The content of the Iranian religious discourse on Israel and Zionism has been shaped, inspired, and influenced by three major sources: (1) the historical confrontation between the early Muslims and Jews of Arabia, as reflected in the Qur'an, mixed with contemporary Arab anti-Zionism; (2) Marxist-leftist anti-imperialism; and (3) European classical anti-Semitism. Information and impressions imported from each of these resources have been embraced by and absorbed into the political Islamic ideology in Iran.

Arab anti-Zionism was known in Iran in the late 1940s through both Sunni and Shi'i personalities. On the Sunni side, the role of the Egyptian Muslim Brotherhood, as well as of the mufti of Jerusalem Amin al-Hosayni, proved significant. On the other hand, Grand Ayatollah Mohammad Hussein Kashif al-Ghita was the first high-ranking Shi'i scholar in Iraq who supported the Palestinian resistance movement led by Ezz-el-din Al-Qassam during 1947–48.[4] It was under such influences that many Shi'i scholars and political activists in Iran—among them Ayatollah Abolqassem Kashani, Ayatollah Mahmoud Taleqani, Ayatollah Khomeini, and Ali Shariati—embraced Arab anti-Zionism and introduced it into the Iranian religious discourse.

Kashani was the first Iranian religious politician to follow Kashif al-Ghita's example of support for the Palestinian people regardless of their belief in the Sunni branch of Islam. Kashani also enjoyed close ties to the mufti of Jerusalem and the Egyptian Muslim Brotherhood. Alongside Mojtaba Navvab Safavi and Seyyed Gholam-Reza Sa'idi, Kashani belonged to a generation of Iranian political thinkers who pioneered a religious anti-Israeli discourse in Iran. Their thoughts were based on a combination of Islamism and nationalism: while Iran had no territorial dispute or specific clash of interests with Israel, these political thinkers tried to replace the concept of a national homeland with that of an "Islamic homeland." They stirred up anti-Israel feelings among Iranians by emphasizing their responsibility toward this "extended homeland," fueling these sentiments whenever necessary by provoking a sense of national pride and making provocative comments about alleged Jewish interferences in Iran's economy.

Later, another Arab anti-Zionist Shi'i cleric became influential in shaping Iranian religious forces' view of Israel: Musa al-Sadr, the prominent Lebanese scholar and politician, who became engaged in Arab-Israeli polemics in the late 1950s. Iran's Shi'i clergy have long had an interest in Lebanon's Shi'i population. Intermarriage between clerical families in both countries had occurred, by the mid-twentieth century, for several generations. Al-Sadr was born in Iran into a clerical family with relatives in Lebanon, which facilitated his acceptance in the latter country. He was a political activist, and like so many clerics of his generation, he trained at Shi'i religious schools in Qom (Iran) and Najaf (Iraq). In 1959 he moved to and spent two decades of his life in Lebanon as a religious and political leader, until his mysterious disappearance in Libya in 1978. During this time, he succeeded in politicizing the Lebanese Shi'i population.[5] As one of the champions of Arab-Shi'i anti-Zionism, al-Sadr, perhaps served as one of the main inspirations of an Iranian revolutionary movement with an anti-Israeli essence. Despite doubts about the extent of the personal friendship between al-Sadr and Khomeini, al-Sadr clearly enjoyed respect among many of Khomeini's closest allies such as Ayatollah Dr. Mohammad Hosseini Beheshti and Taleqani, two major ideologues of the Islamic revolution. Yet his influence on Khomeini himself remains undefined.[6]

Throughout the 1960s, the predominance of leftist discourse in the Middle East, fueled also by Egypt's Gamal Abdel Nasser, affected the language of the Iranian religious forces as well. The communist Tudeh Party had already introduced the concept of anti-imperialism to Iranian society in the late 1940s, but the leftist side of religious discourse began applying it in the 1960s. The influence of the intellectual Jalal Al-e Ahmad's works on religious thinkers and the role of such scholars as Shariati proved decisive in this process. Major events such as the 1967 Arab-Israeli war and the subsequent emergence of the Palestinian resistance movement led by the Palestine Liberation Organization (PLO) were also important to the development of the revolutionary anti-Israeli discourse in Iran. An Iranian-Islamic version of socialism, advocated by Al-e Ahmad and Shariati, provided a fruitful ground for reinforcing religious opposition to Israel on the basis of such modern concepts as "freedom seeking" and in the context of the general clash between the "world oppressors" and the "oppressed." After 1967, Iranian religious thinkers started to use a line of reasoning that portrayed Israel as the representative of Western colonialism and imperialism in the Middle East. In the 1960s and 1970s, when several so-called third world nations in Africa and Asia were striving for independence from colonial rule, the leftist portrayal of the world as divided between oppressors and oppressed appealed to many religious thinkers in Iran, who also opposed the Shah's Western-oriented foreign and domestic policies. In this context, many Iranian leftist and Islamist revolutionaries took Palestinian resistance to Israel as a unifying and sacred symbol of the struggle against oppression and injustice. The leftists considered the West an unjust "imperialist colonizer"; the religious camp likewise called the West the unjust "oppressor." Israel would thus become the perfect target for anger against the West as the representative of injustice.

For those who sought to bridge Islam and socialism, the question of Palestine offered the perfect opportunity to join leftist and Shi'i concepts of justice seeking and opposition to oppression. This may well explain why Palestine became such a preoccupation for Al-e Ahmad and Shariati after 1967. While Al-e Ahmad came from the secular left and gradually moved toward a third-worldist and nativist (Iranian-Islamist) interpretation of socialism, Shariati developed a socialist interpretation of Islam.[7] The two men moved from two opposite ideological sides toward a similar revolutionary standpoint, where their ideas appeared similar on many points, including on Palestine and Israel.

In the Iranian contemporary intellectual sphere, two controversial figures have played the most vital roles in importing and mixing European-style anti-Semitism into religious discourse: Ahmad Fardid (died 1994), and Amir Tavakkol Kambuzia (died 1974), both of whom started speaking out against Jews in the 1950s. European anti-Semitic literature and propaganda had already arrived in Iran in the 1930s, however, when Reza Shah Pahlavi developed cordial relations with Adolf Hitler's Germany as a way to balance British and Russian influence in Iran. At the same time, some Iranian secular writers such as Sadeq Hedayat started to reflect an equally anti-Arab and anti-Jewish perspective in their works,[8] and later, Iranian hard-line nationalist parties, Pan-Iranist and Sumka, adopted the same path at the political level during the 1940s and early 1950s.

In the religious camp, Kashani found himself accused of sympathy for the Nazis, especially given his close relations with the pro-Hitler mufti of Jerusalem, al-Hosayni.[9] As discussed farther in this article, Sa'idi also imported some European anti-Jewish literature, including the *Protocols of the Elders of Zion* to Iran. Yet Fardid and Kambuzia played significant roles in bridging these early contacts between European anti-Semitism and the Islamic movement of the 1960s and 1970s. Neither of these two figures was a Muslim cleric, nor were they even close to Khomeini's circle. Yet they often advocated their anti-Jewish sentiments by widely referring to Islam and the Qur'an, although they had borrowed most of their ideas about Jews directly or indirectly from European resources.

Fardid apparently turned to religion following the Islamic Revolution in Iran.[10] He started to widely use religious terminology to advocate his Heideggerian worldview. His main theory concerned the emergence of an ultimate savior (meister) at the end of the world to free people from the "captivity" of Western liberal democracy. In this context, he found that Khomeini's revolution perfectly fit his ideals. Describing Zionism as "anti-revolutionary" in nature, Fardid called the Iranian Revolution "a world movement" that would prepare the ground for the final revolution of the Mahdi.[11]

Fardid denounced Hitler as "Westernized and evil-spirited," but he regretted, in an implicit reference to the creation of the state of Israel, that the Jews had managed for the most part to use the consequences of Hitler's defeat to their own advantage. Fardid also regretted that the "stubborn" Jews had survived throughout history against Jesus, Muhammad, nineteenth-century European anti-Semitism, and, finally, Hitler, but he hoped that the last promised Shi'i imam, the Mahdi, would eliminate the Jews and that "Islam would no longer be defeated." Highly critical of Western civilization, Fardid believed Zionism was not a product of Western imperialism; rather the Jews themselves had created and now controlled imperialism and colonialism.[12]

Kambuzia, too, warned that the whole of Western civilization was in danger of declining under the "pressure of the insatiable greed" of the Jews, who sought absolute control over the Western world. While acknowledging that six million Jews were massacred by the Nazis, an act Kambuzia denounced as contrary to the principles of Islam, yet he claimed that the Jews deserved to be slaughtered because of their "mal-intentions against their host nations."[13] Mahmoud Dowlatabdi, the famous Iranian writer and intellectual who met with Kambuzia in the mid-1970s, described him as follows:

The main axis of his whole knowledge is the contradiction that he has discovered between Islam and Judaism. He concludes every argument about Judaism being versus Islam. . . . He uses the term "Zionist culture" instead of "colonialist culture" because he believes the former is more appropriate and comprehensive. In fact, he does not consider Zionism a part of the existing colonialist system; [quite to the contrary,] he sees the current colonialist system as a part of Zionism. He analyzes every single phenomenon in the world on the basis of this theory and with regard to Zionism. He is convinced that Jews are responsible for all the destruction and ugliness in the world . . . I realize that he looks on the Jews from Hitler's eyes, not from the perspective of Arab freedom seekers, and not from the perspective of Palestinian refugees.[14]

The legacies of Fardid and Kambuzia have inspired many religious forces committed to the Islamic Republic. Yet neither of them ever denied or questioned the reality of the Holocaust; they recognized that the Jewish people were actually persecuted under the Nazis. Nevertheless, their followers later moved toward the more extreme position of Holocaust denial. The current tendency among some in the Iranian religious elite to deny or underplay the Holocaust certainly constitutes a new phenomenon in the Iranian political discourse on Israel and Zionism.

To conclude this brief introduction, it is also necessary to point out that after the Suez crisis of 1956 and, especially, after the 1967 Arab-Israeli war, Israel itself made efforts to publicly make a direct linkage between the Holocaust, which the state did not officially commemorate during its first years, and the existence and survival of the Jewish state. This "historical" discursive linkage was also echoed by the U.S. government and media. Such attitudes were certainly received in Iran, and they were perhaps one of the elements that led Iranian secular and religious revolutionary intellectuals to see the creation of the state of Israel in the Middle East as the West's reparation for the Holocaust.[15]

Linking Israel and the Holocaust: A Discourse Review

Unlike Khomeini, who generally avoided commenting on the Holocaust, many other religious or leftist political thinkers in Iran analyzed the Palestinian question through the lens of the Holocaust. Among them were Kashani, Sa'idi, Shariati, Al-e Ahmad, Ali Asghar Haj-Seyyed-Javadi, and Reza Baraheni. However, they generally did not question the reality of the Holocaust itself, but rather criticized what they saw as the Zionist "abuse" of the event for justifying the "occupation" of Palestine.

The first political figure who linked the question of Palestine to the Holocaust was Kashani, the prominent Shi'i cleric and Iranian political activist during the 1940s and 1950s. Kashani's earliest reaction to the developments in Palestine concerned the 1947 United Nations (UN) plan for the partition of Palestine. In a public announcement published in January 1948, just a few months before the proclamation of the state of Israel, Kashani regretted that "the big powers of the world" had not learned their lesson from the catastrophic outcomes of the Second World War to support the rights and freedom of the oppressed nations." He added:

It is not clear on what legal and logical basis Palestine is taken as the homeland of the German and Russian and American Jewish immigrants so that [the big powers] vote for its partition. If they want to satisfy the Jews and use them for their own purposes, they would better give them a place and independence in their own countries. In any case, the establishment of the Jewish state will be in the future the source of big troubles for the Muslims of the Middle East, as well as for the whole world.[16]

In January 1948, Kashani called for a public demonstration in support of the Palestinian people, in which he referred to Jews as "unwelcome wanderers" who were used to living by deception and to committing crimes. He said the Jews had been assigned by the big powers to demean and eventually eliminate the Muslims.[17] Kashani later played an important role in persuading the Mossadeq government to shut down Iran's consular office in Jerusalem in 1951.[18]

Another religious anti-Israeli pioneer in Iran was Sa'idi (died 1988), who imported Arab anti-Zionist and European anti-Semitic thought into the Iranian Islamic discourse during the 1950s. Sa'idi was a lesser-known public figure than Kashani, but his role in introducing the Palestinian question into the Iranian religious discourse was perhaps as significant as Kashani's.[19] As a religious writer and translator, Sa'idi had pioneered anti-Zionist publication in Iran since the late 1940s. He had met with al-Ghita in Najaf and was apparently influenced by the ayatollah's opinion on Israel as being "an illegitimate child created and raised by Britain and the United States."[20]

Sa'idi was fluent in Arabic, English, and French, which enabled him to read and understand both Arabic and European anti-Zionist literature. During the late 1940s and early 1950s, he published several articles in *Aa'in-e Eslam* (*Islamic Rites*), a conservative religious weekly, and later in the daily *Neda-ye haq* (*The Voice of Righteousness*), in which he bitterly criticized Iranian Jews for their sympathy for the Zionist cause. After the 1956 Suez war, Sa'idi published his major book with the title *The Danger of the Jew to the Islamic World and Iran*, which consisted mainly of his previously published articles in the above-mentioned journals and also included a Persian translation of the *Protocols of the Elders of Zion* as an appendix, one of the first translations of the text in Iran. According to Sa'idi, his book was aimed at alarming and awakening the Muslims in Iran and elsewhere about the evil plans of the Zionists for the Middle East. He therefore linked the Zionist movement directly to Western imperialist plans in the Middle East:

A close examination of the aggressive plots of the imperialist [powers] against the Islamic countries, part of which have recently been implemented in Palestine, leaves no doubt for anyone that the largest part of the imperialist forces has been employed to extinguish the light of Islam, eliminate the Muslims, and seize their religious heritage. The sly imperialists have assigned the World Zionist movement to execute this plan in Palestine as well as in the Middle East in general, so that the imperialists themselves would not be held responsible for this dangerous operation in the outward appearance.[21]

Sa'idi admired Nazi Germany for the suffering it had inflicted on the Jewish people "as a retribution for their espionage, sabotage, and materialistic greed that are the natural characteristics of all the Jews." He maintained that "the brave decision and action of the Nazi Party in repelling these dirty vandals must be considered punishment from god." But he regretted that Germany's anti-Jewish actions ended up at the expense of Muslims, since "the Jews appeared as the victimized people. Subsequently, they took control over the media in Britain and the United States and manipulated the public opinion in the Anglo-Saxon countries and raised their voice in moaning and groaning that this unwelcome, rejected population must get an allocated nest of their own."[22] Sa'idi clearly linked the idea of the Jewish state to the Holocaust, and his thoughts and writings influenced many religious thinkers and political activists of the younger generation, among them Shariati and Mostafa Chamran.[23]

In the late 1960s, a former Iranian Marxist-socialist intellectual, Al-e Ahmad, also interjected the Holocaust into the Iranian debates on Palestine. Together with Khalil Maleki and some others, he had first welcomed the creation of Israel as an ideal alternative model for the Leninist-Stalinist socialist state. Both Maleki and Al-e Ahmad traveled to the Jewish state in the early 1960s and later published their travelogues in the Iranian press, describing Israel as the ideal manifestation of socialist values. Simultaneously, Maleki, Al-e Ahmad, and their companions were highly critical of the Arab states, which they often described as "backward" and "opportunistic."[24] Their ideas remained the final word on Israel in Iranian intellectual circles for several years. However, as mentioned earlier, Al-e Ahmad gradually moved away from Marxism-socialism and developed his own nativist third-worldist theory. The intensity of the Arab-Israeli conflict, especially in the aftermath of the June 1967 war, further deepened the split between Iranian socialist intellectuals: one side, consisting mainly of former socialists such as Al-e Ahmad, became vehemently hostile to Israel, while the other side, led by Maleki, still avoided blunt criticism of the Jewish state.

Even in the early 1960s, when Al-e Ahmad was still favorably writing of Israel, he related Israel to the Holocaust. He characterized the creation of the Israeli state as a compensation for the West's crimes "paid from the Middle East's pocket," as a bête noire for Arab countries, and as the product of an exaggerated pretension of being wronged, overlaid with ethnocentrism: "I do see in this overly-displayed martyrdom of the Jews following the War massacres, the other side of the coin of Fascism, and basing [one's argument] upon a racism that has taken its place."[25] He added that he supposedly had "a lot of arguments on these aspects of Israel."[26] However, he liked to believe that Israel's close ties to the West were but smart tactics: "Yet, I also see that if you are fated to become a base [for the West], you should learn from Israel for it has sold itself expensively."[27] According to Al-e Ahmad, Israel had successfully pressured the West by overemphasizing the Jewish victimhood and had deceived Western political leaders through short-term political compliance, so that it could use Western financial support to construct its new economy. Therefore Israel could serve as an example for Eastern countries as to how to adopt Western technology while not becoming Westernized:

"In any case, for me as an Easterner, Israel is a quintessential example, among other examples, of how to do business with the West. With the spiritual might of a martyrdom [i.e., the Holocaust], how can we milk Western industries, how can we collect reparations, and how can we use the West's investment monies for the development and prosperity of the country? Thus, for the price of few mornings of political dependency, we can consolidate our newly established undertaking."[28]

In the late 1960s, Al-e Ahmad started to show more interest in Islam in his writings, though he remained highly critical of the Islamic clergy. Whether or not Al-e Ahmad had turned truly religious, he did not seem to have any problem using religious language to support his nativist third-worldist arguments. When the 1967 war broke out between Israel and its Arab neighbors, Al-e Ahmad bridged religion and his version of socialism to stand for "justice" and against Israel. In June 1967, he published an article about Israel, "The Beginning of a Hatred," in which he lambasted Israel and its supporters among Iranian socialists (e.g., Maleki and Daryoush Ashouri):

These days, I regret that I know the Persian language. In the whole Persian press, I did not find a single article . . . that can be said to have been written by an Iranian. If the European intellectual has a guilty conscience for having consented to the [Nazi] killings of the Jews, why should the Iranian intellectual feel guilty, whose queen was Esther and whose vizier was Mordecai and whose holy man was Prophet Daniel? The Iranian conscience must instead be guilty for the fact that Iranian oil fuels the tank[s] and the airplane[s] that are killing his Muslim and Arab brothers. . . . Who has said that the Iranian intellectual's conscience should also be led by Western media?[29]

Al-e Ahmad also accused the leftist intellectuals of having aligned themselves with the Western bourgeoisie in support of Israel:

It has been twenty years that a bunch of bullies, with the aid of international
funds and thanks to such Zionist terrorist organizations as "Haganah," have
occupied the land of Palestine and expelled one million of its inhabitants. It
has been twenty years that [the Jews] are continuously taking Arab territories
inch by inch. . . . By relying on the guilty conscience of Europe and America,
the Jews are treating the Arabs in exactly the same way that the Nazis treated
them. Because Nazism—the perfect product of the Western bourgeois
civilization—burned six million miserable Jews in furnaces, two or three
million Arabs of Palestine, Gaza, and the West of Jordan must today be
displaced and murdered for the sake of the Wall Street capitalists and the
Bank of Rothschild. And since the European intellectuals took part in Hitler's
crimes by not speaking out at the time, they are now yielding the Jews a base
in the Middle East to whip the people of Egypt, Syria, Algeria, and Iraq,
making them never think about fighting against Western colonialism and
never close the Suez Canal to the civilized nations again! Damn on this crappy
bourgeois civilization![30]

For Al-e Ahmad, the Israeli leaders changed from "saints" to "murderers"
after 1967. His earlier hope that Israel's close alliance with the West was but a
"short-term tactic" was about to vanish as he was disappointedly realizing that Israel's ties with the West had rather deep roots. However, as if he still found it difficult
to abjure his image of Israel as a "savior" and an "example" for Eastern people, he
gave Israel advice on what it should and should not do to be accepted among the
peoples of the region:

This is an old argument that questions why we in the Middle East should pay
compensation for a sin that a lunatic committed in Germany and Europe. . . . If
Israel wishes to live in peace in the Middle East, it should stop being a center
of plotting against democratic movements. If Israel wishes to be recognized
by [our] Arab brothers, it should be a relief rather than a further agitation to
the Middle East's sufferings, above all the influence of colonialism and the
exploitation of oil [resources].[31]

Although Al-e Ahmad clearly criticized the West for having paid the compensation
for the Holocaust from the Middle East's pocket, he never actually denied the reality of the Holocaust. He did not find the nature of the Jewish people evil, nor did
he show any sympathy with those who made the Jews suffer. Instead, he directed
his criticism at Zionism, because he claimed that Zionism could easily provoke anti-
Semitism in the region. It seems that Israel's use of military force against its Arab
neighbors and its ambitions to maintain regional supremacy were destroying Al-e
Ahmad's dreams of the country as an "ideal model" of "Eastern identity" to the
extent that he compared Zionism to Nazism: "The problem is that I am afraid that

by their bullying and seeking of the gendarme position in the region, the Israelis will actually provoke a new wave of anti-Semitism. Indeed, Zionism is dangerous because it is the other side of Nazism and Fascism, and it acts exactly like them. For me, 'Haganah' and 'S.S.' are the same."[32]

The socialist critic Baraheni believed that although Al-e Ahmad and the Muslim clergy of Iran ultimately reached a similar perspective in rejection of Israel, their ideas did not derive from the same way of thinking: the clergy's opposition to Israel was based on Islamic ideology, whereas Al-e Ahmad opposed Israel because of his third-worldist views. According to Baraheni, "the clergy believed Israel was an enemy of 'Islam,' and, therefore, they should fight against it. Al-e Ahmad believed that Israel was an enemy of 'Muslims' and that there was no difference between an Israeli [soldier] who opens fire on Palestinians and Arabs and a German S.S. These are two different languages. Jalal, through his own logic, reached the point that the clergy reached by the Shari'a."[33]

For Al-e Ahmad, the world divided into two opposing blocs determined to clash: the "oppressive colonialism" represented by Western imperialism, on the one hand, and the "oppressed colonized nations" represented by the so-called third world countries, on the other. It is true that Al-e Ahmad's language concerning Israel changed dramatically after 1967, but his worldview remained almost the same, as he repeated it similarly in his pro- and anti-Israel articles alike. This is the key to understanding Al-e Ahmad's approach to Israel: he even saw the Jewish people in Israel as the victims and tools, and scapegoats for, Western imperialism. In his first article on Israel in 1964, Al-e Ahmad described the creation of Israel in Palestine as a "compensation paid by Eastern people for Western crimes" and claimed that Muslims and Jews were both victims of this colonial arrangement:

[Israel] constitutes a coarse embodiment of the expiation for the crimes the Fascists committed during the war years in Dachau, Buchenwald, and the other furnaces. Note well: this is a crime, and the perpetrator of this crime is the Westerner, and I, the Easterner, have to pay the price. The Westerner exports the capital and I, the Easterner, provide the base. In this matter, too, I have much to say. Still, if we want to know the truth, Christianity made of Israel a curtain that is stretched out to separate itself from the world of Islam, so that I do not see the real danger—that is how the Arabs were kept preoccupied [i.e., underdeveloped].[34]

From Al-e Ahmad's perspective, the question of Palestine formed part of the historical confrontation between the East and the West, or in today's political language, between the South and the North. He feared that the clash in Palestine would turn into a new "Crusade"—a nonreligious crusade between the oppressed poor and the oppressing rich, in which Muslims represented one side and the Western powers the other.[35]

Seyyed-Javadi was another Iranian socialist who had turned against Israel after 1967. Like other socialist intellectuals, Seyyed-Javadi never advocated the annihilation of Israel or the expulsion of Jews from Israel or the Middle East, nor did he deny the Holocaust. Instead, he believed that Israel must separate itself from the "Zionist bias" and stop being "a local base for imperialism," while starting to collaborate with other nations in the region. Seyyed-Javadi also accused the Western countries for making the Arabs pay "compensation" for Europe's actions during the Holocaust, thereby putting the Jews in a troublesome situation: "The Westerners have abused the oppression that they committed against the Jews throughout the centuries — they were the ones who eliminated six million Jews in the Christian land of Europe during the Second World War alone — for their own political and economic purposes, and this way, not only have they done injustice to the Arabs but they have also betrayed the Jews in the name of friendship."[36]

During the 1960s, the increasing popularity of a worldview emphasizing a global class struggle in which the third world proletariat fought Western exploiters placed the Palestinians as a focal point in global relations. This third-worldist view generally regarded Israel as a tool of Western imperialism and as a colonial settler state. According to Seyyed-Javadi, the Arab-Israeli conflict was rooted in the problematic relationship between the whole region of the Middle East and the West at large. Criticizing the European socialists for their sympathy with Israel, Seyyed-Javadi argued that since "Western socialism is dependent on the Western capitalist economy," it could not support the third world in its struggle "for liberation from political and economic captivity by the West." Seyyed-Javadi believed that the European socialists were in no position to judge fairly the question of Palestine, because "they could not close their eyes to the economic interests that they received from oil." He continued his criticisms of Western leftist intellectuals by referring to their position in the Arab-Israeli conflict as having "the darkest judgments and the most vulgar prejudices": "They have a guilty conscience because six million Jews were slaughtered by the most barbarous and savage means in the civilized Christian Europe of the twentieth century. They feel guilty because His Excellency the Pope kept silent on this slaughter and happily continued his clerical presidency under Hitler's Nazism and Mussolini's Fascism. They are sad because the police forces of the occupied European countries were collaborating with the Gestapo in persecuting and deporting the Jews."[37] In Seyyed-Javadi's opinion, the Israeli people differed from those who had survived the Nazi concentration camps, both given the number of people who survived the Holocaust and from a political perspective: "The Jews of the 1940s were the martyrs of Fascism, but the existing Israelis are some people who have found a reputation and received respect and sympathy at the expense of the lives of those martyrs and the tortures from which they suffered and the embarrassment they caused for Europe. One should always distinguish between the two." He concluded: "While the Jews in diaspora are suffering from anti-Semitic tendencies, today Western colonialism and the state of Israel are using these tendencies to strengthen their own positions in the Arab Middle East and in favor of the goals of Zionism."[38]

Another passionate anti-Israeli member of Al-e Ahmad's former socialist circle was Baraheni, who became well-known in the late 1960s as a socialist writer and critic after he had translated Maxime Rodinson's *Israel and the Arabs*—a classic among leftist analyses of the Arab-Israeli conflict—into Persian.[39] At the core, Rodinson argues that Israel is a colonial creature and that the Western powers are responsible for complicating the situation in the Middle East. According to Rodinson, the West's total support for Israel derives from a guilty conscience caused specifically by the Holocaust. Rodinson's ideas significantly influenced the opinions of Iranian anti-Zionist socialists such as Al-e Ahmad, Seyyed-Javadi, and Baraheni in the late 1960s and early 1970s.

In 1971, Baraheni traveled to Egypt and also secretly visited Lebanon. He later published a travelogue, in which he harshly criticized Israel. He interpreted the link between the Holocaust and the creation of Israel as follows:

The International colonialists—[led by] Britain, United States, and France—have brought us this enormous disaster; they have planted this tower of colonialism in the middle of our territories. The Europeans persecuted and harassed the Jewish people for centuries. A group of Europeans tortured the Jews and another group felt sympathy for them, but they were not ready to accept the Jews either. They chased the Jewish people here and there. The most recent example was the Nazi slaughterhouses and human furnaces. The Europeans considered this people polluted, dirty, and lower than beasts. . . . The Jewish people escaped from Europe and America . . . but colonialism drew their attention to the Arab lands because Europe was not willing to accept the Jews and the United States was implicitly sending signals that the Jews should not settle on the American continent. The land that was chosen [for the Jews] was just in the heart of the Arab nation and Islamic Ummah [i.e., community of Muslim believers]. . . . By building this fortress [i.e., Israel], Europe released itself from the burden of the sins that it had committed against the Jews throughout the centuries. . . . When the United States formally entered the colonial campaign and stood behind Israel in all its actions and dedicated its entire colonial arsenal for this strong fortress of colonialism, it became obvious that the huge, dreadful factory of colonialism, with its all destructive power, had created an Israel against Islam. Christianity is now retaliating against Islam for the Crusades by [using] a people who had once rejected Christ and all Christian ideals.[40]

Like Al-e Ahmad, Baraheni did not mean to support the idea of a "religious" war in Palestine; yet both were convinced that the Muslim world as a part of the "colonized third world" was under attack by the Christian "Western colonialism" in Palestine, and that Zionism was serving as a tool for that purpose.

The most influential Islamist ideologue of the late 1960s and early 1970s was Shariati, who was also known for his strong anti-Israeli stance. Despite his rejection by many Muslim clerics of his time, Shariati played a crucial role in shaping the Iranian religious revolutionary discourse due to his wide popularity among the youth. In an attempt to fill the theoretical gap between religion and modern politics, he borrowed many modern concepts from leftism and introduced them into religious discourse. For example, anti-imperialism, or the perception of the world as divided between the oppressors and the oppressed, ranged among the concepts that Shariati borrowed from the left and reintroduced to Iranian society in the context of Shi'ism.

Shariati asked: if the creation of Israel in Palestine was compensation for the West's crimes against the Jewish people — including its persecution in Germany, Poland, France, Spain, and Russia — why should the Muslims of the Middle East pay the expense of the compensation?

Why should the West and Christianity give away Islamic Palestine as payoff?
Why shouldn't they donate a part of Poland where they put the Jews under
the most terrible torture? Why don't they give up one state of the Federal
Republic of Germany as atonement for the Holocaust? Why should Christianity
compensate for its torture of the Jews during the past two thousand years from
the pocket of Islam? Why should the West pay for its crimes from the empty
pockets of the Middle East nations? Why should the houses and lives of some
hundred thousand of homeless Muslim Arabs be given to the Jews as reparation
for the church's crimes, Europe's sins, and the Nazis' Holocaust? The Jews have
been living in Islamic countries for centuries as if in their homelands and have
been enjoying all social and economic rights.[41]

Shariati regretted that instead of compensating for its past injustice against the Jews from its own resources, the West had put the fate of the Jewish people in the hands of some adventurous militarist leaders and used them as its puppets and its means of torturing the Muslims of the Middle East in the same way that the West had tortured the Jews during the past two thousand years.[42]

Conclusion

President Ahmadinejad's perception of Israel as a direct consequence of the Holocaust shows some similarity to the above-mentioned historical discourse. Although Ahmadinejad had put no particular emphasis on his foreign policy during his presidential campaign, it took him only a few weeks in office to reveal highly controversial ideas on a variety of world issues, most particularly, the Palestinian question and the Holocaust. Some commentators suggest that by initiating a rhetorical attack against Israel, Ahmadinejad intended to turn Iran's foreign policy from "passive" to "active."[43] In this context, his overtly anti-Israeli standpoint was a well-calculated and preemptive move to shock the United States before that country could take any initiatives against Iran. Moreover, at the time, when U.S. troops were present in Iraq and Afghanistan and when Washington was allegedly considering a military attack on Iran, Ahmadinejad's anti-Israeli rhetoric brought greater support for him among the Muslim masses regionally and worldwide, while consolidating Iran's hegemony in the Middle East.

Ahmadinejad launched his discourse on the Holocaust for the first time in December 2005, when in a news conference after the Summit of the Organization of the Islamic Conference (OIC) in Mecca he said: "Some European countries insist on saying that Hitler killed millions of innocent Jews in furnaces, and they insist on it to the extent that if anyone proves something contrary to that, they condemn that person and throw them in jail. Although we do not accept this claim, if we suppose it is true, our question for the Europeans is: Is the killing of innocent Jewish people by Hitler the reason for their support for the occupiers of Jerusalem?"[44] Ahmadinejad asked the Europeans why they did not give a part of their own lands — in Germany or Austria, for example — to "the Zionists" to establish their state in Europe: "If you offer part of Europe [to the Jews], we will also support it and will not say a word against their government."[45] He further suggested, "If you have burned the Jews, why don't you give a piece of Europe, the United States, Canada or Alaska to Israel. . . . Our question is, if you have committed this huge crime, why should the innocent nation of Palestine pay for this crime?"[46] He responded himself: "From the European perspective, the best way to remove the Jews of the whole of Europe was to build up a Jewish camp at the heart of the Islamic region [of the Middle East]. This way, [the Europeans] intended to catch two birds with one stone: To expel the Jews from Europe; and to create a European offspring with a Zionist and anti-Islamic nature at the heart of the Islamic world by invoking the victimhood of Jews."[47]

From Ahmadinejad's viewpoint, the creation of the state of Israel is directly and organically linked to the Holocaust: "The Palestinian people are being suppressed and their lands have been occupied under the pretext of the Holocaust."[48] Ahmadinejad must thus think that by downplaying the Holocaust he is questioning the legitimacy of Israel, because the Holocaust appears as the main justification for the existence of the Jewish state. He also suggests that Israel should be relocated to the West, where he argues that the Holocaust "allegedly" took place, to further pressure Israel's Western supporters.

During his trip to the UN headquarters in New York in 2006, Ahmadinejad held a meeting with the members of the U.S. Council on Foreign Relations. A council member told the Iranian president that he was "totally misled" by thinking that there was any relation between "things going on in Palestine and the Holocaust" and that the Palestinian question consisted of difficult complexities over "territory, history, religion, and belief," and not simply of the Holocaust. To this comment, Ahmadinejad responded:

If the excuse of the Western countries for supporting the occupying regime
of Jerusalem is not the Holocaust, then why are they so overpassioned on it?
What is the benefit of such an overpassioned insistence that the Holocaust
has happened unless to pick its fruits in Palestine? . . . The fact is that some
people from around the world have gathered in Palestine, and have formed a
government in a land belonging to others, and yet, we find such oversensitivity
to a problem which dates back sixty years. . . . In history many cases of genocide
have taken place, but there is no sensitivity about them. The reality is that the
conclusions drawn from the Holocaust are directly influencing the present time
issues. To what thing does the Holocaust relate that when it is questioned some
people get so angry?[49]

In 2006, Ahmadinejad also wrote a letter to then U.S. president George W. Bush—
the first such contact between Iranian and U.S. presidents since the 1979 revolution. In this long and preaching letter, Ahmadinejad touched on the questions of
Israel and the Holocaust. Saying that in Iran, "young people, university students and
ordinary people, have many questions about the phenomenon of Israel," Ahmadien-
jad referred to the "claims" that "six million Jews" were killed in the Holocaust and
continued:

Again let us assume that these events were true. Does that logically translate
into the establishment of the state of Israel in the Middle East or support
for such a state? How can this phenomenon be rationally explained? Mr.
President, I am sure you know how, and at what cost, Israel was established:
many thousands were killed in the process; millions of indigenous people were
made refugees; hundred of thousands of hectares of farmland, olive plantations,
towns and villages were destroyed. This tragedy is not exclusive to the time of
establishment; unfortunately it has been ongoing for sixty years now. . . . Such a
phenomenon is unique, or at the very least, extremely rare in recent memory.[50]

In another letter to the German chancellor, Angela Merkel, Ahmadinejad continued
to link Israel with the Holocaust: "In addition to the people of Germany, the peoples
of the Middle East have also borne the brunt of the Holocaust. By raising the necessity of settling the survivors of the Holocaust in the land of Palestine, they have created a permanent threat in the Middle East in order to rob the people of the region
of the opportunities to achieve progress."[51]

The connection between the creation of the state of Israel and the tragedy
of the Holocaust is highly exaggerated in Ahmadinejad's arguments. The Holocaust
might have reinforced the Zionist cause of providing the Jewish people with a homeland in which they would no longer be a vulnerable minority; but the Zionist movement had originated in Eastern Europe long before the rise of Hitler's National
Socialism, and many Jewish immigrants had already arrived in Palestine prior to the
Second World War. Therefore, the idea of Israel serving as Europe's compensation

for the Holocaust is not, historically speaking, accurate. Yet my article has intended to show that this aspect of Ahmadinejad's arguments has precedent in Iranian anti-Zionist discourse. As discussed above, at least six major Iranian political thinkers preceded Ahmadinejad in linking the occupation of Palestine to the Holocaust in the years prior to the 1979 revolution. It is important to note that such a linkage between the Holocaust and the creation of the state of Israel has also officially been advocated by the Israeli government itself since 1967, and that the U.S. government and media have further repeated and emphasized the point. It should thus come as no surprise that several Iranian political thinkers, from different backgrounds, have considered the creation of Israel as the compensation for the Holocaust and have treated Israel as an expansion of the West and as a representative of Western powers—notably the United States and Britain—in the Middle East. By arguing that "the West should pay the reparation of the Holocaust out of its own pocket" and that "Israel should be relocated to Europe or America," these speakers have actually intended to denounce the West's role in the Middle East and to challenge Western decision makers, as well as public opinion. The dramatic mixture of religion, nationalism, and leftism in Iran since the 1950s has created a type of political psyche that is equally skeptical of Jews and the West. Since most Iranian revolutionary thinkers take for granted that Western powers are responsible for the creation of the Jewish state in the Middle East, Iranian anti-Zionism can catch two birds with one stone when downplaying the Holocaust: it can question Israel's legitimacy and simultaneously put pressure on the West. Like other Iranians quoted above, Ahmadinejad has used Holocaust revisionism as a tool in the broader clash that he envisages between the Muslim world and Western domination.

Notes

1.   Secretariat of the International Conference for the Support of the Palestinian Intifada, *Mavaze'-e saran-e jomhuri-ye eslami-ye Iran nesbat be enqelab va entefaze-ye felestin* (*The Positions of the Leaders of the Islamic Republic of Iran on the Palestinian Revolution and Intifada*) (Tehran: Islamic Consultative Assembly, 2001), 73. Khamenei also referred to the Holocaust when he gave his support to the French historian and writer Roger Garaudy. In a meeting with him in Tehran on April 20, 1998, Khamenei praised Garaudy for his "courage." Later, on March 22, 1999, he stated that the West had contradicted its claimed principles by disregarding Garaudy's right to the freedom of speech only because he had argued that "the Jews have exaggerated about their massacre by Hitler in the Second World War." For a detailed discussion of Khamenei's positions on Garaudy, see Adrien Minard and Michaël Prazan, "La consécration Persane de Roger Garaudy," *Les temps modernes* (*Modern Times*), No. 641 (2006): 29–44. For Khamenei's speech in 1999, see *Mas'aleye felestin va sahyunism: rahnamudhaye maqam-e moazam-e rahbari* (*The Question of Palestine and Zionism: Guidelines from the Supreme Leader*), (Tehran: Sazman-e Tabliqat-e Eslami, 2000), 89.

2.   In his Persian translation of Akram Zu'aytir's *al-qadiya al-filastiniya* (*The Palestine Question*) published in 1963, Rafsanjani argued that the number of Jewish Holocaust victims had never reached six million. He further emphasized, "Of course, we are not pro-

Hitler's murders, but we are arguing that Hitler's actions may not justify the antihuman crimes of the Jews. If one day there is an international trial, both racist parties of Hitlerism and Zionism must be tried and condemned." See Akram Zu'aytir, *Sargozasht-e felestin ya karnameh-ye siyah-e este'mar (The Story of Palestine or the Black Record of Colonialism)*, trans. Akbar Hashemi Rafsanjani (Qom: Chapkhaneh-ye-Hekmat, 1963), 172.

3. Even conservative forces in Iran found Ahmadinejad's comments on the Holocaust inappropriate. For example, an article in *Baztab (Reflection)*, a currently banned conservative online news publication belonging to Mohsen Reza'i, the former chief commander of the Islamic Revolutionary Guards Corps, harshly criticized Ahmadinejad for his words. It argued that Ahmadinejad's comments had damaged Iran's national interests. According to *Baztab*, Iran had no interest in the Holocaust polemics and should refrain from getting involved in that debate. See Sa'id Poursina, "Manfe'e Melli-ye Ma va Da'va-ye Nazism va Sahyunism" ("Our National Interests and the Conflict between Nazism and Zionism"), *Baztab*, January 16, 2006, www.baztab.com/print.php?id=32712.

4. Some sources even allege that Kashif al-Ghita sent a few Shi'a combatants to collaborate with the Palestinian anti-Zionist movement in 1948. He believed that the occupation of Palestine by the Zionists was directly planned by colonialist powers. See Ali Asghar Halabi, *Tarikh-e nehzathaye dini-siyasi-ye mo'aser (History of the Contemporary Politico-Religious Movements)* (Tehran: Zavvar, 2003), 241.

5. For more about al-Sadr and his life, see Fouad Ajami, *The Vanished Imam: Musa Sadr and the Shia of Lebanon* (Ithaca, NY: Cornell University Press, 1986).

6. In their in-depth study of al-Sadr's political life, Houchang E. Chehabi and Majid Tafreshi argue that Khomeini never enjoyed close ties with al-Sadr or his family. According to the authors, the two men had very little in common in terms of their political tastes and strategies: "Their styles could not have been more different: where Sadr was conciliatory and reformist, Khomeini was unyielding and revolutionary. Moreover, relations between the Sadr and Khomeini families had been tense even in Iran." However, the authors admit that al-Sadr and Khomeini "had one thing in common: their political activism and opposition to quietist apolitical clergy, which led them to cooperate occasionally." As evidence, they refer to al-Sadr's support of the Iranian Revolution led by Khomeini. See H. E. Chehabi and Majid Tafreshi, "Musa Sadr and Iran," in Houchang E. Chehabi, ed., *Distant Relations: Iran and Lebanon in the Last Five Hundred Years*, (London: I. B. Tauris, 2006), 137–161.

7. Shariati stated that he believed in a "sort of leftist and progressive interpretation of Islam." See Ali Shariati, *Nameha (Letters)* (Tehran: Qalam, 2005), 91. Yet this did not mean that he believed in Marxism. On the contrary, Shariati quite fervently opposed Marxism and communism. His "sort of leftist" interpretation of Islam simply meant a socialist and revolutionary approach to religion, but Islam still constituted the core of his thoughts.

8. For an example of such perspectives, see, for instance, Sadeq Hedayat, *Haji Aqa (Mr. Pilgrim)* (Tehran: Javidan, 1945).

9. After the arrival of the Allied troops in Iran in 1941, Kashani was formally accused of collaborations with the German agents in Iran by both the British forces and the Iranian government. He was prosecuted from June 1943 forward, but he managed to escape the arrest. After spending several months in hiding, Kashani was finally arrested by the British soldiers and Iranian police in the north of Tehran in June 1944. He spent the next fourteen months at British military bases in the Iranian cities of Arak and Kermanshah. When the war came to an end, the ayatollah was released in September 1945 and finally arrived in Tehran in October of the same year. According to the British and Iranian officials, Kashani was accused of having contacts with a German spy called "Frantz Meir." But the transcript

of parts of his interrogations shows that Kashani's contacts and friendship with the pro-Hitler mufti of Jerusalem had been the main concern of the Allied forces. For a detailed and well-documented account about the Allied accusations against Kashani, see Seyyed Mahmoud Kashani, ed., *Ayatollah Kashani be revayat-e asnad va khaterat* (*Ayatollah Kashani according to Documents and Memories*), vol. 2 (Tehran: Markaz-e Asnad-e Enqelab-e Eslami, 2007), 148, 175. Also see Ghazanfar Roknabadi, *Siyasat, diyanat, va Ayatollah Kashani* (*Politics, Religion, and Ayatollah Kashani*) (Tehran: Mo'asseseh-ye Farhangi-ye Danesh va Andishe-ye Mo'aser, 2000).

10. His critics claim that his dramatic turn toward religion was disingenuous and constituted merely a tactic to consolidate his influence under the new regime and further advocate for his thoughts. One of his main critics is Abdolkarim Soroush, the well-known Iranian philosopher, who once described Fardid as follows: "Fardid was anti-Semitic. He was an anti-Semite in its real term—that is, a kind of anti-Semitism that we have never witnessed in Iran's cultural history. . . . He had learned this anti-Semitism from his mentor, Heidegger, who was undoubtedly a supporter of Fascism and Nazism. . . . [His] attacks on Liberalism derived from [his belief in] Fascism, not Islam or Socialism or anything else." See Abdolkarim Soroush's interview with Maryam Kashani, January 29, 2006, quoted in Aftab News Web site: www.aftabnews.ir/prtewv8e.jh87zi9bbj.html.

11. For Fardid's ideas on the Islamic Revolution, see Seyyed Musa Dibaj, *Ara' va aqayed-e Seyyed Ahmad Fardid, mofradat-e fardidi* (*Ideas and Beliefs of Ahmad Fardid*) (Tehran: Nashr-e Elm, 2007), 85–86, 100, 102–5, 133–34.

12. Ibid., 472.

13. David Menashri, "The Jews of Iran," in Sander L. Gilman and Steven T. Katz, eds., *Anti-Semitism in Times of Crisis*, 367. Also see the daily *Jomhury-e eslami* (Special appendix: *Sahifeh* 31) (October 24, 1985): 15–18.

14. Mahmoud Dowlatabadi, *Safar-e balouch* (*Travel to Balouchestan*) (Tehran: Negah, 2004), 37.

15. See Idith Zertal, *Israel's Holocaust and the Politics of Nationhood* (Cambridge: Cambridge University Press, 2005).

16. Jalaloddin Madani, *Iran-e eslami dar barabar-e sahyunism* (*Islamic Iran versus Zionism*) (Tehran: Soroush, 1983), 19.

17. Ibid., 125–6.

18. After the establishment of the Mossadeq government, Iran officially closed its consular office in Jerusalem in 1952. This was attributed to financial difficulties, but tactically, it was done to satisfy both the domestic religious forces and the Arab countries. Legally, though, the closure of Iran's "mission" in Israel never meant a withdrawal of the "recognition." Although Kashani was then the speaker of the parliament and therefore must have been well aware of such a distinction, he emphasized in advance that Iran would soon "withdraw its recognition of Israel, which did not have any legal basis," and he announced later: "We have withdrawn our recognition of the Jewish state of Israel. Since the past administration was a British puppet, it had recognized Israel. Now all the Islamic and Arab countries must unite for defeating Israel and returning the cities occupied by Israel to their real owners." See M. Dahnavi, *Majmou'eh maktoubat, sokhanraniha, payamha, va fatavi-ye Ayatollah Kashani* (*A Collection of Ayatollah Kashani's Letters, Speeches, Messages, and Religious Decrees*), (Tehran: Chapakhsh, 1982), 2:182.

19. Ebrahim Yazdi and Hossein Shah-Hosseini, former members of the National Front, interviews by the author, Tehran, August 15 and 28, 2005.

20. Seyyed Gholam-Reza Sa'idi, *Khatar-e johud baraye jahan-e eslam va iran* (*The Danger of the Jew to the Islamic World and Iran*), 2nd ed. (Tehran: Me'raj, 1972), 48.

21. Ibid., 12.

22. Ibid., 19.

23. For more on Sa'idi, see his interview, "Ostad Gholamreza Sa'idi, hozur-e haftad saleh dar masir-e ehyaye tafakkor-e dini" ("Master Gholamreza Sa'idi, Seventy Years of Presence in the Path of Revitalizing the Religious Thinking"), *Kayhan farhangi* (*Cultural Kayhan*), No. 19 (1985): 3–12.

24. For an example of Maleki's criticism of the Arabs, see his editorial note "Mas'aleh-ye a'rab va esra'il" ("The Arab-Israeli Question"), *Nabard-e zendegi* (*The Life Battle*), January 1959, 32–33. For Al-e Ahmad's early opinion on the Arabs, see Jalal Al-e Ahmad, *Safar be velayat-e Ezra'il* (*Travel to the Land of Israel*), ed. Shams Al-e Ahmad (Tehran: Ravaq, 1984), 59–60, 62–63.

25. Al-e Ahmad, *Safar*, 51.

26. Ibid.

27. Hamid Dabashi, *Theology of Discontent: The Ideological Foundations of the Islamic Revolution in Iran* (New York: New York University Press, 1993), 68.

28. Al-e Ahmad, *Safar*, 52.

29. Al-e Ahmad, *Safar*, 91–92. Esther, the sacred biblical character who saved the lives of several thousands of Jews in Persia, was married to the Persian king Xerxes (Khashayarshah in Persian; he ruled from 486 to 465 BC). Esther's uncle, Mordecai, became a powerful figure at the king's court after Xerxes ordered Haman, his powerful minister, to be hanged for plotting against the king. Mordecai played an important role in rescuing the Jews who were supposed to be murdered by their enemies. Daniel, the great Jewish prophet during the first diaspora, is buried in Shush, an ancient region in southwestern Iran. His shrine is considered a holy place by Iranians, and many Muslim pilgrims visit his tomb for blessings.

30. Ibid., 89–90.

31. Ibid., 92.

32. Ibid., 99.

33. Reza Baraheni, *Safar-e mesr* (*Travel to Egypt*), 2nd ed. (Tehran: Nashr-e Avval, 1984), 143.

34. Dabashi, *Theology of Discontent*, 86.

35. Al-e Ahmad, *Safar*, 96.

36. Ali Asghar Haj-Seyyed-Javadi, "Dar in suye madar-e 45 darajeh" ("On the Other Side of 45° Orbit"), *Negin* (*Bezel*), June 1967, 5.

37. Ibid., 7.

38. Ibid., 69.

39. Maxime Rodinson, *A'rab va esra'il* (*Israel and the Arabs*), trans. Reza Baraheni (Tehran: Amirkabir, 1969).

40. Baraheni, *Safar*, 141–43.

41. Ali Shariati, *Asaar-e goonegoon* (*Various Works*), pt. 2 (Tehran: Agah, 2003), 635.

42. Ibid., 636.

43. See Hooshang Amirahmadi's analysis in this regard, "Iran's President on Israel and the Holocaust," *American-Iranian Council Update*, Vol. 3, No. 38 (2006): 1–6.

44. Islamic Republic of Iran News Agency (IRNA), December 8, 2005, quoted in Robert Tait, "Israel Should Move to Europe, Says Iran's Leader," *Guardian* (December 9, 2005), www.guardian.co.uk/world/2005/dec/09/iran.israel.

45. Ibid.

46. CNN International, December 15, 2005, quoted in the *Jerusalem Post*, online edition, May 16, 2006, www.jpost.com/servlet/Satellite?cid=1145961353170&pagename=JPost%2 FJPArticle%2FPrinter.

47. BBC Persian Web site, January 2, 2006, www.bbc.co.uk/persian/iran/story/2006/01/060102 _mv-ahmadi-dialogue.shtml.

48. Mahmoud Ahmadinejad, interview with NBC, New York, September 19, 2006. For the full transcript of the interview, see "NBC Exclusive: Ahmadinejad on the Record," *NBC Nightly News*, www.msnbc.msn.com/id/14911753.

49. The full text of Ahmadinejad's address and the question and answer session before the US Foreign Relations Council is published on the English page of *Mahmoud Ahmadinejad's Personal Memos*, October 1, 2006, www.ahmadinejad.ir.

50. For the full text of Ahmadinejad's letter to Bush, see "La lettre de Mahmoud Ahmadinejad à George W. Bush," *Le Monde*, December 19, 2006, www.lemonde.fr/iran-la-crise-nucleaire/ article/2006/05/09/la-lettre-de-mahmoud-ahmadinejad-a-george-w-bush_769886_727571 .html.

51. See "Full Text of Pres. Ahmadinejad's Letter to German Chancellor," *Fars News Agency*, August 28, 2006, english.farsnews.com/newstext.php?nn=8506060558.

Revolution, Trauma, and Nostalgia in Diasporic Iranian Women's Autobiographies

Nima Naghibi

Twenty years after the 1979 Iranian Revolution, Gelareh Asayesh and Tara Bahrampour published autobiographical accounts of their childhoods in Iran, recounting the effects of the revolution on their lives and their painful transitions to life in the diaspora. Published in 1999, Asayesh's *Saffron Sky: A Life between Iran and America* and Bahrampour's *To See and See Again: A Life in Iran and America* are at the forefront of what has now become a veritable phenomenon of diasporic Iranian women's autobiographical writing in English.[1] Their memoirs are the first of a plethora of texts by a generation of Iranian American women writers, most of whom experienced the 1979 revolution in pre- or early adolescence and who emigrated to the United States with their families. A decade after the publication of these books, we continue to witness a profusion of autobiographical narratives by Iranian women written in English.[2]

These texts form part of a genre, the autobiography, discouraged as recently as the early 1990s in Iran, as Farzaneh Milani and Afsaneh Najmabadi observe, particularly for women, as it suggested an immodest disclosure of the private.[3] The questions I want to investigate concern the sudden popularity of these memoirs.[4] Theorists of autobiography and life writings have discussed the historical distinctions between autobiography and memoir: the genre of autobiography was established in the late eighteenth century; it operated within an evolutionary model of per-

Radical History Review

Issue 105 (Fall 2009)   DOI 10.1215/01636545-2009-005

© 2009 by MARHO: The Radical Historians' Organization, Inc.

sonal development and was generally understood as a superior form of self-reflexive exercise. Memoirs, on the other hand, were perceived to make fewer intellectual demands of the reflecting subject. Autobiography was seen as a more masculine genre, while memoir was often associated with the feminine.[5]

In this paper, I will be using the terms "autobiography" and "memoir" inter-changeably, as the contemporary abundance of nonfictional self-reflexive narratives tend to challenge the traditional generic and gendered distinctions between the two categories. What interests me most about this particular wave of Iranian memoirs is that they are being produced by a generation of authors whose childhood or early adolescence the 1979 revolution interrupted. Thus the predominant sentiment in these texts, nostalgia for a lost childhood, is deeply bound up with a nostalgia for a lost (prerevolutionary) nation or home. In her compelling book, *The Future of Nostalgia*, Svetlana Boym defines nostalgia as "a mourning for the impossibility of mythical return, for the loss of an enchanted world with clear borders and values."[6] The desire to return and restore one's imagined past is what Boym calls "restorative" nostalgia which seeks to rebuild the crumbled ruins of an imagined past. But the autobiographical Iranian texts I am discussing here also engage with what Boym terms "reflective" nostalgia which "dwells in *algia*, in longing and loss, the imperfect process of remembrance."[7] I would like to trace in these works how the twinning of private, familial memory with public memory through revolutionary rupture and trauma frames these writers' nostalgic recollections of Iran. The overlapping of pri-vate and public memory, restorative and reflective nostalgia, shapes their subjectivi-ties and determines their relationships to their host country, the United States, as well as their perceptions of their former home, (prerevolutionary) Iran.[8]

The first part of this essay will focus on *To See and See Again* and *Saffron Sky*. Both of these autobiographies can be considered in terms of what Gillian Whit-lock calls "generational" narratives produced mostly by a generation of women who experienced the trauma of the revolution at "a critical moment of becoming in their personal histories."[9] What binds these texts is the shared experience and articulation of the revolution as a traumatic event, as a wound inflicted during a key period in the authors' personal development. Understanding the revolution as trauma shows us the ways in which "trauma is not locatable in the simple violent or original event in an individual's past, but rather in the way that its very unassimilated nature—the way it was precisely *not known* in the first instance—returns to haunt the survivor later on."[10] Thus the very fact that the traumatic event is unassimilable at the moment of its occurrence explains the continued outpouring of autobiographies thirty years after the revolution. Further, these particular writers appear to be working through their trauma through the cathartic process of "scriptotherapy," a process that Suzette Henke has argued renders the role of the analyst obsolete.[11] These texts thus consti-tute a "gathering of the wounded," a working through revolutionary trauma, and the disclosure of memories marked by the events of the revolution: the loss of home and culture, shaped by the nostalgia that scars life in the diaspora.[12]

The second half of my essay examines Azadeh Moaveni's *Lipstick Jihad: A Memoir of Growing Up Iranian in America and American in Iran.*[13] While the author shares with Asayesh and Bahrampour a nostalgia for prerevolutionary Iran, hers is generated by and mediated through family narratives told in the diaspora. Moaveni's text thus calls attention to the fact that "memory . . . is not tied to the individual who experienced a given event, but dispersed and transmitted to subsequent generations."[14] Moaveni's nostalgia for the "home" country, then, is mediated by "postmemory." As Marianne Hirsch describes it, postmemory constitutes a very powerful type of memory since it does not refer to or draw on a person's actual past experiences; rather, it is a memory refracted through the lens of a preceding generation marked by trauma.[15]

These autobiographies offer a sharp contrast to the culture of self-effacing female modesty that resonates among Iranian women and that is also consistent with Western stereotypical perceptions of Middle Eastern women. Perhaps in part because of their previous absence, Iranian women's autobiographies have become phenomenally popular in the West. A number of critics, myself included, have argued that these texts invite and encourage the Western imperial gaze, offering Westerners a glimpse into the presumably forbidden world beneath the veil.[16] The thirst in the West for these autobiographies appears unquenchable, and the prevailing interest in what Graham Huggan calls the "ethnic autobiography" invokes a history of a prurient Western impulse to unveil the secrets of a feminized East.[17]

Indeed, the genre of the Middle Eastern woman's memoir has become a highly marketable commodity, particularly in the post–9/11 context. There are highbrow iterations like Azar Nafisi's *Reading Lolita in Tehran: A Memoir in Books* and *Things I've Been Silent About: Memoirs,* as well as the more popular books, nowadays many of them by Afghan women.[18] This latter group of texts is often ghostwritten, raising important questions about voice and representation. Most of these books have covers with tantalizing photographs of abject veiled women who promise to reveal themselves in their tell-all narratives. The texts promise the Western reader access to the East, a promise that invokes a long history of colonial desire to unveil the simultaneously eroticized and abject Muslim woman. This colonial history to know and therefore to own the Orient needs to be understood as part of a civilizational discourse that categorizes nations along an axis of evolutionary development and provides "evidence" for foreign and imperial intervention. This civilizational discourse also forms part of a narrative of universal human rights, and tell-all memoirs have to negotiate their ambivalent positioning within a genre of political engagement and rights discourse, within which they can serve as "a soft weapon."[19]

On the one hand, the autobiography can render human the dehumanized and convey the fullness of voice and presence to those denied their rights. But, as Whitlock argues, it can also be used as "a soft weapon because it is easily co-opted into propaganda. In modern democratic societies propaganda is frequently not the violent and coercive imposition of ideas but a careful manipulation of information in the engineering of consent."[20] Any critical engagement with Iranian women's memoirs thus needs to take into account their complicity as "soft weapons"; it is not an accident that these autobiographies prove so popular in the West. These books—their publication, their marketing, and their popularity—speak to their complicity with a system of knowledge production that markets and packages the exoticized and simultaneously reviled East for the consumption of the West. And by marketing the East in this way, as a place both inviting and threatening, these texts lend their implicit support to colonial intervention.

However, more binds this grouping of texts than covetous imperial eyes. The memoir, I would argue, has become the "genre du jour" in the West. Leigh Gilmore identifies this phenomenon as part of "the therapy-driven 'culture of confession'" in which we currently live.[21] The current surge in Iranian women's memoirs can be understood in terms of what she identifies as the convergence of the "culture of confession and the culture of testimony" in contemporary Western society. Certainly, these memoirs can be situated in relation to our society's compulsive use of social networking technologies such as Facebook and Twitter to document and broadcast the minutiae of our daily existence.[22] But these texts share another element: the experience of the Iranian Revolution, and of the challenges of exilic life, as an emotional wound or rupture to women's subjectivity. These autobiographies tend to portray the revolution as an individual and collective trauma colored by a powerful nostalgia for the prerevolutionary era. The central sentiment they foreground is that of loss: deeply personal memories intertwined with the rupture of a cultural and national identity effected by the 1979 revolution. Katharine Hodgkin and Susannah Radstone have observed that "memory in the public sphere—is inseparable from discourses of national identity. Memory, then, both underpins and undermines the national narrative."[23] In the case of contemporary Iranian women's autobiographies, personal memoirs enter the political sphere by bringing to the fore questions of home and nation, identity and belonging.

While both Asayesh's and Bahrampour's texts are marked by nostalgia and a longing for prerevolutionary Iran, filtered through childhood memories, a significant difference between their texts is captured by their choice of coordinating conjunctions in their titles. While Bahrampour writes of a life in Iran *and* America, situating herself as a more or less fluid border crosser, Asayesh indicates the pain of cultural dislocation and liminality as she lives a life *between* Iran and America. Asayesh's memoir offers a painful exploration of self, a poignant meditation on diasporic life. She turns her focus inward in her book, reflecting on her relationship to Iran, to the United States, to her husband and her children. *Saffron Sky* is an internal exploration of a loss of cultural identity, and more acutely, of herself. Asayesh's text is structured around the theme of departures and arrivals, leave-takings and homecomings. *Saffron Sky* begins with a chapter entitled "The Return," in which she writes of going back to Iran after a fourteen-year absence and of experiencing this return to

Iranian culture through the senses: "The taste of pomegranate juice, the sight of sheep on a city street, the way a pail is made . . . these are the details that define our lives. In forgetting them, I had forgotten my own face. Here in Mashad, little by little, I am restoring the contours of my identity."[24]

The second chapter, entitled "Homecoming: America," underscores the irony of her homecoming to a place in which she feels dislocated. Indeed, the book is structured so as to emphasize the sense of in-betweenness to which the title draws attention. These two chapters are followed by another in the center of the text entitled "Homecoming: Iran." Both chapters on homecoming convey a sense of unease with the notion of claiming home in a single location. The book thus ends with an aptly titled chapter, "In Between," illustrating the quintessential diasporic condition: the inability to choose one side over the other and the challenges of enduring "unhomeliness" everywhere. This final chapter captures Asayesh's dilemma as an Iranian American: she is a product of both cultures and nationalities, but every occasion is marked by loss. Her experiences as a new parent, for instance, are tinged with apprehensions about the incursion of Americanness into her life, and the attendant eviction of her Iranian identity. She writes of her efforts to teach her daughter, Mina, how to speak Farsi, and of her panic when the child dilutes her vocabulary with English: "Anxiety seizes me, for I know that language is the lifeblood of culture. Language is the self, reflected and clothed in nouns and verbs and adjectives. Without Farsi, the Iranian in Mina will shrivel up and die. Even as I think this, I know that my greatest fear is of my own inner shriveling, not Mina's. In guarding Mina's heritage, I guard my own, for they are linked."[25] Asayesh's determination to maintain linguistic and cultural continuity between her Iranian past and her American present is expressed through a nostalgic longing for the Iran of her childhood, a childhood, and historical period, aborted by the rupture of revolution.

In their work on nostalgia and memory, theorists such as Boym, Hirsch, and Leo Spitzer have traced the origin of the word *nostalgia* to a Swiss medical thesis published in 1688. The word comes "from the Greek *nostos*, to return home, and *algia*, a painful feeling."[26] The disease of nostalgia was diagnosed as "a debilitating, sometimes fatal, medical affliction," and its cure was generally understood to be a return to one's original homeland.[27] Although nostalgia is no longer pathologized in the same way, its association with a lost homeland, or a sense of loss "of a more general and abstract type, including the yearning for a 'lost childhood,' for 'irretrievable youth,' for a vanished 'world of yesterday'" continues.

Only in her chapter on childhood does Asayesh represent an uncomplicated connection to one nation or home: Iran. This chapter, entitled "Childhood," offers a nostalgic look at a childhood of pure pleasure and a life rich with family relationships and connections, one in which she is possessed by a sense of wholeness that eludes her in the United States. Her move to the latter country, and her break from her Iranian girlhood and cultural mores, is captured poignantly in the following chapter entitled "The Break." Here she describes herself as a young girl who goes on her first date with an American, and who makes the bold decision of breaking the rules of (gendered) behavior by putting her arm around the young man's waist: "I can still remember, as if it were seared into the palm of my hand, the cool silk of his jacket, the forbidden heat of the body beneath. I can still remember the moment when I let go of that girl from Iran."[28] Interestingly, this final break with Iranianness coincides with a quintessential "loss-of-innocence" moment that signifies her departure from a home—associated with childhood simplicity, coherence, and national belonging—to an "away-from-home" state equated with the confusing experiences of nascent adulthood, as well as severance from the original culture or nation.

Theorists of the nation have addressed the concept of home as both physical location and imaginative space; their formulations of citizenship and belonging have been taken up by postcolonial and feminist scholars interested in questions of self and other, home and away, center and margin. Scholars studying the culture of childhood have also explored this figuration of the nation as home, arguing that the home/nation, often associated with the maternal, is frequently represented as the natural space of the child. Any transgression out of this space, any move away from home, is marked by deep anxiety because it leads to the space of the unknown, a terrain laden with the anxieties of adolescence and entry into adulthood, and the accompanying loss of childhood innocence.[29]

In point of fact, Asayesh's heartrending description of her sense of loss and dislocation on arriving in the United States is deeply bound up with the loss of childhood innocence: "In America childhood seemed to end early, to be replaced by a cultivated cynicism that masked both vulnerability and immaturity. . . . Going to high school in America felt like a violation of my childhood, an abrupt and painful loss of innocence."[30]

Her comments confirm the place of exile as profoundly unnatural and disruptive to the organic wholeness of the state of childhood; exile corrupts and abridges what is perceived as a pure experience and stage of life protected from the complex world outside the home.[31] While Asayesh explains the diasporic condition as a loss of childhood innocence and of cultural belonging, an ambivalent location of self across national borders, her narrative also invokes an idealized representation of childhood and of the child's place within the home and the nation. This nostalgic formulation and equation of childhood with memories of home and a sense of belonging is found in both Asayesh's and Bahrampour's texts; their poignant sense of loss and deep nostalgia is bound up with a sense of the permanent loss of childhood and of Iran-as-home. As they adapt to their new lives in the United States, they negotiate their own nostalgic childhood memories with the nostalgia of their parents' generation for an Iran left behind.

In *To See and See Again*, Bahrampour's announcement to her parents that she is returning to Iran for a visit elicits a swift and sharp response from her mother:

"She turns to me, trying to be calm, but there is a bitterness in her voice that I have never heard before. 'What are you looking for? Your childhood? You can't get that back.'"[32] Her brusque reaction can perhaps be explained by an apprehension of the repercussions of what Bahrampour may be seeking: perhaps the mother fears that by revisiting the place of her childhood, Bahrampour is moving away from her current home and reclaiming a past and a cultural identity to which her (American) mother no longer has access. Throughout her book, Bahrampour offers nostalgic anecdotes and remembrances of her childhood friends and of the games they played. The book even ends with a poignant description of one of those games:

[The game] calls for four people to stand beside four trees in a wide-open square of grass. The fifth one stands in the center, and at a signal we run, trying to switch trees without the middle person getting there before us. The pattern is circular and endless. After each run, someone is always left floating in the middle of the lawn. The floater cries out and the rest of us pick a direction and run blindly until we hit a tree and whip our arms around it. We stop with a jerk, breathless, relieved to be holding on to the solid trunk. And then we look around to see where we are.[33]

The text concludes with this description that reorients the reader back to an irretrievable past, and to a game that has ambivalence and unbelonging built into its very structure. While Bahrampour's text, like Asayesh's, offers a nostalgic recollection of her idyllic childhood in Iran, her relationship to her diasporic identity is more celebratory than Asayesh's as suggested by the subtitle of her book. The use of the coordinating conjunction *and* suggests an embrace of the two cultures rather than a fraught relationship between the two. This idea is further illustrated by the fact that Bahrampour herself is a product of both cultures, with an American mother and an Iranian father. Rather than feel out of place in either context, she moves freely across borders—performing the occasional social gaffe in Iranian contexts, where the rules of social behavior are at times more prescribed than in American ones.

Like Asayesh's, Bahrampour's recollections of her prerevolutionary childhood in Iran border on the idyllic, but there is an awareness that her childhood experiences were not typical. During a reunion with an old friend from Iran, the daughter of American professors, Bahrampour is initially startled to hear herself referred to as an expatriate, but accepts the relative accuracy of the description:

That day at breakfast Carla illustrated my own expatness with a story I hadn't remembered, an indication of how separate, at the age of four, we already felt from those around us. One day we begged to dress up like Iranian women, so Mama bought a length of black cloth and made us two little chadors. We draped them over our heads and squatted silently against a wall the way we had seen Iranian women do in the street. We already knew we would never wear chadors in our real lives; no matter how many dark, draped women we passed on the

sidewalk, we would end up in minidresses and tights like our mothers. Ours was
an expat game. You don't see children of immigrants to America dressing up as
Americans for a day; they make sure to dress American every day.[34]

Nevertheless, Bahrampour claims Iran as her home, just as she claims America as
her home, meanwhile recognizing the differences between her family's postrevolutionary exilic experience and those of other Iranians: "When we finally left, we were
not immigrants to America either. Three of us had been born there; four of us spoke
perfect American English. Landing in America, we went straight to Grandma and
Grandpa's backyard swimming pool in the hills."[35]

　　Bahrampour recognizes that she cannot uncomplicatedly claim a diasporic
identity; although her parents were forced to choose one home over another, both
places were, in a way, equally home to them. At the same time, the transition to
the United States was not entirely smooth, and Bahrampour writes of the pain of
displacement and dislocation filtered through the emotions of adolescence. She
recounts her coming to terms with her Iranian identity as she embraces her American side, emphasizing the revolutionary trauma and sense of permanent loss experienced by Iranians of her generation, particularly those who were in preadolescence
at the time of revolution: "Strangely, [a sense of displacement] seems strongest in
Iranians my own age. Those young enough to have adjusted to America but old
enough to still remember Iran seem to have the most difficulty choosing their cultural allegiances, perhaps because they were too young to have made their own
decisions about staying in Iran or leaving."[36]

　　The feeling of cultural alienation was heightened by the political climate
in the United States in 1980; this was the time of the hostage crisis and of overwhelming anti-Iranian sentiment in the United States. The yellow ribbons Americans pinned to their clothes and tied around trees signified support for American
hostages in Iran, but they also worked as divisive symbols of true-blood American patriotism, bringing some members of society together, while excluding others.
These ribbons were part of a visible campaign that drew clear lines in the sand,
demarcating good from evil. This was also the time that the popular band Vince
Vance and the Valiants released a song, "Bomb Iran," to the tune of the famous
Beach Boys' "Barbara Ann."[37]

　　Thus Iranians fleeing the trauma of revolution arrived in the United States
to suffer the trauma of American xenophobia during the hostage crisis. Seen from
this vantage point, the overwhelming number of autobiographies in the postrevolutionary period illustrate Kai Erikson's argument about the social dimension of
trauma and its possibilities for creating community.[38] As Asayesh and Bahrampour
work through their personal and public memories, they are initiating, through their
recounting of trauma on individual and national scales, "a kind of empathic 'sharing'
that moves us forward, if only by inches."[39]

Revolution and Postmemory

Moaveni's *Lipstick Jihad* needs to be considered slightly apart from the works of Asayesh and Bahrampour. While Moaveni's text, like Asayesh's and Bahrampour's, is interlaced with nostalgic memories of Iran, Moaveni's longing for "home" precedes her visit to the country that she sees for the first time at the age of five. Her trip recements her nostalgia for an Iran mediated through an earlier generation's memories and yearning for an elusive homeland. Her book thus begins critically self-aware of her mediated relationship to Iran: "I was born in Palo Alto, CA, into the lap of an Iranian diaspora community awash in nostalgia and longing for an Iran many thousands of miles away. As a girl, raised on the distorting myths of exile, I imagined myself a Persian princess, estranged from my homeland—a place of light, poetry, and nightingales—by a dark, evil force called the Revolution. I borrowed the plot from Star Wars, convinced it told Iran's story."[40]

Moaveni's nostalgia for Iran is mediated through postmemory, a term that "specifically describes the relationship of children of survivors of cultural or collective trauma to the experiences of their parents, experiences that they 'remember' only as the narratives and images with which they grew up, but that are so powerful, so monumental, as to constitute memories in their own right."[41] Moaveni's text illustrates the productive ways in which this concept can be applied to the specifics of an Iranian situation. Her longing for an idealized prerevolutionary Iran constitutes a nostalgia transmitted by the generation that preceded her, the generation that lived through the traumatic revolutionary years in Iran and through the ordeal of the hostage crisis in the United States.

What the three autobiographical texts have in common, then, is a description of the diasporic condition as loss—a loss of childhood, a loss of cultural identity, and a loss of (national) home. Moaveni's mediated nostalgia for Iran manifests itself through a longing for a childhood and home to which she did not have access except briefly during a visit to Tehran as a child, a trip romanticized through her memories of climbing mulberry trees in an "orchard . . . so dense that I could scramble from the limb of one tree to another, plucking the plump, red berries as I went along. . . . The trees stretched out as far as I could see, a glorious forest of mulberries, ripe for my picking."[42] This pastoral scene of idyllic childhood colors her self-representation and understanding of her Persianness and shapes her relationship to a country that she has never physically inhabited but that occupies her imagination throughout her growing years in Northern California. It is this imaginative inhabiting of Iran that inspires her "return" in a chapter entitled "Homecoming."

When she moves to Tehran at the age of twenty-four as a *Time* magazine correspondent in 2000, Moaveni becomes acutely aware that her relationship to Iran has been mediated through the memories of a wounded, diasporic generation that has glorified and glamorized the prerevolutionary era and vilified the postrevolutionary period: "Iran, as it turned out, was not the Death Star, but a country where people voted, picked their noses and ate French fries."[43] It is thus Moaveni's "rootless nostalgia" and postmemory that propels her "home" to Iran.[44] The idea of "going home" to a place mostly foreign to her is an example of the ways in which the conditions of exile, of a persistent longing to return to the home country, are conjoined with the effects of trauma, an event experienced "belatedly, in its repeated possession of the one who experiences it."[45] It is indeed this very belatedness of the traumatic experience that gives rise to the concept of postmemory: "Perhaps it is *only* in subsequent generations that trauma can be witnessed and worked through, by those who were not there to live it but who received its effects, belatedly, through the narratives, actions and symptoms of the previous generation."[46] Moaveni, born and raised in the West, bears the marks of such a mediated and belated traumatic experience, through postmemory, as she writes:

> We were all displaced, whether internally, on the streets of Tehran, captives
> in living rooms, strangers in our own country, or externally, in exile, sitting
> in this New York bar, foreigners in a foreign country, at home together. At
> least for now, there would be no revolution that returned Iran to us, and we
> would remain adrift. But the bridge between Iran and the past, Iran and the
> future, between exile and homeland, existed at those tables — in kitchens, in
> bars, in Tehran or Manhattan — where we forgot about the world outside. Iran
> had been disfigured, and we carried its scraps in our pockets, and when we
> assembled, we laid them out, and were home.[47]

A defining feature of most diasporic narratives is an embrace of the ambiguous, ambivalent space of the border. But in these texts, the diasporic experience tends to focus on the trauma of revolution and on the loss of childhood, home, and cultural identity. The impulse in particularly Asayesh's and Moaveni's texts is less about celebrating the state of "unbelonging," to which Bahrampour appears to have reconciled herself, than about repeated attempts to lay claim to an elusive Iranian identity. Asayesh's efforts to reproduce Iranian culture on a small scale — by renovating a room in her house in the traditional Iranian style, by ensuring that her American husband and her children speak Farsi, by returning regularly to Iran for long visits with her family — are indicative of her efforts to bring "home" into the "away." Through these efforts she recreates a version of Iranian culture and identity for her and her children to inhabit in their own domestic space in the United States.

Moaveni's choice to live, work, marry, and have a child in Iran perhaps constitutes her way of accessing an Iranianness no longer available to a nostalgic diasporic Iranian community in California. Rather than celebrating the diasporic position of the border, then, Asayesh and Moaveni work toward resituating themselves within ethnic and national boundaries through attempts to resolidify their Iranian national and cultural heritage. A critical diasporic cultural politics focuses on a creative tension between the home and the host country, interrogating the concept of the nation-state that tends to emphasize borders and locating and celebrating a border space that facilitates the production of hybrid cultural forms.[48] But at this particular historical juncture, the wounds of revolution are still fresh, and we remain at the preliminary stages of capturing and processing a sense of loss before we can redefine our diasporic subject positions through the possibilities of revolutionary trauma.

However, as we begin this process of working through the trauma of revolution, a process identified by Dominick LaCapra as an ability "to recall in memory that something happened to one (or one's people) back then while realizing that one is living here and now with openings to the future," we can see the possibility of trauma as a productive wound, one that compels a reconfiguration of Iranian national and gendered identities.[49] In the Iranian context, the radical rupture in the political, social, and cultural fabric of the nation effected by the revolution can enable, and indeed already has enabled, alternative forms of self-imagining. The redefinition of the nation, of culture, and of gender roles are represented as both rupture and possibility in Iranian women's writings, positioning Iranian women in the diaspora as key players in the process of reimagining Iranian women's subjectivities through revolutionary trauma.

Notes

I am grateful to the anonymous reviewers for their insightful comments on an earlier version of this article.

1. Gelareh Asayesh, *Saffron Sky: A Life between Iran and America* (Boston: Beacon, 1999); and Tara Bahrampour, *To See and See Again: A Life in Iran and America* (New York: Farrar, Straus and Giroux, 1999).
2. A handful of examples include Davar Ardalan's *My Name Is Iran: A Memoir* (New York: Henry Holt, 2007); Firoozeh Dumas, *Funny in Farsi: A Memoir of Growing Up Iranian in America* (New York: Villard, 2003), and *Laughing Without an Accent: Adventures of an Iranian American at Home and Abroad* (New York: Villard, 2008); Farideh Goldin, *Wedding Song: Memoirs of an Iranian Jewish Woman* (Lebanon, NH: Brandeis University Press, 2003); Roya Hakakian, *Journey from the Land of No: A Girlhood Caught in Revolutionary Iran* (New York: Crown, 2004); Afschineh Latifi, *Even After All This Time: A Story of Love, Revolution, and Leaving Iran* (New York: HarperCollins, 2005); Nahid Rachlin, *Persian Girls: A Memoir* (New York: Penguin, 2006); Marjane Satrapi, *Persepolis: The Story of a Childhood* (New York: Pantheon, 2003), and *Persepolis 2: The Story of a Return* (New York: Pantheon, 2004).
3. See Farzaneh Milani, *Veils and Words: The Emerging Voices of Iranian Women Writers* (Syracuse, NY: Syracuse University Press, 1992); and Afsaneh Najmabadi, ed., *Women's Autobiographies in Contemporary Iran* (Cambridge, MA: Harvard University Press, 1990).
4. Shusha Guppy's *The Blindfold Horse: Memories of a Persian Childhood* (London: Heinemann, 1988) and *A Girl in Paris: A Persian Encounter with the West* (London: Heinemann, 1991), are the exceptions here.
5. In *Veils and Words*, Milani makes an opposite claim, suggesting that in Iran, men tended to write memoirs, drawing on public, historical events, while women's autobiographical writing (an underutilized genre that began to emerge in the mid-twentieth century) turned the gaze inward and drew on personal experiences (207).
6. Svetlana Boym, *The Future of Nostalgia* (New York: Basic Books, 2001), 8.
7. Ibid., 41.
8. Nancy K. Miller has argued that "memoir writing . . . participates in an important form

of collective memorialisation, providing building blocks to a more fully shared national narrative." See her "Reading Spaces: 'But Enough About Me, What Do You Think of My Memoir?'" *Yale Journal of Criticism* 13 (2000): 424.

9. Gillian Whitlock, *Soft Weapons: Autobiography in Transit* (Chicago: University of Chicago Press, 2007), 164.

10. Cathy Caruth, *Unclaimed Experience: Trauma, Narrative, and History* (Baltimore: Johns Hopkins University Press, 1996), 4.

11. Suzette Henke, *Shattered Subjects: Trauma and Testimony in Women's Life-Writing* (New York: St. Martin's, 2000).

12. I am borrowing the evocative expression "gathering of the wounded" from Kai Erikson's "Notes on Trauma and Community," in *Trauma: Explorations in Memory*, ed. Cathy Caruth (Baltimore: Johns Hopkins University Press, 1995), 187.

13. Azadeh Moaveni, *Lipstick Jihad: A Memoir of Growing Up Iranian in America and American in Iran* (New York: Public Affairs, 2005).

14. Katharine Hodgkin and Susannah Radstone, "Transforming Memory: Introduction," in *Contested Pasts: The Politics of Memory* (New York: Routledge, 2003), 27.

15. Marianne Hirsch, "Surviving Images: Holocaust Photographs and the Work of Postmemory," *Yale Journal of Criticism* 14 (2001): 5–37.

16. See Niki Akhavan et al., "A Genre in the Service of Empire," ZNet, February 2, 2007, www.payvand.com/news/07/feb/1007.html; Roxana Bahramitash, "The War on Terror, Feminist Orientalism, and Orientalist Feminism: Case Studies of Two North American Bestsellers," *Critique: Critical Middle Eastern Studies* 14 (2005): 221–35; Catherine Burwell, "Reading Lolita in Times of War: Women's Book Clubs and the Politics of Reception," *Intercultural Education* 18 (2007): 281–96; Hamid Dabashi, "Native Informers and the Making of the American Empire," *Al-Ahram Weekly On-line*, June 1–7, 2006, weekly.ahram.org.eg/2006/797/special.htm; Anne Donadey and Huma Ahmed-Ghosh, "Why Americans Love Azar Nafisi's *Reading Lolita in Tehran*," *Signs: Journal of Women in Culture and Society* 33 (2008): 623–46; Fatemeh Keshavarz, *Jasmine and Stars: Reading More than Lolita in Tehran* (Chapel Hill: University of North Carolina Press, 2007); Negar Mottahedeh, "Off the Grid: Reading Iranian Memoirs in Our Time of Total War," *Middle Eastern Report Online*, September 2004, www.merip.org/mero/interventions/mottahedeh_interv.html. See references to Nafisi in Nima Naghibi and Andrew O'Malley, "Estranging the Familiar: 'East' and 'West' in Satrapi's *Persepolis*," *English Studies in Canada* 31 (2005): 223–47; and in Nima Naghibi, *Rethinking Global Sisterhood: Western Feminism and Iran* (Minneapolis: University of Minnesota Press, 2007).

17. Graham Huggan, *The Post-colonial Exotic: Marketing the Margins* (London: Routledge, 2001).

18. Azar Nafisi, *Reading Lolita in Tehran: A Memoir in Books* (New York: Random House, 2003), and *Things I've Been Silent About: Memories* (New York: Random House, 2008). A smattering of examples of the popular works include: *Zoya's Story: An Afghan Woman's Struggle for Freedom* (2002); *My Forbidden Face: Growing Up under the Taliban; A Young Woman's Story by Latifa* (2001); and *Behind the Burqa: Our Life in Afghanistan and How We Escaped to Freedom (by Sulima and Hala)* (2002).

19. See Whitlock, *Soft Weapons.*

20. Ibid., 3.

21. Leigh Gilmore, *The Limits of Autobiography: Trauma and Testimony* (Ithaca, NY: Cornell University Press, 2001), 2.

22. Ibid. An extreme manifestation of this navel-gazing phenomenon is Gordon Bell's Microsoft-sponsored My Life Bits project, in which Bell scans and uploads every piece of communication

(e-mails, phone calls, scribbled notes) he has received throughout his entire life. The obsessive recording and digitizing of all his communications also spill over into the visual terrain as he continually photographs himself; this bizarre project is a radical example of our obsession with documenting and making public the (often mundane) details of our lives.

23. Hodgkin and Radstone, "Transforming Memory," 170.
24. Asayesh, *Saffron Sky*, 22.
25. Ibid., 213.
26. Marianne Hirsch and Leo Spitzer, "'We Would Not Have Come Without You': Generations of Nostalgia," in *Contested Pasts: The Politics of Memory*, ed. Katharine Hodgkin and Susannah Radstone (New York: Routledge, 2003), 82.
27. Ibid., 82. Boym defines algia as "longing" and nostalgia as "a longing for a home that no longer exists, or has never existed." See Boym, *The Future of Nostalgia*, xiii.
28. Asayesh, *Saffron Sky*, 113.
29. My thanks to Andrew O'Malley for his insights on discourses of childhood and the home.
30. Asayesh, *Saffron Sky*, 103.
31. See Mavis Reimer's edited collection *Home Words: Discourses of Children's Literature in Canada* (Waterloo, ON: Wilfrid Laurier University Press, 2008), for various conceptualizations of home and childhood in Canadian children's literature.
32. Bahrampour, *To See and See Again*, 201.
33. Ibid., 357.
34. Ibid., 354.
35. Ibid., 355.
36. Ibid., 348.
37. This ugly chapter in American history reared its head again when the Republican presidential candidate Senator John McCain made a glib reference to "Bomb Iran" on a campaign stop in South Carolina in April 2007. In response to an irate audience member who wanted to know what he was going to do regarding the "obvious" Iranian "threat," McCain's response was to sing "Bomb Iran." His offhand allusion to this inflammatory song was posted on YouTube.com and attracted much criticism.
38. Erikson, "Notes on Trauma and Community," 185.
39. E. Ann Kaplan, *Trauma Culture* (New Brunswick, NJ: Rutgers University Press, 2005), 37.
40. Moaveni, *Lipstick Jihad*, iv.
41. Hirsch, "Surviving Images," 9. Although Hirsch uses the term in her work on Holocaust survivors and their descendants, she states that she does not intend to "restrict the notion of postmemory to the remembrance of the Holocaust" (11).
42. Moaveni, *Lipstick Jihad*, 3.
43. Ibid., iv.
44. Hirsch and Spitzer, "We Would Not Have Come Without You," 85.
45. Caruth, *Trauma: Explorations in Memory*, 4.
46. Hirsch, "Surviving Images," 12.
47. Moaveni, *Lipstick Jihad*, 246.
48. Nasrin Rahimieh's recent "Border Crossing" offers a poignant exploration of the politics and poetics of the in-between by theorizing her own border crossings from Iran to the United States, Canada, and back to the United States, where she currently resides. Her analysis grapples with the critical questions of citizenship and belonging, trauma and memory that preoccupy the current generation of Iranian American women writers. See her "Border Crossing," *Comparative Studies of South Asia, Africa, and the Middle East* 27 (2007): 225–32.
49. Dominick LaCapra, *Writing History, Writing Trauma* (Baltimore: Johns Hopkins University Press, 2001), 21–22.

Figure 1. Theory of Survival, announcement card. Design by Navid Ghaem Maghami.
Photograph by Leila Pazooki

The Theory of Survival

An Interview with Taraneh Hemami

Behrooz Ghamari-Tabrizi

Taraneh Hemami was the guest curator of an exhibition she called Theory of Survival at the Yerba Buena Center for the Arts in San Francisco. The exhibition, which ran from July 19 to August 24, 2008, attracted considerable attention from the local media and the Iranian American communities in the Bay Area. The exhibit included the work of three other Iranian artists: Reza Aramesh, based in London; Gita Hashemi, based in Toronto; and Leila Pazooki, based in Berlin. Each contributor presented a variety of multimedia and installation pieces through which they addressed the experiences of different generations of Iranians who participated in the revolutionary movement of the 1970s and 1980s and its aftermath. The title of the show, Theory of Survival, is a conspicuous reference to a 1969 revolutionary pamphlet, *The Necessity of Armed Struggle and the Refutation of the Theory of Survival*, a manifesto promoting Marxist-Leninist urban guerilla warfare against the Shah's regime. The author of the pamphlet, Amir Parviz Pouyan, was one of the founding members of the underground Fadāʾiyan-e Khalq (Devotees of the People) organization established in 1970. In his pamphlet, he advanced a thesis about "two absolutes": "[Workers] presume," Pouyan wrote, "the power of their enemy to be *absolute* and their own inability to emancipate themselves [to be] *absolute*." Furthermore, he asked: "How can one think of emancipation while confronting absolute power with absolute weakness?"[1]

He had hoped that a campaign of assassinations of high-profile figures would expose the regime's military and security vulnerabilities to the masses, who in

Radical History Review
Issue 105 (Fall 2009)   DOI 10.1215/01636545-2009-006
© 2009 by MARHO: The Radical Historians' Organization, Inc.

turn would overthrow their tyrants. It is evident now how flawed Pouyan's strategy was. Moreover, the masses (the majority of them unfamiliar with Pouyan's thesis) remained unresponsive. By 1976, only two years before the commencement of large-scale protests that culminated in the 1979 revolution, the entire founding leadership of Pouyan's Fadā'iyan were either killed or jailed. Although the guerilla movement (and a host of other Marxist or Marxist-influenced organizations) did not directly spark the 1979 revolution, it did leave a profound mark on Iranian sensibilities and historical memory. Thousands of young people participating in the protests during 1978–79 were inspired by the selfless revolutionary fervor of the Fadā'iyan and the ideals of a just, classless society for which they were willing to die.

Behrooz Ghamari-Tabrizi: *Let me first thank you for agreeing to this interview and for allowing us to share some of the images of the exhibition with our readers. How did the idea of this exhibition come about?*

Taraneh Hemami: For the past few years I have been engaged in collecting memories and memoirs from the Iranian community in the Bay Area.[2] The process began as a need for me to make sense of my history and to forge connections to the stories of the community, as well as a celebration of surviving the most difficult years of our migration. The collected material became an embracement of our history as a community, in all its pride and flaws, as well as a reservoir for generations to come, a connection between past and present.

In 2006, CrossConnections, the collective project I was directing at the California College of the Arts, attempted to expand its collection of archives to include historical material for a four-day event entitled We Are Here: An Archive in Progress.[3] As a response to our open call to the community, Parviz Shokat, a long-time local activist, brought to our attention a basement full of boxes of Iranian books, posters, newspapers and periodicals that belonged to Bonyad-e Farhang (Culture Foundation), a small organization that had attempted to create a public library for the community but had to close its doors within a year due to lack of funding. There had been attempts to find a home for the books and other documents for years, and some were donated to the UC Berkeley library as well as the Hoover Institute at Stanford; however, most had been collecting dust and had been damaged in the many moves over the past thirty years. The majority of the material was from the library of the Iranian Students Association of Northern California that had been active from 1964 to 1984 and included a large array of publications printed outside of Iran and reflected the political sensibilities of the Iranian student organizations worldwide.

Our two-week process for We Are Here allowed for a first round of cleaning, sorting, archiving, and displaying of the materials. It was heartbreaking to have to return the material to the boxes without making them accessible to the public. I ended up feeling quite responsible for preserving this material as history. As most publications in Iran have been censored throughout time, it was important to hang onto the alternative history this material represented. In the following year, trying to find a home for the books in a public collection, I met Hirad Dinavari from the Library of Congress, who immediately became an advocate for the collection.

I was able to create another opportunity for the books to come out of their hiding through a one-month collective residency at the Lab, a four thousand–square feet of alternative art space in San Francisco. The large space made it possible to sort and organize the entire collection and to make a short list for the Library of Congress from which they could make their final acquisition decision. Artists were invited to come in for the duration of the residency to respond to the material in different forms, from drawings to performance and video. The general public also had limited access to the material for the duration of the residency. Our audience and participants were primarily Iranian, since most of the material was in Persian. It was during this residency that I was offered an exhibition opportunity as part of the triennial Bay Area Now 5 at Yerba Buena Center for the Arts (YBCA). As a reflection of the global nature of the Iranian student movement, I proposed a collective response by Iranian diaspora artists to these political publications, intended as an exchange and connection between the artists engaged in discussions, dialogues, and cocreations. We wanted to share this engagement with audiences through exhibition and performances.

BGT: *The title of the exhibition, Theory of Survival, conspicuously refers to Amir Parviz Pouyan's pamphlet. As you know, Pouyan's manifesto is about the "refutation of the theory of survival." Did you have a parody of Pouyan in mind?*

TH: During the process of organizing and sorting the material for We Are Here, I had invited a number of friends to help, since most of the artists involved had little knowledge of the history of the period and needed help from across generations to elucidate the material. This process led to exchange of stories, myths, and histories and created a conducive environment for raising questions and trying to revisit this critical era through the documents.

The title occurred to me as I came across a few copies of the book in the boxes and discovered its role in initiating a movement that had inspired so many to sacrifice their lives. They risked everything in the prime of their youth for the dream of justice and equality. The violence that followed the 1979 revolution and the establishment of an Islamic Republic, the disillusionments, the defeat, and the disappointment, would end up defining this generation living in the shadow of conflict, terror, and war. What I find interesting is theorizing the survival of an ideology which itself refuted the theory of survival.

There was also the material survival of the theory in the form of the books we found in the damp basement. There were remembered stories about smuggling of the banned books inside the country, of hiding them in basements, under piles of dirt, burning them to elude the authorities, and destroying the evidence of ever being moved by the dream of a just society and sacrifices made toward this goal. For most who experienced this history there followed a story of migration. Migration demands letting go of a settled home, a stable identity, extended family, networks and connections, and the knowledge of the world around you. Migration demands letting go of possessions, relationships, in many cases language, and connectivity. To survive, you let go. What has survived as memories are the hopes of a generation, which can be gleaned through the pages of material that had been stored in boxes.

BGT: *There was a passage in the exhibition's description posted on the YBCA Web page that caught my attention. It says, "The artists that guest curator Taraneh Hemami has chosen to work with collectively investigate the archives of the past while exploring notions of devotion, salvation, victory, freedom and survival." These are such powerful, existential words. Could you elaborate on these themes?*

TH: Loss fills the pages of these newspapers, flyers, and books, page after page of headshots; young faces arresting your gaze, those who have lost their lives for their devotion to an ideology, becoming martyrs for their beliefs, for their truth. In this endless list of names are reflected countless differences but a shared ideal of being free. As we delved deeper into the materials, we ended up with more questions about notions of sacrifice, action, reward, and belief. The archives reflected changed, fractured, and defeated ideologies, and the process through which their significance is altered through time.

BGT: *One of the main themes of the exhibition, which was also evident in Leila Pazooki's split video installation, is what happens to ideologies when they cross borders. Am I right to think that your goal here is to see how the postrevolutionary generation of immigrant Iranians relates to this past? Do you also see the exhibition as a commentary on nostalgia?*

TH: There are layers of connection between this title and the materials and the artists who traveled across oceans to engage with them. Crossing characterizes how different and at times competing ideologies in the sixties and seventies traveled from all around the world to Iran. Liberation movements around the globe deeply influenced Iranian university students, both inside and outside the country. The rapid modernization of the country had created an educated elite who traveled extensively and followed the Western trends — in fashion, art, and ideals in politics — and many of whom came into conflict with the monarchy. In effect, however, this conflict led to a revolution that in many respects generated unanticipated results. Over the past thirty years, we have seen so many different kinds of border crossing that has shaped the lives of Iranians, particularly those who left the country. The question we pondered was what role these ideologies that define the life of a generation now play in their lives. To the postrevolutionary generation, the collected material at the exhibit is a primary source of information about and illumination on an era that has had a defining role in shaping their identity and yet has been almost completely erased from public memory.

BGT: *These installations dealt with an overtly political topic. I wonder whether you also intended at the same time to transcend its underlying politics. Let me be clearer: Am I correct in assuming that in your exhibit the books, posters, flyers, and pamphlets present mere objects evoking memories of a generation, somehow stripped of their actual content?*

TH: I find the specifics of the archives interesting on so many levels. They represent another side of the story, of the history—aspirations and hopes of a generation. The visual, written language, the politics and philosophy of the pamphlets and publications reflect the specifics of this moment in Iranian history which brought along new and diverse sets of political, cultural, and artistic influences through the agency of Iranian students abroad, whether in Köln [Cologne], Germany, Milan, Italy, Washington, D.C., or Berkeley, California.

   The materials are containers of memory and relics of a past. For so many Iranians who experienced exile, the material becomes symbolic of a particular trend of the revolutionary fervor, which paradoxically resulted in their permanent departure from "home." They are silenced dreams, and at the same time are evidence of the resolve of members of a generation, their successes and failures. They are the stories behind the exodus of a few million Iranians. They also represent what was intentionally erased by the Islamic Republic in its concerted efforts to transform Iran by monopolizing the production of public images of Iran, the Iranian Revolution, and Iranians.

BGT: *As scholars, we often rely on words and narratives to communicate our ideas. Many of us unlock a variety of conceptual issues with which we are concerned through the act of writing. I wonder how much of this exhibit was shaped through the act of its production. How did this project affect you?*

TH: The piece is a product of its process—an evidence of the evolution that continues its passage through one phase to another, from the act of collecting to connections that have been forged with artists, scholars, friends, and the Iranian diaspora community. The installation became an experiential narrative of the process of its production. From discovering the materials, hauling-unpacking-archiving, to documentations and reproductions to a process of reengaging with the ideologies and driving force of the material, by relearning, rearranging, and rewriting—as in Gita Hashemi's performance/installation *Ephemeral Monument*, writing on a blackboard, a teach-in constantly renegotiating a persistent unresolved quest.

   The installation at YBCA became a reflection of the stories that were shared between the artists, as well as the past participants and audiences, a reflection on the histories that the material revealed. The books were arranged in temporary shelves inside a wall, exposed only in a few sections, suggesting that they belonged to another time. Language created another degree of separation for those who were not able to read the texts. But at the same time, the inability to read the text forced them to look for other familiar connections. The archive becomes impenetrable if not for images and signs that gain significance in revealing its content and shaping its narrative.

Inviting the audience to respond to the material by writing on a chalkboard, the visitors gravitated to the board. In Reza Aramesh's rereading of a historical ideology, at various intervals during the crowded reception all throughout the spaces of the larger YBCA, ten young volunteers recited William Z. Foster's *The Twilight of World Capitalism*, alluding to the intricacies of communication—repeated lessons of history and ideology lost in the cacophony of voices.

BGT: *This was a collaborative work. Can you elaborate on some of the ideas and concerns you discussed with your collaborators?*

TH: There were many layers of collaborations. The first phase of the project brought together a number of Bay Area Iranian artists for a collective project during the residency at the Lab. In contrast to a traditional exhibition, it was designed as a space of gathering, a library, a research lab, a photo studio, and an open stage for expression. The project was as much about learning to work together as a community as it was about learning about where we had come from and understanding our own history as a diaspora community. Every attempt was made to facilitate an open dialogue, to connect people and ideas, curiosities, and histories. The approach was experimental, with open participation, and was focused on removing boundaries between audience/art while fusing the material and the works produced. Termeh Yeghiazarian's series, for instance, invited audiences and past members of the student organization to pose as live models for her portraits entitled *Anonymous Hero*, alluding to many faceless, nameless "heroes" of that particular generation. Ali Dadgar's tracings of news and public images, lists, slogans, and historical data there were altered in a humorous way, reinterpreting the histories they represented. Darvag Theater group also collaborated by creating a short performance for the closing event, where they spontaneously recited key historical speeches intercepted with revolutionary slogans with members of the group standing discreetly among the audience.

In the second phase at YBCA, we presented materials that were focused on political publications exclusively, and our communication was limited to written and verbal (Skype) dialogues focusing on the era, and each individual artist's connection to the specifics of that moment in Iranian history. To create a meaningful connection with our non-Iranian audiences of YBCA's BAN5, we offered information and posed questions, inviting their participation by adding their voices, questions, and opinions, trying to bridge the gap that the lack of cultural knowledge and language barrier could create.

BGT: *How was the exhibition received by the public?*

TH: What I find interesting in the experiences of the past few exhibitions is the hunger for understanding, both among those who were familiar with the cultural and political context of that period and those who were not. The Iranian visitors and participants most often expressed interest in an open dialogue on the scope and the approach of the exhibition, in documenting stories, in understanding and learning from them. For those who were not familiar with the context, the projects were most effective when they were experienced viscerally, when the conceptual-ideological concerns crept under their skin while reflecting on these entangled relationships and parallel histories. It was quite telling to see the second group participating much more in voicing their thoughts and emotions on the blackboard.

Figure 2. Taraneh Hemami, installation detail, Yerba Buena Center for the Arts, 2008. Photograph by Jahanshah Javid

Figure 3. *What Happens to Ideologies When They Cross Borders?*, Leila Pazooki, installation, Yerba Buena Center for the Arts, 2008. Photograph by Taraneh Hemami

Figure 4. Taraneh Hemami, installation detail, Yerba Buena Center for the Arts, 2008. Photograph by Taraneh Hemami

Figure 5. Taraneh Hemami, installation detail, Yerba Buena Center for the Arts, 2008.
Photograph by Taraneh Hemami

Figure 6. Taraneh Hemami, installation detail, Yerba Buena Center for the Arts, 2008.
Photograph by Taraneh Hemami

Figure 7. Theory of Survival, installation detail, Yerba Buena Center for the Arts, 2008.
Photograph by Taraneh Hemami

Figure 8. Theory of Survival, Yerba Buena Center for the Arts, 2008. Front wall: Taraneh Hemami;
back wall: Leila Pazooki. Photograph by Taraneh Hemami

Figure 9. Theory of Survival, Taraneh Hemami, installation detail, Yerba Buena Center for the Arts, 2008. Photograph by Taraneh Hemami

Figure 10. Taraneh Hemami, installation detail, Yerba Buena Center for the Arts, 2008. Photograph by Taraneh Hemami

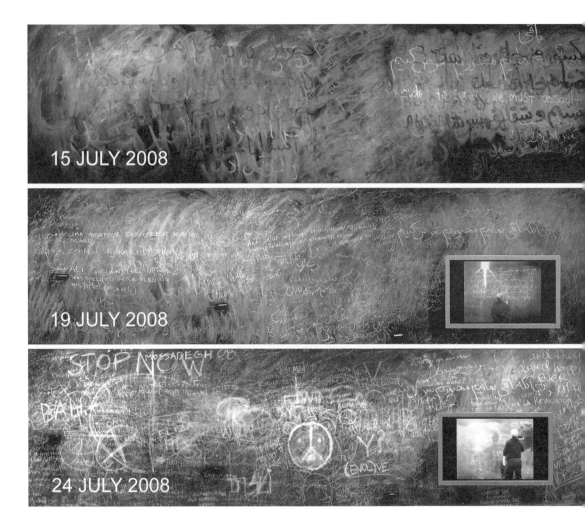

Figure 11. *Ephemeral Monument*, Gita Hashemi, performance and participatory installation, 19' x 6', Yerba Buena Center for the Arts, 2008. Photograph by Gita Hashemi

Notes

1. Amir Parviz Pouyan, *Zaroorat-e mobarezeh-e mosalahaneh va rad-e teory-e bagha* (*The Necessity of Armed Struggle and the Refutation of the Theory of Survival*) (n.p.: n.p., 1969), 4. Pouyan was born in 1946 in Mashad and killed by the security forces during a clash in the western part of Tehran in 1971.
2. Hall of Reflections, Remembrances of the Iranian Immigrants, 2001–present.
3. CrossConnections, engaging the Iranian diaspora community in an intergenerational, creative dialogue about issues of cultural identity, preservation, and representation, 2005–present.

Memory, Mourning, Memorializing

On the Victims of Iran-Iraq War, 1980–Present

Behrooz Ghamari-Tabrizi

In the early summer of 2006, while talking to an Iranian veteran of the Iran-Iraq war, I realized that he used a conscious present tense in his description of the war. I pointed out my observation to him. "When did it end," he smiled glaringly, "how come nobody told us about it?"

In September 1980, exploiting the chaotic postrevolutionary circumstances, Iraqi forces invaded large territories in southern and southwestern Iran. They occupied the oil-rich regions and hoped that in addition to their swift military victories, with a halt in oil production the Iranian economy would collapse and the new regime surrender. Along with his then NATO and Warsaw Pact supporters, Saddam Hussein believed that his quick victory, besides settling old border disputes between the two countries, would contain the Islamic Republic and end its leaders' aspiration of exporting their revolution to neighboring nations. Hussein and his supporters had miscalculated the power of the revolutionary zeal and patriotic fervor of an entire nation. Hundreds of thousands of volunteers were mobilized, trained, and sent to the fronts during the first months of the war. Iraqi victories turned out to be short-lived. Not only did Iranian military and militia forces halt Iraqi advances but they also recaptured most of the occupied territories. By the end of 1982, the old borders were restored; yet for a variety of political and ideological reasons, neither side was willing to end the hostilities.

Radical History Review

Issue 105 (Fall 2009)   DOI 10.1215/01636545-2009-007

© 2009 by MARHO: The Radical Historians' Organization, Inc.

In early 1984, it became evident that the fighting had grown into a long war of attrition. By then, the Iranian side had already recaptured all the territories seized earlier by the Iraqis. However, the Iranian military command had concluded that they needed to establish a buffer zone inside Iraq as a safeguard against future attacks. But the val-Fajr and Kheibar offensives in 1983 and 1984 to capture the Iraqi city of Basra and to control the Basra-Baghdad Highway failed to achieve that goal. The casualties of the war continued to mount. The val-Fajr-5 offensive in February and March 1984 turned particularly deadly for the Iranian side, as the Iraqis with their heavy artillery, French- and Soviet-made helicopter gunships, and extensive use of chemical weapons reportedly killed more than 40,000 Iranians in a four-week period.

The war, which at its inception had threatened the existence of the postrevolutionary regime, was thus transformed into a vehicle for the consolidation of the Islamic Republic's power. The dominant factions that exploited it as a state-building tool now had to face the reality that the country's mounting casualties, in addition to war's enormous economic price tag, could cost them their very existence.[1] With its political legitimacy at stake, and no opposition to blame, the regime could no longer sustain its prevarications on terminating the war.

Although world powers were indirectly involved in the eight-year war, neither the Reagan administration nor the Soviet Union saw any benefit in the continuation of a war of attrition. International pressure to end the conflict reached its peak during the so-called tanker wars, when the hostilities directly threatened the free flow of oil from the Persian Gulf. For the first time, American warships took on the responsibility of protecting tankers in the Persian Gulf. They directly responded to threats of the disruption of oil exports from the region. From early 1987 onward, the United States, with its forces in the region and its ultimatum for a final resolution at the United Nations (UN) Security Council, insisted that it would no longer tolerate the continuation of the war.

On July 20, 1987, the UN Security Council unanimously passed Resolution 598, urging Iraq and Iran to accept a cease-fire, withdraw their forces to internationally recognized boundaries, and settle their frontier disputes through negotiations held under UN auspices. Iraq agreed to abide by these terms if Iran followed suit. Iran, however, neither accepted nor rejected the resolution, instead demanding amendments that condemned Iraq as the aggressor and calling on all foreign navies to leave the Persian Gulf. None of the Iranian demands fell on sympathetic ears.

For the Islamic Republic, the final impetus for making peace with Hussein stemmed both from a domestic calculation and from international pressures. The war had become the one, and perhaps the only, medium through which the state managed to perpetuate the revolution and to nurture its legitimacy. The conceptualization of the conflict as the "war against blasphemy," as Prime Minister Mir Hossein Musavi put it, and its ultimate purpose as "the defense of the honor of the Qur'an and Islam," as the speaker of the Majlis (Parliament), Akbar Hashemi Rafsanjani called it, had stifled public debate on its real objectives and the means for ending the war.[2] By 1987, however, it became evident that exploiting the war to maintain the unity and legitimacy of the republic had become an untenable strategy.

In less than nine years, Iran's population had grown by more than 14 million. Now, more than half of all Iranians were under the age of fifteen, the largest age group in the emerging demography of a nation weary of war and with fading memories of the revolution. As Shahram Chubin, one of the leading historians of the war, observed in 1988:

> After seven years, the momentum of the war has not yet been exhausted. However, in the past year there has been a marked change in the tempo of the war, domestic politics of Iran, and what might be called psychological expectation. Within Iran there has been a quickening of the pace of domestic politics, as if the war was in its last phase and the domestic decks needed to be cleared for action. The Islamic Republican Party has been dissolved, conscription broadened, an anti-profiteering campaign initiated, a financial *jihad* proclaimed, a new will for Khomeini submitted. . . . The sense of urgency is unmistakable and derives as much from the pressures of the war as it does from anticipation of Khomeini's immanent demise.[3]

This sense of urgency intensified when the U.S. navy attacked Iranian ships and oil platforms in October 1987 and April 1988. The fear of direct confrontation with the American forces in the Persian Gulf, against the backdrop of rising political factionalism within the Islamic Republic and popular discontent, forced Ayatollah Ruhollah Khomeini's close advisors to encourage him to accept Resolution 598 unconditionally. The pressure on Khomeini intensified on July 3, 1988, when the USS *Vincennes* shot down an Iranian passenger plane, killing all 290 passengers on board. Iran Air flight 655, the Boeing 747 en route from Bandar Abbas to Dubai, was apparently mistaken for a much smaller and sleeker F-14 fighter plane. Whatever the circumstances and intentions behind the event, its result was unambiguous.

Three weeks later, in one of his most remarkable speeches, Khomeini accepted the terms of Resolution 598. He referred to the cease-fire as a "poisonous chalice" that *had* to be drunk:

> Accepting the UN resolution was truly a very bitter and tragic issue for everyone, particularly me. Only a few days ago, I was in support of the policy of the sacred defense, and saw the interests of the country and the revolution in the continuation of the war. But for reasons about which I cannot speak now,

and which will be clarified with the help of God in the future, at this juncture, I regard [the cease-fire] to be in the interest of the revolution and of the system. God knows that had it not been for the desire to sacrifice our selves, honor, and credibility for the sake of Islam and the Muslims, I would never have agreed to this. Death and martyrdom would have been more bearable to me. But what is the solution except that all of us should submit to the satisfaction of the Divine Will. . . . How unhappy I am because I have survived and have [to drink] the poisonous chalice of accepting the resolution.[4]

Khomeini died a few months later in June 1989. No one felt the bitterness of the poison he had spoken of more acutely than the hundreds of thousands of veterans on their homecoming. As depicted in Mohsen Makhmalbaf's masterful 1989 film, *The Marriage of the Blessed*, they returned to discover that the revolutionary values they had upheld and shielded on the war fronts were now pronounced outdated, even un-Islamic, by the same leaders who had called on them to defend it with their lives. They came back only to realize how oblivious residents of urban centers had grown to their plight. For the nouveaux riches of Tehran and other major cities, the revolution was over.[5]

In a nuanced scene, Makhmalbaf shows this contradiction between the state of mind of the veteran and the postwar realities of everyday life. In a scene in the office of an adjuster, Haji, the protagonist, experiences a flashback when the tapping of the typewriter keys, finalizing a real-estate transaction, melds in his mind and on the screen with his memories of battlefields. With a generic name, Haji symbolizes an entire generation of devoted Muslim revolutionaries now disillusioned and disowned. At Haji's wedding, Makhmalbaf abandons allegories and allows the bridegroom to sabotage the ceremony and divulge his inner crisis in a cathartic breakdown. Speaking through a loudspeaker from a balcony, framed like the supreme leader, Haji addresses the guests first satirically poking fun at their newfound riches: "Guests with mismatched socks are welcome. Guests with mismatched cars are welcome. Guests with mismatched wives are welcome." He then turns bitter, angry, and political: "Eat the food robbed from the poor. Robbed food is delicious. Robbed food is delicious, Robbed food is delicious."

Millions of soldiers, volunteer militias, and revolutionary guards came back from the war; hundreds of thousands of them were wounded, a significant number permanently disabled. Tens of thousands had been exposed to chemical weapons: thirty-six thousand of them required prolonged treatment, and nearly eight hundred of them have since died.[6] More than two hundred thousand were killed. In the absence of a Persian word for *war veteran*, the language made do with a creative neologism, *jānbāzan* (literally, those willing to sacrifice their lives).

With the end of the war, the newly elected president Hashemi Rafsanjani aimed to curtail the revolutionary mores and ideological outlook that had dominated the country and to begin a period of *towse'eh-gera'ei* (growth-oriented planning). In a Friday prayer sermon on November 9, 1990, for the first time the president directly challenged the foundational ideology of postrevolutionary Iran. In what Mohammad Quchani has called the "manifesto of the white collar *hezbollahis* [the partisans of God]," Hashemi Rafsanjani transformed the revolutionary virtues of the *homo Islamicus* — selflessness, austerity, and perpetual discontent — into a post-revolutionary ethos of the prosperous, joyful, and content subject.[7] The *mostaz'af* (disinherited) no longer represented the symbolic or the real power of the republic. In the new era, the *mostaz'af* became the *āsib-pazir* (vulnerable), a pathology to be overcome. After the war, the modus operandi of Hashemi Rafsanjani's adminis-tration became incongruous with the modus vivendi of the old *hezbollahis*. In his manifesto, the president chastised those *hezbollahis* who praised asceticism over indulgence in what life could provide, "God's blessed offering [*ne'mat*]," he scolded the backward-looking masses, "is for the people and the believers [to devour]. Ascet-icism and disuse [*sic*] of holy consumption will create deprivation and a lack of drive to produce, work, and develop."[8]

He further ridiculed the old revolutionary *hezbollahis* for their lack of hygiene and of proper etiquette in public. "Being a revolutionary," he admonished them, "does not mean that one has to live in poverty." In a direct reference to the veterans' discontent, he declared: "There is nothing un-Islamic about the accumula-tion of wealth." Those who advocated the idea that "religion does not give serious consideration to production and proliferation of society's wealth . . . are propagating an un-Islamic viewpoint."[9] He left nothing opaque about how he intended to close the first chapter of the postrevolutionary regime by ending the wartime mentality and institutions of governance. "God has created in human beings an ornamental and beauty-seeking sense," Hashemi Rafsanjani advised the crowd during a Friday prayer, "with a disdain for ugliness."

Seeking beauty is a pillar [of Islam]. Now, if we object to beautiful sights,
it is tantamount to fighting nature, something that God did not want. . . .
We suffer from a culture in which the style of living and the appearance of
priests and *hezbollahis* should be unpleasant and ugly. If it becomes a cultural
phenomenon that being a *hezbollahi* means looking unbearable, this is a sin and
Islam has fought this. . . . It would defame Islam. . . . Luxury should exist, but
not overt luxury. . . . We have religious decrees that you must wear perfume,
comb your hair, comb your beard, and wear a clean outfit. The Prophet himself
looked at his reflection in water to make sure that he was presentable before
his guests.[10]

The president's remarks further antagonized the war veterans and deeply scandal-ized the revolutionaries who had remained powerful in the parliament and were by no means ready to hang up their revolutionary garb. Hashemi Rafsanjani swiftly introduced a cabinet of *kārshenāsān* and *motekhassesin* (experts and specialists) to the parliament and maneuvered his way into getting the majority of deputies' vote of confidence, even though only four of the twenty-two ministerial jobs went to clerics. More generally, he embarked on a campaign to move the center of decision making from the dusty and unsightly quarters of the clerics to the clean, bright, and fragrant offices of his technocratic allies.

The contradiction that the volunteered veterans, with their revolutionary ide-als, faced in the cities gave rise to a new grassroots and highly organized movement against what they described as the "Western cultural invasion." The *hezbollahis*, who fought against the Iraqi invasion and against opposition parties in the early days of the revolution, now found themselves in direct conflict with the post-Khomeini regime. For the first time, this group organized itself to fend off the cultural assault of capitalism and of its corrupt sympathizers within the ruling coalition. The new group named itself Ansār-e Hezbollah (Companions/Helpers of the Party of God) and began publishing a biweekly called *Shalamcheh*.[11] In an interview in 1998, Mas'ud Dehnamaki, the group's forthright spokesperson, recalled, "Ansar-e Hezbol-lah did not exist before 1989; the group came together around that time to defend the values [of the revolution] and fight those who betrayed it."[12]

Hashemi Rafsanjani's reinvention of the revolutionary discourse and his technocratic cadres, whom Quchani calls "necktie revolutionaries," gave rise to an emerging civil society and a consumer middle class.[13] His policies fomented a breach between the postrevolutionary nouveaux riches and the masses of *mostaz'afin* as well as the millions of veterans of the eight-year war. Two factions opposing Hashemi Rafsanjani followed different strategies in mobilizing people against his policy of *bāz-sāzi* (reconstruction). The antirepublican absolutists raised the flag of Islam and designated themselves as the only true Muslims genuinely committed to revolutionary ideals. They successfully coupled the *maslahat* (expediency)-driven pragmatic political philosophy of the new republic and its secularist undertone with the pauperization of *mostaz'afin*, the foot soldiers of the revolution and the war. This strategy bore fruit in the presidential election of 2005, as whose victor emerged a former Revolutionary Guard and the son of a blacksmith, Mahmoud Ahmadinejad.

In contrast, recognizing the significance of constructing a new postwar polit-ical philosophy, many of the former "Jacobins" emphasized the republican core of the revolutionary ideal. They did not defend Hashemi Rafsanjani's growth machine and considered political reform and republicanism as the precondition of social justice for the disinherited. They sought to advance their cause through theological interventions in promoting religious and political pluralism. They found the most comprehensive theological articulation of their political agenda in the new voice of Abdolkarim Soroush, and the most amenable constituents in the growing numbers of the urban youth and women, students, and many secular intellectuals. Said Hajjarian, one of the leading ideologues of the reform movement, gave this project a strategic political voice, which resulted in the landslide victory in 1997 of Mohammad Khatami in the presidential election.

Not only did the eight-year-long "sacred defense" play a constitutive role in the emergence of the postrevolutionary regime but its legacy also continues to inform the political strategy of competing factions. As the tables at the end of this article show, people of all walks of life fought and were killed during the Iran-Iraq war. White- and blue-collar workers, teachers and students, the young and the old, the educated and the illiterate, rural and urban masses all partook in what they believed was a "sacred defense" (see tables 1–3). Although the state affords entitlement programs and benefits to veterans and their families, these services have been progressively diminishing since the end of the war. In many cases, eligibility for services has been turned into a device for party politics and the political mobilization of the veterans.

Wars leave lasting marks on the political and social circumstances of every nation through the ways in which they are remembered, the ways in which these remembrances are contested in public, and the ways in which their legacies are mourned and memorialized. In the following section we offer some photographic images that capture distinct moments of mourning and remembrance.

Table 1. Iranian soldiers killed during the war based on occupation

Occupation	Number	Percentage
Public sector	115,080	52.9
Private sector	39,001	17.9
Clergy	3,117	1.4
University student	2,895	1.3
High school student	36,898	16.9
Homemaker	3,432	1.6
Retired	300	0.1
Children (under 10)	2,503	1.2
Other	14,263	6.7
Total	217,489	100

Source: Holy Defense Week Special, *Iran*, September 22, 2003

Table 2. Iranian soldiers killed during the war based on education

Education	Number	Percentage
Elementary and lower	80,668	37.1
Middle school	55,677	25.6
High school	66,334	30.5
College	8,061	3.7
Seminarian	3,117	1.4
Unknown	3,632	1.7
Total	217,489	100

Source: Holy Defense Week Special, *Iran*, September 22, 2003

Table 3. Rural-urban distribution of Iranian soldiers killed during the war

Residence	Number	Percentage
Urban	147,336	67.7
Rural	70,153	32.3
Total	217,489	100

Source: Holy Defense Week Special, *Iran*, September 22, 2003

The photographs in this section were taken by Melissa Hibbard and Hamid Rahmanian at Behesht-e Zahra (Zahra's Paradise) on the southern outskirts of Tehran. Thousands of deceased Iranian soldiers of the Iran-Iraq war are buried in a sixteen-block section of this enormous cemetery.

Figure 1. Three girls reading the Koran, 2007, by Melissa Hibbard. Image courtesy of the artist

Figure 2. Untitled, digital print, 2007, by Hamid Rahmanian. Image courtesy of the artist

Figure 3. Untitled, digital print, 2007, by Hamid Rahmanian. Image courtesy of the artist

Figure 4. Untitled, digital print, 2007, by Hamid Rahmanian. Image courtesy of the artist

Figure 5. Untitled, digital print, 2007, by Hamid Rahmanian. Image courtesy of the artist

Figure 6. Untitled, digital print, 2007, by Hamid Rahmanian. Image courtesy of the artist

Figure 7. Untitled, digital print, 2007, by Hamid Rahmanian. Image courtesy of the artist

Figure 8. Untitled, digital print, 2007, by Hamid Rahmanian. Image courtesy of the artist

Figure 9. By Melissa Hibbard. Image courtesy of the artist

Notes

1. Because Iran purchased much of its arms on the international black market, estimates on the economic cost of the war vary significantly. In his speech to the Iranian parliament, Musavi stated that "some 30 percent of the 1983–1984 budget . . . was spent on the war effort. Expenditures were 14 percent higher in 1984 than in the previous year." Quoted in Bahman Baktiari, *Parliamentary Politics in Revolutionary Iran: The Institutionazation of Factional Politics* (Gainesville: University Press of Florida, 1996), 119–20. Three years later, in 1987, the prime minister put the expenditure at "52 percent of the total allocations for the government to military and security affairs" of the war. See Shahram Chubin, *Iran and Iraq at War* (Boulder, CO: Westview, 1988), 123–38. Hooshang Amirahmadi, "Economic Reconstruction of Iran: Costing the War Damage," *Third World Quarterly* 12 (1991): 26–47, has offered one of the most plausible sets of figures. He estimated that by 1987, the cost of the war had reached $18 billion; its total economic cost topped $309 billion.

2. Chubin, *Iran and Iraq at War*, 81.

3. Ibid., 252.

4. Ruhollah Khomeini, *Sahifeh-ye nur* (*Collected Declarations of Imam Khomeini*), vol. 20 (Tehran: The Organization of the Islamic Revolution's Cultural Documents, 1992), 238.

5. The disillusionment of veterans was depicted in many other films of the "holy defense" genre. The two notable ones are: Ebrahim Hatamikia's *The Glass Agency* (1998) and Jafar Panahi's *Crimson Gold* (2003).

6. See the following tables for a complete survey of the human costs of war. For the victims of chemical weapons, see Shahriyar Khateri and Mohammad Heidarian, *Jānbāzān-e shimiā'i: Tārikhcheh, āmār, khadamāt* (*Veterans Exposed to Chemical Weapons: History, Statistics, and Services*) (Tehran: Jānbāzān Engineering and Medical Sciences Research Center, 2004), 14.

7. Mohammad Quchani, *Yaqeh sefid-hā* (*The White-Collars*) (Tehran: Naqsh-o-Negar, 2000), 121–32.

8. Quoted in Mehdi Moslem, *Factional Politics in Post-Khomeini Iran* (Syracuse, NY: Syracuse University Press, 2002), 144.

9. Quoted in Daniel Brumberg, *Reinventing Khomeini: The Struggle for Reform in Iran* (Chicago: Chicago University Press, 2001), 161.

10. Quoted in Moslem, *Factional Politics*, 145.

11. This is a reference to the Shalamcheh Valley in the Iranian southwest in which Karbala 8, one of the final war campaigns, turned into one of the bloodiest last-ditch efforts to push into Iraqi territory before Khomeini's acceptance of UN Resolution 598.

12. Quoted in Hojjat Martaji, *Jenāh-hāy-e siyāsi dar Irān-e emruz* (*Political Factions in Contemporary Iran*) (Tehran: Shafi`i, 1999), 39.

13. Mohammad Quchani, *Yaqeh sefid-hā* (*The White-Collars*) (Tehran: Naqsh-o-Negar, 2000).

The Revolution Will Not Be Fabricated

Minoo Moallem

The other side. Must have. Must be.
Must have been a side. Aside from.
What has one seen.
This view. What has one viewed
—Theresa Hak Kyung Cha, *Dictée*

Nationalisms are invented, performed, and consumed in ways that do not
follow a universal blueprint.
—Anne McClintock, *Imperial Leather: Race, Gender, and Sexuality in the
Colonial Contest*

On cite toujours Marx et l'opium du peuple. La phrase qui précède
immédiatement et qu'on ne cite jamais dit que la religion est l'esprit d'un
monde sans esprit. Disons donc que l'Islam, cette année 1978, n'a pas été
l'opium du peuple, justement parce qu'il a été l'esprit d'un monde sans esprit.

We always quote Marx [and religion] as the opium of people, but what we don't
cite is the phrase that follows immediately that religion is the spirit of a world
without spirit. Let us say therefore that Islam, in the year of 1978, was not the
opium of the people precisely because it was the spirit of a spiritless world.
—Michel Foucault, "Iran: Révolution au nom de Dieu"

The discourse of revolution constitutes an important part of modernity, one marked
by the humanism of the French Revolution, which united as one force or one nation

Radical History Review
Issue 105 (Fall 2009)   DOI 10.1215/01636545-2009-008
© 2009 by MARHO: The Radical Historians' Organization, Inc.

those who did not suffer with those who were "malheureux" (wretched), of the high classes with the low people.[1] However, the third world anticolonial and anti-imperialist revolutions that imprinted the political sphere of the twentieth century in Latin America, Africa, Asia, and the Middle East have not been systematically examined in relation to modernity, colonialism, and postcolonial formations. In addition, the question of revolution has been continuously addressed from within a modern Western epistemology that relies extensively on notions of the "philosophy of history" and the "rights of man" for understanding the revolutionary spectacle and the birth of the nation-state. As Hannah Arendt argued, these narratives describe revolutions in its modern philosophical understanding of "the whole realm of human action, not in terms of actor and the agent, but from the standpoint of the spectator who watches a spectacle."[2] Reflecting on the Iranian Revolution requires an epistemological shift away from Eurocentric and modernist approaches that attempt to assimilate revolutionary temporality into linear narratives of "freedom" and "unfreedom"—especially when it comes to an analysis of women and gender issues—through the guidance of the party, the avant-garde classes, or secular revolutionary groups.[3]

If one rejects the assimilation of the Iranian Revolution into Western comfort zones that seek to explain it through the presence of a political avant-garde or within stage theories of progress, it is impossible to understand it without directing one's attention to specific cultural and religious forces able to mobilize social institutions based on Islamic nationalism and transnationalism.[4] In addition, the teleological ideas legitimating or condemning the Iranian Revolution and its outcomes not only have failed a number of Iranian scholars and activists in understanding the revolution and its aftermath but also have created space for the convergence of nationalism and imperialism in their desire to contain conflicts and contradictions. For example, an identification with a militarized imperial gaze targeting Iran for an imperialist military and nonmilitary intervention has been crucial in the emergence of new modes of control and surveillance that involve local and diasporic Iranians as collaborators, as the latter are invested in the authority of vision and of technologies of surveillance couched in terms of "participatory democracy." (For a while, on its home page, Zamaneh—a Western-funded Iranian diasporic radio station and Web site—depicted a young man with a camera filming the viewer; the caption said, "Everyone can participate.")[5] Such participation has created a space for the mediation of native informants as they take part in the fantasy of violence as a site of liberation. In this context, the question is how to challenge the narratives of resistance reified as the everyday practices of militarism.[6]

The Revolutionary War

Growing up in the aftermath of the CIA coup d'état of 1953, I joined many other Iranians in challenging not only the dictatorship but also normative notions of gender and sexuality based on the modernization of patriarchal relations.[7] The modern dictatorship established after the coup d'état was camouflaged as the Iranian way of joining the family of nations, the civilized West, and the modernized world, yet it was haunted by the ghost of a lost opportunity to establish a national democratic state. The grandiose celebration of the glorious past of the Persian Empire and its pre-Islamic origin by the Pahlavi regime concealed the loss of what was abjectified during nation formation in the context of colonial modernity and civilizational imperialism, the trauma of the coup d'état, and the humiliation of an emasculated male elite.

It did not take long for my generation to realize that we were in the midst of an imperial and national war. Before long, the dictatorship became viciously invested in the militarization of Iranian society, making army service mandatory and expanding surveillance technologies into every aspect of political life through a heavy investment in the expansion of the secret police, SAVAK, and the prison industry. However, in the late 1960s and early 1970s, the Pahlavi regime was subjected to my generation's desire for liberation—including that of many women—because of which we declared a revolutionary war against the state. The spectacular violence of the state soon replaced the sluggish violence of the post–coup d'état years and became productive of a revolution. The revolution demanded that we take sides in opposing the dictatorship and its imperialist allies.

The emergence of a militant Islamist movement did not have much to do with the return of Islam as an incarnation of a fixed tradition opposed to modernity; rather, it was a by-product of modernity and postmodernity. As I have argued before, we should not underestimate the conditions, scales, and meanings of modern nationalism, transnational third-world revolutionary movements, and gender identities, as well as the expansion of information technologies as they articulated with the inflections of Shi'a Islam for contemporary political use. Modern forms of state violence became productive of revolutionary militant subjectivities. Indeed social revolutions are very important events of the twentieth century, especially in the context of Third World countries, and have been sources of hope, despair, romanticism, and anger. In this context, the technologies of vision, along with gender performance—meaning the ways in which one displays one's body as a surface on which disciplinary technologies of masculinity and femininity, including fashion, modesty, clothing, body shape, and the like, are practiced—proved central to the formation of a modern gendered citizen-subject in Iran and its mobilization in pre- and post-revolutionary Iran.[8]

In this short essay, I would like to very briefly address several components of the Iranian Revolution, meaning the revolution as an event in its singularity, the revolution as experienced by the subjects who participated in it or to whom the revolution occurred, and the effects that the event of revolution has produced in subjects who participated in it.

While an understanding of the revolution as an event enables us to examine a multiplicity of subject positions and the formation of a "they" during the revolution beyond the desire of any individual or group, the full complexity of the revolution as an event cannot be grasped because most of the time the narrativization of the revolution entails a beginning and an end, in this case the overthrow of the Pahlavi regime, the revolutionary moment, and the postrevolutionary establishment of an Islamic Republic. In this narrativization the revolution becomes a spectacle of events, events that have been eventualized through totalizing representational practices. The revolution thus becomes prior to its subjects and agents. While the revolt of the subjects against the unbearability of submission to an order is undeniable in the event of the revolution, a homogenization appears when the event is eventualized, because the contradictions are resolved in the narrative and the forces of homogenization succeed the forces of differentiation. This has proven particularly costly for women in the case of the Iranian Revolution since in the spectacle of the revolution, women's agency was either domesticated or marginalized, if not erased. There is still very little written on what women fought for or on how their involvement in the revolutionary events differed from that of men. While a number of Iranian women who participated in the revolution courted revolutionary figures such as Leila Khaled and Jamileh Bupasha, the significance of these figures for their political mobilization remains unexamined. As I have argued elsewhere, the possibility of women committing to revolutionary acts in the spectacle of revolutionary events and in the Islamic transnationalist recounting of the tragedy of Karbala was replaced by an inclusion/domestication of women as wives, mothers, and sisters in the Islamic community of *Ummah*. However, the politicization, inclusion, and domestication of women in the *Ummah* in the Islamic nationalist discourse have effectively integrated women as citizen-subjects in the Islamic state, allowing political negotiations around gender and women's issues in the postrevolutionary context.

In other words, the mobilization of the Islamic *Ummah* has functioned as a catalyst for the inclusion of women as active citizens of the Islamic state while simultaneously domesticating them in their belonging to the *Ummah*. This politicization and integration of the private and the public spheres in the Islamic Republic both responded to the crisis of the modernizing nation-state in regulating and disciplining gendered spaces and in turn put into crisis modern forms of citizenship in their reliance on a number of dichotomies including traditional/modern, needs/rights, difference/equality, and religious/secular. These changes have certainly had a number of unexpected consequences for the regulation of gender identities and Islamic femininities and masculinities.[9] The disjuncture between Iranian women as willing subjects and citizens of the postrevolutionary Islamic State and a homogenized notion of Muslim women and their fragmentation and contradiction in what constitutes gender difference or gender equality has created fertile ground for a plurality of positions vis-à-vis women and gender issues in Iran, challenging essentializing and foundationalist interpretations of Islam.[10]

The story of the revolution as an event through the experience of those who joined it—from women to oil workers, students to ethnic and religious minorities, and rural people to the army—or to whom the revolution happened is much more complicated, requiring a nuanced microanalysis of a broad spectrum of multiple subject positions, locations, dislocations, and relocations without the possibility of grasping what emerged and departed with the event of the revolution. In other words, the eventualization of the Iranian revolution and its representation from a multiplicity of locations are still widely open to writing and reflection.

Death, Revolt, and Sexuality

Mara bebus, mara babus
Baraye akharin bar
Tora khoda Negahdar
Ke miravam besuy-e sarnevesht

Kiss me, Kiss me
for the last time
May God protect you
I am heading towards my destiny
—From a legendary revolutionary love song sung by Hassan Golnaraghi in the post-1953 coup d'état era[11]

In reflecting about the effects of the revolution, one needs to think about death, revolt, and sexuality.[12] What connects this triadic mapping is the relationship between the body, power, and knowledge, sexuality being central here to the ways in which subjects are made and enabled to transform themselves by constituting themselves as subjects of desire.[13] This has perhaps been the most enduring effect of the Iranian Revolution for gender and women's issues both in Iran and in the diaspora.

In Iran, the formation of a revolutionary subject occurred in relation to two concomitant processes: the transgression of disciplinary boundaries in terms of the modern homogenization and gendering of people's experience; and the potential to exercise power through the construction and legitimization of a particular knowledge closed to the control of the West and the Westernized local elite. Two important moments articulate these processes: first, the possibility of death as a radical site of subjectivity; and second, the channeling of revolt into a revolution by muting or glossing over the idea that the needs of the self differ from or are opposed to love of the Islamic *Ummah,* love of the revolution, love of the motherland. In the first instance death becomes a site of revolt, the right to intervene in life, a moment at which, in Foucauldian terms, "death now becomes, in contrast, the moment when the individual escapes all power, falls back on himself and retreats, so to speak, into his own privacy."[14] In the revolutionary context, while modern structures of power tend to hide death by making it a private matter, the revolutionary subject makes it a public matter in the day-to-day theater of revolution. For example, in the context of the Iranian Revolution, the Shi'i rituals of Muharram and the tragedy of Karbala provided space for the subjects of the revolt to take over the sovereign power of the state, which has the right, according to Michel Foucault, "to make live and to let die [à faire vivre et à laisser mourir]."[15] However, in the Islamic nationalist and transnationalist narrativization of the revolution, this moment is discursively assimilated and transferred to a second moment, where through a dialectical logic all conflicts (read politics) are reduced to a fundamental antagonism—war, conflict, and death become the object of the state and of civil order. In modern territorial nationalism the nation and the state function in conjunction with each other. However, in the case of Islamic nationalism in Iran, the notion of Ummah goes beyond territorial nationalism and includes all Muslims, especially those oppressed by the Western powers. After the establishment of the Islamic Republic, and especially in the context of the Iran-Iraq war and its aftermath, the concept of Ummah became a site of tension and contradiction between Islamic nationalism within the territorial boundaries of Iran and Islamic transnationalism. This contradiction has created a productive tension between the limits of both nationalism and religion in defining the Ummah as a unified entity or an imagined community.

As a result, death as a radical act of revolt is recuperated and assimilated into the state agenda and the constitution of the gendered and willing subject-citizens that give their lives for the sake of the nation, the Islamic *Ummah*, the state, and the homeland.[16] This radical shift from the subjects of revolt to the subjects of an Islamic *Ummah* has had a number of consequences. For example, the convergence of a warrior masculinity with the act of revolt as sacrificial in the postrevolutionary era (especially during the Iran-Iraq war) transferred attention from the body and the self to the fraternal community of the *Ummah*. As a result, the opportunity for an interrogation of the value of one's life or death eroded as the revolt of the subjects became narrativized in the linear time of the revolution as it was consumed by the state.[17] Indeed, what was put outside the limits of the revolutionary discourse, including issues of the body and of sexuality, continues to haunt the Islamic Republic.

Whose Collective Will?

The Iranian Revolution reflected the collective will of a people that refused subordination to Western control, similar to a number of anticolonial, anti-imperialist, and nationalist movements; but they also refused to be ruled by those local forces that for many years determined their political destiny. The revolt of subjects against the unbearable opened up a complex intellectual realm in Iran in the postrevolutionary era that continues to influence what has come to be established as an Islamic Republic. It also continues to have an impact on the question of what constitutes an Islamic republic at all, and what it means to be a Muslim, an Iranian, a gendered subject, a citizen of a state that rules in the name of religion. In addition, the creation of a postrevolutionary state established a continuity between pre-Islamic and Islamic

Iran and a hybrid sense of identity linking both national and religious discourses. This form of continuity has been productive of a new crisis in challenging both gender issues and the glorifying notions of a pre-Islamic Persia and in investing in the Islamic discourse and its claim of equality within difference. This process has been contradictory given that the challenge of the West led to a search for a certain style of existence rooted in local knowledge or an Islamic "morality style" (in Foucault's terminology) familiar to people. The very establishment of a state in which an Islamic morality becomes common to everyone, both by force and by choice, itself provides fertile ground for new forms of national and transnational consumerism, including Islamic fashion, religious tourism, business opportunities based on gender segregation, and the like.[18]

The Iranian Revolution puts in crisis the idea of revolution through a number of different processes: (1) the interruption of the existing juridical and disciplinary processes, especially those rooted in the Western humanist traditions; (2) the articulation of a political will through the discourse of religion; (3) the mixing of revolutionary symbols, icons, and ideas from other modern revolutions (e.g. China, Russia, Cuba, and Algeria) with Islam and Shi'ism;[19] (4) the potential transformation of this political will into the universality of the state, in this case, the establishment of an Islamic state; (5) the penetration of what were depicted as barbaric Islamic traditions in European colonial discourse into so-called civilized institutions and constitutions;[20] (6) the stylization of gendered political subjects by indigenizing masculinity and femininity through religion and Shi'ism; and (7) the imposition of an Islamic "morality style," in its Foucauldian sense, via state power.

The implication of an ethno-religious imaginary and its gendered components as essential to what appealed to masses of young and educated Iranians and led to the revolt of a nation against oppressive powers needs to be interrogated further. Indeed, the Western notion of revolution as progressive transformation or, as Foucault has put it, defined by an internal autodialectical historical discourse[21] is at stake here and needs to be opened up to the investigation of the formation of revolutionary subjects as historical subjects able to ensure the existence of the nation as a gendered imagined community.

In lieu of a conclusion one could raise a number of questions: What are the limits of those social revolutions that take place in spaces of political mobilization powerfully defined and contained by the state apparatus? Can we be at all sanguine about social revolutions without falling into the trap of believing in "evolved" institutions after the revolutionary period? Was the Iranian Revolution caught up in the sovereignty of the nation-state articulated and institutionalized via the establishment of an Islamic Republic? Could we, in light of the Iranian Revolution, make the claim that the Western idea of revolution is in crisis? What if the subject of revolt exceeds modern politics of visibility invested in all kinds of nationalism, religious or secular?

Notes

The title of this essay is borrowing from the title of Gil Scott-Heron's famous song "The Revolution Will Not Be Televised." Gil Scott-Heron is an important figure in black popular music.

1. Hannah Arendt, *On Revolution* (1963; New York: Penguin, 1990), 85. In her great discussion of compassion and the French Revolution, Arendt refers to Dostoyevsky's Grand Inquisitor who, like Robespierre, was attracted to the suffering masses "not only because such attraction was indistinguishable from lust for power, but also because he had depersonalized the sufferers, lumped them together."
2. Ibid., 52.
3. The myth of progress persists more than any other modern myth because of its gender components. We constantly use gender signifiers to talk about progress, development, and democracy.
4. While located in the particular context of Iran and influenced by Islamic nationalism and transnationalism, the Iranian Revolution was cross-fertilized by other revolutionary symbols, icons, and discourses from the Russian Revolution to the Chinese Revolution to various other anticolonial and national revolutions in other parts of the world, including Latin America and North Africa.
5. A number of Iranian television programs, magazines, and Web sites in the diaspora have invested in the mission of "saving Iran" from the Muslim fundamentalists, often using gender signifiers as a site of distinction between the "oppressed Iran" and the "liberated diaspora." Such notions have become an obstacle for the interrogation of patriarchal gender discourses and practices at work not only in Iran but also in the diaspora. For an insightful critique of native informers and the politics of empire, see Hamid Dabashi, "Native Informers and the Making of the American Empire," *al-Ahram Weekly Online*, no. 797, June 1–7, 2006, weekly.ahram.org.eg/2006/797/special.htm.
6. Members of a number of Iranian diasporic communities, who either left Iran after the revolution as counterrevolutionaries or were displaced because of their political ideologies, have become involved in the project of a regime change in Iran, with the direct and indirect support and intervention of Western powers, especially the United States.
7. Elsewhere I have argued that modernization did not challenge patriarchy but transformed it and made it possible for the heteronormative family to become a partner to the state. See Minoo Moallem, *Between Warrior Brother and Veiled Sister: Islamic Fundamentalism and the Cultural Politics of Patriarchy* (Berkeley: University of California Press, 2005).
8. For a further discussion, see ibid.
9. For a detailed and everyday account of these negotiations, see *Zanan* (*Women*), various issues published between 1992 and 2007 (unfortunately, *Zanan* was banned after this date). Also, a number of Iranian feminist scholars have written about these negotiations and changes. Among others, see Haleh Afshar, *Islam and Feminisms: An Iranian Case Study* (New York: St. Martin's Press, 1998); Ziba Mir-Hosseini, *Islam and Gender: The Religious Debate in Contemporary Iran* (Princeton, NJ: Princeton University Press, 1999); Moallem, *Between Warrior Brother and Veiled Sister*; Homa Hoodfar, "The Women's Movement in Iran: Women at the Crossroads of Secularization and Islamization," in *Women Living under Muslim Law: International Solidarity Network* (Paris: The Women's Movement Series, No. 1, Winter 1999), 3–46.
10. For a further discussion of this argument, see Minoo Moallem, "Muslim Women and the Politics of Representation," *Journal of Feminist Studies of Religion* 24 (2008): 106–10.

11.   "Mara Bebus" ("Kiss me") was the most popular revolutionary love song in the post-coup d'état years in Iran. The singer, Golnaraghi, was not a professional and did not sing any other songs after this song. For many years (even after the SAVAK, or secret police, released the identity of the songwriter) people believed that it was written by one of the leaders of the military network of the Tudeh Party (the pro-Soviet Communist Party of Iran) in jail on the eve of his execution. The song was courted by masses of people because it expressed a strong desire for love, lust, and life at a time when one was destined to die.

12.   As Foucault stated: "Now it is over life, throughout its unfolding, that power establishes its domination; death is power's limit, the moment that escapes it; death becomes the most secret aspect of existence, the most 'private.'" Michel Foucault, *The History of Sexuality: An Introduction*, vol. 1, trans. Robert Hurley (New York: Pantheon, 1978), 138.

13.   See Foucault, *History of Sexuality*, vol. 1 and Jacques Derrida, *The Gift of Death*, trans. David Wills (Chicago: University of Chicago Press, 1995).

14.   Michel Foucault, *Society Must Be Defended: Lectures at the Collège de France, 1975–1976*, trans. David Macey (New York: Picador, 1997), 248.

15.   Ibid., 241.

16.   A radical shift occurred between women's militancy during the revolution and after the Iran-Iraq war (1980–88). The Islamic state limited women's participation to behind the war front (*posht-e jebheh*), as a result of which only men participated actively in the war as combatants.

17.   This is not to suggest that what was put outside the limits of the revolutionary discourse has lost its appeal.

18.   I am referring to Foucault and his use of "morality style" to talk about the behavior of individuals in relation to the rules and values recommended to them. See Michel Foucault, *The Use of Pleasure: The History of Sexuaity*, vol. 2, trans. Robert Hurley (New York: Vintage, 1990), 25. See also Michel Foucault, "Inutile de soulever?" ("Is It Useless to Rebel?") in *Dits et écrits* (*Interviews and Writings*), vol. 3 (Paris: Gallimard, 1994), 790–94.

19.   For example, in *Between Warrior Brother and Veiled Sister*, 102–6, I show how the concept of the Mostaz'af, or powerless, was in intertextuality—that is, reinforced by a buildup of meanings and images referring to each other—with modern secular concepts of the left, including the proletariat: *ranjbaran* (laborers), *karegaran* (workers), and *dehghanan* (peasants). In his interview with Claire Brière, Foucault refers to the differences between the Iranian revolution and the Chinese revolution; see Claire Brière and Pierre Blanchot, *Iran: La révolution au nom de Dieu; Suivi d'un entretien avec Michel Foucault* (Paris: Éditions du Seuil, 1979), 232. An intertextual reading of the revolutionary discourses, terminologies and practices and their transnational circulation needs more scholarly attention.

20.   In *Between Warrior Brother and Veiled Sister*, 31–57, I have elaborated on the Orientalist discourse vis-à-vis Persia as an important site of othering by Western powers that was used to justify Western intervention in the Iranian political sphere in the twentieth century.

21.   Foucault, *Society Must Be Defended*, 216.

Has Iran's Islamic Revolution Ended?

Saïd Amir Arjomand

Though the rise of a faction of hard-liners forged by revolution and war, and profess-
ing loyalty to the original spirit of the Islamic Revolution and its charismatic leader,
Ruhollah Khomeini, had been signaled by their capture of the entire thirty seats of
Tehran's Municipal Council in 2003 and of the seventh Majles (Parliament) in 2004,
the general assumption shared by many Iranian and outside political analysts until
the election of Mahmoud Ahmadinejad in 2005 was that the revolution had ended.
Different commentators variously ended it with the victory of pragmatism and the
former president Akbar Hashemi Rafsanjani's program of economic reconstruction
in 1989, following the end of the Iran-Iraq war, or with the rise of the reform movement during the 1997–2005 presidency of Mohammad Khatami. The assumption
that the revolution has ended is still widely held by sociologists and political scientists, largely because of a serious misunderstanding of the revolutionary process in
a paradigm in the sociology of revolution called the "anatomy of revolution."[1] I shall
argue that the prevalent conception of the revolutionary process in that paradigm as
a sudden convulsion in the body politic likened to a passing fever that breaks with
the return to normalcy is too restrictive to be able to account for revolutionary institution building. The construction of a new political order is a much more long-term
process and involves what I have called constitutional politics.[2] In a perceptive commentary on Ahmadinejad's election, Fred Halliday spoke of a "twenty-years spasm"
typical of all great revolutions. Halliday's new anatomical metaphor, the spasm, is
unfortunately suggestive of an even greater degree of irregularity and ephemerality
than fever, and therefore proves just as misleading.[3] In fact, neither the elimination
by 1983 of the other factions participating in the initial revolutionary coalition nor

Radical History Review
Issue 105 (Fall 2009)   DOI 10.1215/01636545-2009-009
© 2009 by MARHO: The Radical Historians' Organization, Inc.

the death of Khomeini as its imam and charismatic leader in June 1989 meant the end of the Islamic Revolution. These significant markers rather signaled the beginning of a prolonged struggle among the children of the revolution over his heritage. The raucous struggle to define, structure, and control the new Islamic political order set up by Khomeini among different factions of his followers has a logic that can be understood as the consequence of the revolution. The revolution cannot be said to have ended while that struggle for the definition of the political order continues.

The French Revolution was quite atypical in that a charismatic leader capable of holding and consolidating power and exporting the revolution did not emerge until 1799, a decade after its beginning. The anatomy-of-revolution paradigm ousted the view of some earlier historians who considered Napoléon the child of the revolution, the exporter of its values abroad and their institutional consolidator at home. Not only did it sever the French Revolution's link to Napoléon but it also gave it the extremely short life span of five years, which is more in line with the anatomical analogy for revolution as that which breaks quickly and results in the return of the postrevolutionary polity to "normal" conditions. The revolution was said to begin with the prominence of the moderates in 1789, continue with the rise of the radicals and the reign of terror, and end with the return of the moderates in Thermidor/July 1794. This paradigm still dominates our thought and the terminology of the sociology of revolution; consequently, the sequence identified by the anatomical metaphor has been loosely applied to the coming to power of the "moderates" in Iran at the beginning of the revolution, and again to the ascendancy of Hashemi Rafsanjani. The Islamic Revolution in Iran was seen to go through the typical cycle of the rule of the moderates (1979–80), taken over by the radicals (1981–88), and finally a "Thermidorian" return to more moderate rule and a consolidation of the revolution at the end of the war with Iraq.

The typical sequence of the succession of the moderates by the radicals and the Thermidorian return of moderation, even in its extended and more rigorously formalized pattern sketched by Jack Goldstone, does not allow for the examination of the institutional consequences of revolutions.[4] Furthermore, this paradigm obscures the identity of the historical revolutionary actors. The agents of Thermidorian moderation are not the same persons or group as the moderates of the initial phase of the revolution. In my forthcoming book, I call them the "pragmatists," best exemplified by the former president Hashemi Rafsanjani. As distinct from the original 1979 moderates, they are transformed radicals. The transformation of the radicals can take different directions and proceed in different sequences. Some radicals become pragmatists, while others, together with some pragmatists, can turn to reformism as an evolution of pragmatism and/or in contrast to it. The best example of the radicals becoming reformists through pragmatism is another former president, Khatami, and Abdulkarim Soroush and Akbar Ganji can be mentioned as examples of radicals becoming reformists directly. And there is yet a further possible stage in the long-term revolutionary process: the return of revolutionary radicalism and an emergent and fairly distinct group associated with it. This final possibility is fully realized in Iran under Ahmadinejad and with the recent rise of the group I call the "hard-liners" and define by their loyalty to the martyrs of the revolution and by the advocacy of return to revolutionary radicalism.

Moderates, pragmatists, and hard-liners so conceived can be differentiated on the basis of two criteria: the revolutionary justification of violence, and the importance of ideology as a factor in revolutionary solidarity. The identities of revolutionary groups are, furthermore, not fixed. As revolutions proceed, some radicals renounce the legitimacy or utility of violence and become pragmatists or reformers. Others persist in the revolutionary justification of violence and its use and become hard-liners. The grip of ideology on the revolutionaries may also be loosened as it gradually ceases to serve as the basis of revolutionary solidarity. At the beginning of the revolution, ideology as a motive force unifies groups with little shared life experience. As the revolution proceeds, and is complemented by war in many cases, as in Iran, the revolutionary career and life experience of the winners become the basis of their group solidarity and identity. Some renounce ideology altogether and become pragmatists or reformists, while others assign it secondary place as a value—just a symbol for revolutionary solidarity that is more solidly based on the shared life experience of revolutionary careers. This latter group of revolutionaries insists on the categorical and uncompromising loyalty to the revolution and becomes hard-liners.

As ideology receded in importance for both the pragmatists and the hard-liners in Iran, it became a mere ancillary to two kinds of solidarity born out of two different kinds of formative life experience. As the life experiences of the clerical ruling elite and the lay second stratum in revolutionary Iran differed significantly, the character of their solidarity evolved in different directions. The clerical solidarity of the ruling elite emerged from a preexisting esprit de corps of the religious professionals produced in the madrassas and only later seasoned by the revolutionary struggle under their charismatic teacher, Khomeini. The revolutionary solidarity of the agitprops that formed the lay second stratum of the Islamic Republic of Iran had no comparably uniform preexisting educational and professional basis, but was steeled by the decisive experience of the decade of revolution and war into an insider, or to use the expressive Persian adjective, *khodi* (one of us), solidarity.

The revolutionary power struggle takes much longer than the revolutionary process suggested in the works on the anatomy of revolution. It is much more drawn out because it merges with the constitutional politics of succession to the charismatic leadership of the revolution and therefore requires a long-term perspective. In the complementary framework with a long-term perspective developed in my forthcoming book, postrevolutionary institution building and the construction of a new political order are considered the long-term consequences of revolution. This revisionist sociology of revolution shows that the return of the hard-liners is not as anomalous as it seems and suggests that the group is much more accurately described as (revolutionary) hard-liners, as they purport to recover the original purity of the Islamic Revolution. Parallels can be found in other important revolutions, notably those of Mexico and Russia.[5]

The parallel with the Russian Revolution regarding the dominance of hard-liners thirty years after 1917 is quite striking. After the failure of the export of revolutionary policy in the early 1980s, the most aggressive phase of Iran's foreign policy occurred with the ascendancy of the hard-liners among the Revolutionary Guards under Ahmadinejad nearly three decades after the Islamic Revolution of 1979 — roughly the same time span that separated Stalin's export of the Marxist-Leninist revolution from the Bolshevik revolution of 1917. After the period of "socialism in one country" and its accommodating so-called hedgehog foreign policy, Stalin decided to tilt the balance against the pragmatic technocrats under Georgy Malenkov, who had been gaining influence steadily until 1945, by promoting the hard-liners' "party revival" and return to ideological orthodoxy championed by Andrei Zhdanov and, after his death in 1948, by Mikhail Suslov. The peak of Soviet expansionism and aggressive foreign policy thus came in 1947–48, a full three decades after the Bolshevik revolution. Externally, victory during the Second World War enormously enhanced the international position of the Soviet Union, and its aggressive foreign policy paid off handsomely. An era of the most spectacular export of the Marxist-Leninist revolution to Eastern Europe and Asia was thus inaugurated in Stalin's last years. Moderate expansionism was pushed by increased cartelization long after Stalin's death and under favorable international conditions created the third world liberation movements, and they did not come to an end until the death of the hard-liner Suslov in 1982.[6]

The regime set up by Khomeini in his attempt to institutionalize his charismatic authority as the leader of the Islamic Revolution had a mixed constitution consisting of three elements: theocratic or clericalist, republican or democratic, and populist and egalitarian centered on social justice. The emergence of the system of collective rule by clerical councils with the constitutional amendments of 1989 and its consolidation after Khomeini's death can be considered the institutionalization of his clericalist heritage. The attempt to develop the republican or democratic elements of Khomeini's constitutional heritage was not made until nearly a decade after his death, however, and it generally ended in failure, except for the creation of the local and municipal councils. Elsewhere I have offered an analysis of the rise and fall of Khatami and of the reform movement as a struggle for the definition of the political order, or what I call constitutional politics.[7] This postrevolutionary power struggle took place at two connected levels. At one, it was a struggle between two factions among the children of the Islamic Revolution, only recently divided into reformers and hard-liners. With the rise of the Basij (mobilization) militia and the Revolutionary Guards since 2004 and the Ahmadinejad presidency, the last group of the children of the Islamic Revolution turned politicians have sought to appropriate the final element of Khomeini's constitutional heritage, one not previously claimed by either the clerical ruling elite or the reformers. Claiming to follow the line of the imam (i.e., Khomeini's teachings), they took what was left — namely, populism and social justice — and championed it as proof of their unflinching loyalty as the children of the Islamic Revolution of 1979.

In the constitutional politics of Iran after the death of Khomeini, which can be considered the (basically) peaceful extension of the violent revolutionary power struggle of 1979–82 and the war of 1980–88, different social groups rallied behind the three sets of principles identified as Khomeini's heritage, as these were the only open avenues for political participation. In my forthcoming book I demonstrate that the contradictions among three heterogeneous principles of the Constitution of 1979 — namely, theocratic government, the rule of law, and participatory representative government — can explain the confrontation between the supreme leader, or clerical monarch, Ayatollah Khamenei, and President Khatami from 1997 to 2005. The ayatollah stood for the first principle, and aligned behind him were the conservative clerics who came to power as a result of the Islamic Revolution and are in control of the revolution-generated system of collective rule by clerical councils, foundations (*bonyāds*), and foundation-supported unofficial groups, including the thuggish Helpers of the Party of God, the judiciary, and the commanders of the Revolutionary Guards and its Mobilization Corps. The president stood for the last two principles, which fused together his new political discourse of the rule of law, democratic participation, and civil society. As children of the Islamic Revolution, Khatami and his supporters called this fusion of the rule of law and democratic participation the 'republicanism' of the political regime founded by Imam Khomeini. Behind Khatami were the technocrats for reconstruction, the reformist and excluded clerics, and the disenfranchised middle classes. The battlefield was slanted against the president and his supporters by the Constitution and by the rhetoric of the Islamic Revolution.

The new phase of constitutional politics opened by Ahmadinejad's espousal of populism and social justice introduces a new configuration of social forces. Following Gaetano Mosca's idea that revolutions give birth to a new political class, I examine the latest phase of Iranian constitutional politics in the context of the shift in the center of gravity of Iran's emerging political class from the clerical elite to what Mosca called the second stratum that runs the administration, and in the case of Iran is primarily drawn from the military-security elements of the revolutionary regime.[8] The military-security second stratum was initially promoted by the supreme leader, but now it controls the Majles and the presidency while adopting its own institutional bases, notably the million Basijis in active duty. Ahmadinejad won election as the mayor of Tehran in 2003 in part by declaring he has a "Basij mentality" and has propounded the "Basij culture" as the panacea for Iran and the world, and his populism—including regular provincial tours and programs in social justice—appeals to the urban poor neglected by Khatami and the reformists.

Constitutional politics also involved vested and evolving institutional interests and made for a power struggle at the institutional level. The political control and protection of the regime thus became the most important function of the Guardian Council as the gatekeeper to all elected offices during the Khatami presidency, eclipsing its constitutionally defined responsibilities. The Basij organization briefly assumed the new function of delivering votes as the political machine of the Islamic Republic of Iran after 2003. After capturing the state with Ahmadinejad's presidency, however, the hardliners, counting on the continued strong support of the Secretary of the Guardian Council, Ayatollah Jannati, decided to act directly through the Ministry of Interior, which set up the polling stations and counted the vote. The Basij militiamen were kept for the task for which they had been trained to replace the haphazard Helpers of the Party of God: suppression of protest.

Thirty years after the Islamic Revolution of 1979, the astounding voter turnout followed by a week of massive demonstrations in reaction to the preposterous fraud perpetrated by the Ministry of the Interior in the election of June 12, 2009, had two important consequences from our point of view. It revealed a fault line separating the clerical and the military-security elements of the new political class, and it immediately rekindled the revolutionary power struggle between the reformists and the hardliners. Ahmadinejad appears to have succeeded in unifying the key elements in the military-security second stratum to assume the leadership of Iran's new political class to at least go along with the electoral putsch of June 12, 2009. But the putsch created considerable tension between the military-security second stratum and the ruling clerical elite and its aftermaths have seriously strained the orchestrated unity of the two components of Iran's new political class.

Already by midday on June 12 Ahmadinejad's Web site called the election the beginning of the "Third Revolution," no doubt meaning it would mark the victory of the hardliners and the ascendancy of the military-security second stratum of Iran's new political class. The clerical monarch, Ayatollah Khamenei, immediately congratulated his man without waiting. Remembering how handsomely his determination in stemming the tide of reformism after another massive electoral victory in 2000 had paid off, Khamenei stood firmly behind the fraudulent official results and ordered the suppression of the massive peaceful protests. The two reformist candidates, Mousavi and Karrubi, denounced the electoral fraud as a coup d'état aiming at the destruction of the "republicanism" of the regime established by Imam Khomeini and told their supporters to repeat from the rooftops the cry of "God is Great!" which they claimed as their own as Islamic revolutionaries of 1979.

A revolution worthy of the name is not a passing fever to give way to nature's warming with any Thermidor. Nor does the revolution die with its charismatic leader. The short-term power struggle as a process in which Saturn devours his children merges into a more drawn-out struggle among the children of the revolution for the definition of the new political order. It merges with the constitutional politics of postrevolutionary reconstruction, which will not be complete as long as contending factions in the generation that made the revolution can claim that the heritage of its charismatic leader has been betrayed or remains unrealized. The Islamic Revolution will end when the claim to Khomeini's allegedly unfulfilled heritage can no longer be plausibly made in Iranian constitutional politics or be backed by effective force.

Notes

This theme has been developed in my forthcoming book, *After Khomeini: Iran under His Successors.*

1. The work most frequently cited in this connection is Crane Brinton's famous *Anatomy of Revolution* (New York: Norton, 1938). An earlier formulation of this pattern can be found in Lyford P. Edwards, *The Natural History of Revolution* (Chicago: University of Chicago Press, 1927).

2. See S. A. Arjomand, "Constitutions and the Struggle for Political Order: A Study in the Modernization of Political Traditions," *European Journal of Sociology/Archives européennes de sociologie* 33 (1992): 39–82: and S. A. Arjomand, introduction to *Constitutional Politics in the Middle East*, ed. Arjomand (London: Hart, 2008), 1–10.

3. Fred Halliday, "Iran's Revolutionary Spasm," *Open Democracy* (2005), www.open democracy.net/globalization-vision_reflections/iran_2642.jsp. The metaphor is not misleading with regard to the Islamic Revolution in Iran alone. Just think of the Russian Revolution. It is more than plausible to argue that, without the so-called "spasm" of the Russian Revolution under Joseph Stalin, which I would place thirty and not twenty years after 1917, there would have been no second wave of the export of the Marxist-Leninist revolution and its historical expansion throughout the world.

4. See Jack A. Goldstone, "The Comparative and Historical Study of Revolutions," *Annual Review of Sociology* 8 (1982): 187–207.

5. For Mexico, see Alan Knight, "The Modern Mexican State: Theory and Practice," in *The Other Mirror: Grand Theory through the Lens of Latin America*, ed. M. A. Centeno and F. López-Alves (Princeton, NJ: Princeton University Press, 2001), 177–218. This essay brings out the appropriateness of a long-term perspective for the analysis of the Mexican Revolution in particular.

6. See Jack Snyder, *Myths of Empire: Domestic Politics and International Ambition* (Ithaca, NY: Cornell University Press, 1991), 244–52.

7. See S. A. Arjomand, "The Rise and Fall of President Khātami and the Reform Movement in Iran," *Constellations* 12 (2005): 504–22.

8. Gaetano Mosca, *Elementi di scienza politica* (*Elements of Political Science*), 2 vols. (Bari: Laterza, 1939).

The Revolution and the Rural Poor

Djavad Salehi-Isfahani

Thirty years on, there seems to be doubt as to whether the Iranian Revolution of 1978–79 has fostered deep social change. A recent book by Farhad Nomani and Sohrab Behdad (2006) offers a perspective from the left based on a detailed review of the evidence on changes in the structure of employment in postrevolution Iran.[1] It finds little evidence of change in class structure and, as its subtitle suggests, concludes that the revolution did not matter. Thomas Friedman, by no means an Iran expert, has also offered a very negative assessment of the revolution as a "nation building enterprise," calling it "an abject failure."[2] Others have called into question the revolution's promise to eradicate poverty and bring about prosperity and equity. One can read in the *Washington Post* (false) claims that as late as 2003 average incomes in Iran were only one-fourth of their level before the revolution,[3] and elsewhere reports of increasing poverty and inequality.[4]

These overarching accounts of social and economic stagnation are very misleading. Although Iran's economic progress since the revolution has left much to be desired, claims about rising poverty and dire economic conditions are highly exaggerated. In fact, after a sharp drop in the 1980s, the Iranian economy has been growing steadily since the mid-1990s at about 5 percent per year, and per capita incomes in 2008 fully caught up with their prerevolution peak. As a result, poverty has been falling for the past fifteen years and has been in the single digits for several years.[5] To be sure, the Iranian Revolution set lofty goals not only for improving the lot of the poor but also for eliminating social inequities. Initially, the postrevolutionary state was able to reduce income inequality, reversing the rise in inequality that had occurred just before the revolution as a consequence of the oil boom of the

Radical History Review

Issue 105 (Fall 2009)   DOI 10.1215/01636545-2009-010

© 2009 by MARHO: The Radical Historians' Organization, Inc.

1970s and the Shah's policies.[6] But, significantly, it has not been able to go beyond that: over the past two decades, economic inequality has remained fairly stable, rising and falling slightly with the price of oil, despite substantial changes in policy ranging from the nationalization of banks and large enterprises in the first decade of the revolution to market-based reforms under the Rafsanjani administration. For whatever reason, the goal of greater equity in incomes has so far eluded the Islamic government.

Yet deep and lasting social change has occurred in Iran, though away from the sight of those focused mostly on the more affluent urban areas. Improvements in basic health, education, and infrastructure have taken place nationwide, in particular in poorer rural and urban areas. Despite a rapidly rising population, since the 1980s infant mortality has been cut by half and life expectancy increased by about ten years.[7] The percentage of undernourished citizens has been reduced to 5 percent, which is close to the Republic of Korea's 3 percent rate and much lower than Pakistan's 19 percent or India's 21 percent.

Improvements in the quality of life in rural areas have been particularly impressive, potentially removing an important source of overall inequality. Until the late 1960s, when the Shah's land reform program put an end to the traditional land tenure system, feudal landlords had exploited rural inhabitants economically and treated them as second-class citizens. Although Iranian society has never had formal delineations on par with those in India or a class structure as in feudal Europe, the lines between the *ra'iyat* (sharecropper; literally, "subjects") and *arbāb* (landlord; literally, "master") were sharply drawn by social custom. Mohammad Eslami-Nadoushan, who grew up in a landowning family in a village, describes these relations in the 1940s in his biography:

> Wealth was not so much the issue; what was more ghastly was the arrogant and domineering posture that someone who belonged to the class of *arbāb* and feudal lords [*khān*] would display. The *arbāb* demanded to be greeted by his *ra'iyat*, addressed him harshly, and if necessary, did not shy away from beating him. It was common for the ruling class to believe that peasants and the poor were created as an underclass as God had wanted. . . . The members of this group, male or female, turbaned or not, old or young, wealthy or poor, even those who could not read or write, believed that they had rights superior to others.[8]

In other words, as in any class society, one's social position was largely inherited, and mobility through income and education was rare. Although the Shah's reform program had given peasants land and thereby increased their wealth and income, coming from above, it did not provide them with a new identity to go with the land. The newly liberated *ra'iyat* class still knew who they were and did not consider themselves full citizens. Even the many landless rural residents who migrated to the cities in the 1970s could not easily shed their identity. While no longer *ra'iyats*, they remained *dehātis* (villagers), a pejorative term still used in Iran to refer to people with poor manners or crude taste.

For the rural underclass, the revolution provided a fast track to full citizenship, even though they had not contributed much to its success. The supposedly popular nature of the revolution, its rejection of modern and urban values and manners (women were required to wear the *hijab* and men were not to wear ties in public after the institution of the Islamic Republic), and Ayatollah Ruhollah Khomeini's addressing the poor as the inspiration for the revolution, greatly helped rural Iranians begin to feel like real citizens. These psychological factors were soon complemented by real improvements on the ground. Soon after the revolution, the Reconstruction Crusade (for rural areas) extended electricity and other basic services to villages and expanded educational facilities. Such urban symbols of modernity as sending girls to school, watching television, and even drinking (previously considered un-Islamic) became more common in rural areas. Rural electrification was the first basic service to arrive and later allowed schools and health clinics to function. In 1977, only 16.2 percent of rural homes had electricity; by 1984 the number had jumped to 57.1 percent, and by 2004 to 98.3 percent. This had a quick and considerable impact on village life: the percentage of rural homes with refrigerators increased from 7.6 percent in 1977 to 35.5 percent in 1984 and to 92.4 percent in 2004; television ownership went from 3.2 to 26.6 to 89.1 percent.[9] However, these improvements in basic services at times came with a deterioration in social and gender relations following the intrusive enforcement of religious mores, such as the Islamic dress code and changes in family law that lowered the age of marriage and required women to obtain the consent of their husbands or fathers to go to school or work.

More fundamental rural development started in 1985, when the government launched its rural Health Network System (HNS), which substantially lowered fertility and mortality rates and laid the foundation for rural modernization. By then, recruitment for the war with Iraq in rural areas had increasingly integrated the rural population into the revolutionary ranks. As a result, the government felt highly motivated to improve rural conditions. The health network included a carefully designed delivery mechanism that eventually established over eighteen thousand rural clinics (Health Houses) in larger villages, with services extending to many more smaller villages and hamlets dispersed across Iran's tough terrain. Health Houses only employed health workers (*behvarz*) from the same villages and offered active services, meaning that every woman of childbearing age would be visited at least once a year.

Rural clinics, with family planning as part of their mandate, had been initiated during the Shah's reign, but, like his other key programs—the literacy and health corps—the message they delivered lacked the necessary credibility to either affect behavior or help rural people shed their *ra'iyat* identity. At the time, the literacy and health corps generally comprised disaffected urban young (mostly) men sent to civilize the hinterland. While many succeeded in establishing a good rapport with their rural "subjects," they did not live or work there as equals. As a result, the Shah's literacy and family-planning programs had a limited effect on fertility and the schooling of girls in rural areas.

New theories of economic development emphasize change in family demographic behavior as a precondition for the transition to long-term growth.[10] This stands in contrast to both the traditional growth theory that emphasizes physical capital accumulation, and the Marxist emphasis on change in the relations of production, both of which concern the behavior of firms. By contrast, the more recent theories of development contend that change in the relations of procreation is necessary to take advantage of technological advancements: individual families must transform from producers of children to producers of human capital.

This type of change has now been completed in Iran. In rural areas, fertility has declined from about eight births per woman to about two in the past two decades, and the average years of schooling for rural women born after 1980 have doubled compared to those born around 1970. These changes came only after a turnabout by the government in its policy toward family planning. In the context of the new emphasis on family behavior and human capital, the spread of the HNS has not only set in motion the modernization of the rural population but has also made them full partners in Iran's new economy.

The family-planning program has won international praise for its innovativeness and its impact.[11] High-fertility countries wish to imitate it, but there are certain aspects of Iran's program that may not be reproducible because they have to do with the nature of the revolution. Skeptics of "rural development from above" have argued for a long time that rural development programs must respect the hierarchy of needs of the local population.[12] Family-planning programs often fail this test because, even when they are included in a broader health-delivery system, the poor see them as ways to limit their numbers, rather than as ways to improve their lot. In Iran, the Islamic government did not face this problem. The revolution's leaders employed strongly pro-poor rhetoric and, more important, when the revolutionary government started its health-delivery system in rural areas, it was still condemning family planning as a relic of the Shah's regime. Only four years later, in 1989, did the government make an about-face and adopt an antinatal posture, officially adding family planning to the HNS tasks. Before that it had brought electricity, paved roads, piped water, and health services in an order almost exactly corresponding to the perceptions of the rural poor concerning their own needs.

Another aspect of Iran's revolution, its Islamic ideology, also may have helped the transformation of the rural family by removing an ideological barrier to the education of girls. Commentators have argued that by separating boys and girls in schools, and by enforcing Islamic codes of behavior in public spaces, the Islamic government made it easier for religiously conservative families to send their girls to school.[13] Perhaps this is the reason why the expansion of girls' education in rural areas has been twice as fast as that of boys: females born in the 1960s had only about 40 percent of the years of schooling of their male counterparts, whereas their 1980s cohorts have closed that gap to 90 percent.

In my view the most impressive and lasting effect of the Islamic Revolution on social change has been bridging the gap in development status between rural and urban areas. This is particularly important if the country continues along a path on which individual votes and voices increasingly matter. At a time when Iranian politics appears to be in the grip of populism with an emphasis on redistribution, a rapidly expanding, undereducated rural population might threaten social stability. On the other hand, a rural population with greater resources devoted to education, both on account of low fertility and greater access to schools, may decide to eschew populism in favor of social democracy. Iranian society has now entered a phase in which those on the lower rungs of the social ladder are quite ready to place their hopes on equality of opportunity, rather than push for the equality of outcomes. The postrevolution expansion of health and education have brought the poor's dream of equality of opportunity that much closer to reality, but, lacking access to productive employment and unable to marry, their educated youth have reason to be very skeptical.[14] The challenge for the Islamic government is now to help ease the transitions of these youth to adulthood, so that they and their families can continue to view an investment in education as the way to attain social and economic mobility.

Notes

1. Farhad Nomani and Sohrab Behdad, *Class and Labor in Iran: Did the Revolution Matter?* (Syracuse, NY: Syracuse University Press, 2006).
2. Thomas Friedman, "Sleepless in Tehran," *New York Times*, October 28, 2008.
3. Afshin Molavi, "Economic Ills Fuel Iranian Dissent," *Washington Post*, July 8, 2003.
4. See, for example, Jahangir Amuzegar, "Iran's Third Development Plan: An Appraisal," *Middle East Policy* 12 (2005): 46–63. For an opposing view, see Djavad Salehi-Isfahani "Poverty, Inequality, and Populist Politics in Iran," *Journal of Economic Inequality* 7 (2009): 5–24.
5. This is based on the international poverty line of $2 per day per person (equal to about $3 per day in 2006). Higher poverty lines naturally lead to higher poverty rates, that is, a greater proportion of the population with less than that level of income. For more details, see Salehi-Isfahani, "Poverty, Inequality, and Populist Politics in Iran."
6. The Gini coefficient increased by about ten points in just a few years, from 0.45 in 1972 to 0.55 in 1976, indicating a substantial increase in inequality.
7. Mohammad Jalal Abbasi-Shavazi, et al., "Trends and Emerging Issues of Health and Mortality in the Islamic Republic of Iran," in United Nations Economic and Social Commission for Asia and the Pacific, *Emerging Issues of Health and Mortality in the Asian and Pacific Region* (New York: United Nations Population Fund, 2005), 147–160.
8. Mohammad Eslami-Nadoushan, *Rouz-ha: Sargozasht* (*Days: A Biography*), vol. 3 (Tehran: Yazdan Publishers, 2006), 42.

9.   Salehi-Isfahani, "Poverty, Inequality, and Populist Politics in Iran."

10. For a nontechnical statement of this view, see Robert E. Lucas, "Industrial Revolution: Past and Future," Federal Reserve Bank of Minneapolis, 2003 Annual Report, www .minneapolisfed.org/publications_papers/pub_display.cfm?id=3333, accessed May 9, 2009.

11. Mohammad Jalal Abbasi-Shavazi, Meimanat Hosseini-Chavoshi, and Peter McDonald, "The Path to Below-Replacement Fertility in Iran," *Asia-Pacific Population Journal* 22 (2007): 91–112.

12. Paulo Freire, *The Pedagogy of the Oppressed*, trans. Myra Bergman Ramos (New York: Continuum, 2007).

13. Golnar Mehran, "The Paradox of Tradition and Modernity in Female Education in the Islamic Republic of Iran," *Comparative Education Review* 47 (2003): 269–86.

14. See Djavad Salehi-Isfahani and Daniel Egel, "Youth Exclusion in Iran: The State of Education, Employment, and Family Formation," Wolfensohn Center for Development, Brookings Institution, September 2007, www.brookings.edu/papers/2007/09_youth _exclusion_salehi_isfahani.aspx.

Postrevolutionary Persian Literature

Creativity and Resistance

Kamran Talattof

Persian literature after the 1979 revolution has been inspiring, entertaining, and even cathartic and it has, as it did in the prerevolutionary period, both influenced events and been influenced by societal changes. This body of contemporary literary works can help us understand how postrevolutionary events unfolded, how those events affected lives, and how the Iranian Revolution influenced the way in which art and ideology are produced and consumed.

In the years immediately following the revolution, Persian poetry declined, both in terms of volume and of reception. Committed leftist revolutionary poets such as Ahmad Shamlu, Hamid Mosadeq, Siyavosh Kasrai, or Mehdi Akhvan Sales, who had inspired social change among students and ordinary people in the decades prior to the revolution, lost their key motivation after the fall of the Shah. In addition, a number of these poets also either lost their lives (e.g., Said Soltanpur) or went into exile (e.g., Esmail Khoi), or they simply changed their method of social and cultural participation (e.g., Shamlu). A few, such as Simin Behbahani, continued to be productive in poetic endeavors, but even she espoused new approaches and became an advocate of women's rights and civil society in her literary and social activities. Several years later, poetry regained some of its past glory and many poets such as Qaysar Aminpur, Shams Langrudi, Mohamd Mokhtari, Sayed Ali Salehi, and Hasan Hosayni began focusing their aesthetic efforts on cultural, social, and political issues of their day. The poetry of some of the members of the older generations, such as Forugh Farrokhzad, posthumously gained a new significance due to the rise of

Radical History Review
Issue 105 (Fall 2009)   DOI 10.1215/01636545-2009-011

women's literary discourse in the late 1980s. In fact, since then, many new women poets have adopted the feminist literary discourse, expressing their dismay with those imposing social restrictions. Banafsheh Hejazi, Pegah Ahmadi, and Maryam Haydari have lamented the gender gap and traditional understanding of women's roles. In addition to such discursive shifts in women's poetry, the narrative element in so-called New Poetry (free verse or modern poetry) has received more emphasis since the revolution. That even holds true in the case of the contemporary poems written in classical forms such as the *ghazal* (lyric), which seems to have made a noticeable comeback as well.[1]

A number of poets have chosen to reflect the dominant state ideology. Among these poets, only a few have gained any literary recognition. Ali Garmarudi and Tahereh Safarzadeh, who actually began their careers in the prerevolutionary period, feature as the most prominent. But many younger poets were also inspired by the Iran-Iraq war to produce a sort of ideological poetry that has become known as "the poetry of war."

In recent decades, Persian poetry has flourished on the Internet and thus now reflects global topics and approaches. The appearance of electronic versions of classical poetry has inspired more poetry lovers to contribute to this surge. Many collections of both new and old Persian poetry have been translated into other languages.

The postrevolutionary period has witnessed a rise in writing and interest in short stories, novels, and drama after an initial lull right after the revolution. Many writers who had established their reputation before the revolution, as well as newer authors, found fiction an effective genre to portray the dramatic and sometimes devastating events unfolding in front their eyes. However, the early years were marked by the publication of Mahmud Dowlatabadi's *Kalidar*, which even though written before the revolution still found a great readership in the early 1980s.[2] The ten-volume novel depicts life and class issues in northeast Iran, highlighting the peasants' struggle and urban petit bourgeois despair. In it, the intellectuals—Muslim or not—unite in the fight against landlords, capitalists, and the oppressive forces that support them.

Like Dowlatabadi, Hushang Golshiri began the decade with a number of similar works. Even though the time for such themes had ended, the prose style of Dowlatabadi and Golshiri continued to influence the next generation. A new wave of energetic and creative fiction writers gave rise to new ideas, themes, and styles and began to dominate the field. Besides Abas Ma'rufi's pioneering postrevolutionary novel *Sanfoni-e mordegan* (*Symphony of the Dead*; 1987), Reza Barahani's *Razha-ye sarzamin-e man* (*The Secrets of My Land*; 1987), Sharnush Parsipur's *Touba va ma'na ye shap* (*Touba and the Meaning of Night*; 1988), and Ebrahim Yunesi's *Gurestan-e ghari ban* (*Strangers' Graveyard*; 1994)—about the history of Kurdish resistance—proved influential. Two novels were written about the Iran-Iraq war: *Zemestan-e 62* (*Winter of 62*; 1987), by Esmail Fasih, and *Zamin-e sukhteh* (*In the*

Burned Land; 1982), by Ahmad Mahmud. Later on, the publication of *Nakhl-ha-ye bi sar* (*Headless Palm Trees*; 1989), by Qasem Farasat, and *Ahu-ye Kuhi* (*Mountain Deer*; 1991), by Mahumd Golabdarehi, stand out as notable achievements.

Other promising authors in these decades include Bijan Najdi, Shahriyar Mandanipur, Mohamad Rahim Okhovat, Abu Torab Khosravi, Ahmad Dehqan, and Amirhasan Cheheltan, as well as many women authors such as Moniru Ravanipur, Ghazaelh Alizadeh, Zoya Pirzad, Farkhondeh Aqai, Fataneh Hajsayed Javadi, Nazi Safavi, Fahimeh Rahimi, Nasrin Sameni, Nasrin Qadiri, Parinush Sani'i, Qodsi Nasiri, Belqis Soleimani, Nahid Tabatabai, and Shohreh Vakili. Many of these authors have also published collections of short stories. Some, such as Ma'rufi, Mahshid Amirshahi, Parsipur, and Goli Taraqi, have continued to write in the diaspora. Postrevolutionary fiction writers often depict themes such as politics, struggle, prison, family, migration, moral issues, historical events, love — as always in a highly metaphorical language. But they also use styles such as realism or magical realism.

As the female names above indicate, women fiction writers in fact dominate the literary scene in terms of their readership (reflected in the number of the reprintings of their novels), their social impact (reflected in their connection with broader women's movements), and their preoccupation with such urgent issues as gender relations, individuality, sexual inequality, and the problematics of identity, especially female identity.[3]

Some fiction writers, of course, have supported the state religious discourse in one way or another, or at least at one time in their career. The most important names to be mentioned here include Mohsen Makhmalbaf and Reza Rahgozar. The former is also a prolific filmmaker, while the latter actively attempts to challenge the secular literary tradition, especially the one represented by the works of Sadeq Hedayat; otherwise he writes for children.

Some of the most prominent playwrights and dramatists immigrated during the early years after the revolution due to the harsh political situation. G. H. Saedi died in exile. Others such as Akbar Radi, Bahram Bayzai, Marziyeh Meshkini, Naser Irani, and Abbas Kiarostami who remained in Iran continue to work closely with the Persian cinema and theater industries. In recent decades, many more writers — Mohamad Charmshir, Qotbadin Sadeqi, Sharmin Maymandinejad, Azam Brujerdi, Davud Mirbaqeri, and Sadeq Ashurpur, to name a few — have joined the list of playwrights.

After the Iranian Revolution, humor and satirical writings grew with the publication of journals such as *Ahengar, Asghar Aqa,* and *Gol Aqa.* They transcended the boundaries to which older journals such as *Towfiq* succumbed. Soon these journals came under attack, and some of their prominent writers such as Hadi Khorsandi and Ebrahim Nabavi ended up working in exile. Now they manage popular humor and satire Web sites, such as Hadisara.com and Nabavionline.com. In Iran, Ruya Sadr, with works such *Bist Sal ba Tanz* (Twenty Years with Satire; 2002) or her work on the renowned satirist Kayumars Saberi, is a pioneer in the scholarship on humor and satire, working within the boundaries set by the state.

Children's literature has thrived in the postrevolutionary period. In addition to still productive, experienced writers such as Ali Ashraf Darvishiyan and Qodsi Qazinur, a host of new names has appeared in the field. Hushang Moradi Kermani, who wrote *Qeseh-ha-ye Majid* (*Majid's Stories*) in 2001, stands as an example. The Database on Culture and Literature of Iranian Children (Bank-e Itelaat-e farhang va adabiyat-e kudakan-e Iran) by the Center for Children's Culture and Literature is a large project that holds numerous literary works and a substantial number of documents. The Center for the Intellectual Development of the Children and Youth (Kanun-e Parvaresh-i Fekri-e Kudakan va Nowjavanan) has likewise continued to be active and productive within the framework provided by the state. Banafsheh Hejazi ably explains the scope and characteristics of the contemporary Iranian children's literature in her *Adabiyat-e Kudakan va Nowjavanan* (Literature for Children and Youth; 1995). The messages and overall mission of these works vary depending on the author's social and cultural orientation. However, the tensions between secular and religious tendencies, liberal and fundamental interpretations of Islam, and independent and public publishing manifest themselves in the processes and products of literary works written for children.

The growth in literary activities can also be measured by the increase in the number of literary critics and the amount of literary criticism produced in essay and book format. In addition to the more experienced literary critics and scholars such as Shafi'I Kadkani, A. Zarinkub, Mohamad Hoquqi, A. A. Dastghabe, M. A. Sepanlu, M. J. Puyandeh, Mohamad Mokhtari, Reza Baraheni, Daryush Ashuri, and Farj Sarkuhi, a number of other thinkers have become prominent. These include Babak Ahmadi, Hasan Abedini, Sirus Shamisa, Mansur Rastegar Fasai, Hasan Mirabadi, Shams Langrudi, Mashiyat Elahi, Kamyar Abedi, and others.

Many of these authors have contributed to literary journals, whose number also multiplied after the revolution, despite the demise of some of the most influential titles. These journals include *Adineh, Donya-ye Sokhan, Gardun, Kelk, Ayeneh, Takapu, Bokhara, Jahan-e Ketab, Negah-e Now, Ketab-e Mah, Faslnameh Honar, Goharan, Karnameh, Mofid, Adabiyat-e Dastani, Golestaneh, Jong-e Esfahan,* and *Adabestan.* However, many university- and state-sponsored journals from the past carried on or reemerged. These have been accompanied by the appearance of a few literary encyclopedias (and concordances) including *Daneshnameh-i Adab-e Farsi* (1996–), *Daneshnameh-i Zaban va Adab-i Farsi* (Encyclopedia of Persian Literature; 2005–), and *Daneshnameh-i Zaban va Adab-i Farsi dar Shebh-e Qarah* (Encyclopedia of Persian Language and Literature in the Indian Subcontinent; 2005). The latter has been published and managed by the Farhangestan-e Zaban-e Farsi (Academy of the Persian Language). Despite the academy's many activities and online resources, it cannot quite seem to keep up with the pace of literary production.

The journals *Adineh, Donya-ye Sokhan, Gardun,* and *Kiyan,* all of which the authorities closed down directly or indirectly by imposing severe limitations, played a significant role in keeping alive literary and creative activities inspired by modern topics and thought in the 1980s, when almost all secular and progressive thinkers came under attack. They not only published works on issues such as democracy, freedom of expression, civil society, peace, and justice but also promoted translation activities that kept Iranians informed about world literature. Among them, *Ayandeh* was the first that inspired hope and encouraged other journals such as *Adabestan, Amuzesh Adab-e Farsi, Kelk,* or *Takapu.* Other journals, such as *Kiyan, Zanan,* and *Majaleh-e Film,* indirectly played roles in the rise and growth of literary output. And it should be mentioned that the number of journals that appear, thrive briefly, and then vanish at the hands of the judiciary or of other governmental bodies is simply astonishing. No matter what their focus, many of these journals publish translations of Western and Latin American literary works. These journals and the translation of Western books constitute an aspect of Iranian literary history that has yet to be analyzed in terms of its vital impact on domestic literary production.

Independent literary establishments and scholars have created a number of literary awards. These include the Gardun's Award (the first of its kind), Karnameh, Yalda, the Golshiri Award, the Year's Book Award, Mehrgan, the Association of Authors and Critics' Award, and many more. The Award in Poetry goes exclusively to women authors. They all often struggle for sponsorship and survival. The ceremonies provide a forum in which experienced writers see each other and meet members of the new generation. The journalists, whose numbers also increased enormously under the reformist government, report these events in the many newspapers that have been allowed publication. The state has created a few awards such as the Chehreh-ha-ye Mandegar, which can be awarded to a literary author or an artist for great contributions to their field.

A number of events have had enduring effects. These include the revival of the Association of Iranian Writers (after being closed and having its members persecuted a few times during the early years of the revolutionary period), the establishment of the Tehran International Book Fair, and the creation of the International Arts Exhibition of Tehran. The formation of a few literary institutes and the addition of new academic departments of literature at universities also helped enhance literary activities. These included the Council for the Promotion of the Persian Language and Literature (Shoray-e Gostaresh-e Zaban va Adabiyat-e Farsi), the Iranology Foundation (Bonyad-e Iranshenasi), as well as others.

However, three incidents proved pivotal in terms of sociopolitical consequences on all literary and intellectual activities.[4] The first was women's rallies against the mandatory veiling codes in 1980, after which many women joined literary communities to write about their plight. The second was an open letter titled "We Are the Writers" composed by 134 writers in 1994 in which, for the first time, they publicly and bravely criticized the ruling elite's suppression of writers and its failure to move society forward. The letter broke a taboo. It read, "The identity of the writer, the nature of his/her work, as well as writers' collective presence have become subject to unpleasant treatment."[5] Abbas Marufi, author of *Symphony of the Dead* (1987) and the editor of *Gardun*, was one of the authors of that letter. The third pivotal event was the murder of Mohamad Mokhtari, Mohamd Jafar Puyandeh, and Majid Sharif (all members of the Association of Iranian Writers) in 1998, along with the assassination of nearly eighty other writers, critics, reformist intellectuals and politicians over several years as a part of what became known as the "chain murders" in Iran. When the crimes were revealed as being the work of some official agents, many joined in public condemnation of the hard-liners whose ideology was seen as responsible.

Thus all these publications and literary activities, often shaped by the literary movements of their time, have, as in the past, been connected with the broader intellectual and ideological movements in society. This exciting and creative body of work provides valuable insight into the contemporary social and cultural history of Iran.

Notes

1. For information about the rise of feminist literary discourse, see Kamran Talattof, *The Politics of Writing in Iran: A History of Modern Persian Literature* (Syracuse, NY: Syracuse University Press, 2000).
2. Mahmud Dowlatabadi, *Kalidar* (Tehran: Farhang-i Mu'asir, 1979).
3. Examples of the reprints of the works of women novelists that have been on the top of best-seller lists include *Bamdad-e Khomar* by Fataneh Hajsayed Javadi (thirty-eight times), *Cheragh-ha ra Man Khamush Mikonam* by Zoya Pirzad (twenty-two times), and *Dalan-e Behesht* by Naazi Safavi (twenty-two times).
4. The Iran-Iraq war was a devastating event, but its direct impact on literature has thus far been an increase in the number of works written in support of the defense against the invaders and in praise of state ideology.
5. The letter was widely circulated in many journals. For a translation of its text, see "We Are the Writers: A Statement by 134 Iranian Writers," trans. Hammed Shahidian, *Iranian Studies* 30 (1997): 291–93.

Reflections on Literature after the 1979 Revolution in Iran and in the Diaspora

Persis M. Karim

One of the most interesting effects of the Iranian Revolution of 1979 (and here I would like to indicate that I am using the term *Iranian* as opposed to *Islamic*) is that it has given rise to dramatic and unprecedented literary productivity. Although writers and intellectuals did play a role in the movements and events that led up to the revolution, their output and influence after the establishment of the Islamic Republic has been notable both in terms of production and impact. Both inside and outside Iran, writers have taken the opportunity to reflect on and write about the changes and tensions that have shaped Iran's postrevolutionary society and, for those who chose to leave Iran for other parts of the world, about the challenges of remaking their lives elsewhere. Nowhere is this more evident than in the emergence of a vibrant postrevolution literature dominated by women both inside and outside Iran.

Given that Iran's literary tradition has for nearly a thousand years been shaped and dominated by men, the presence of women authors in the period before the revolution was spotty at best. With the exception of a handful of female poets and writers like Parvin E'tesami, Forugh Farrokhzad, Simin Daneshvar, and Simin Behbehani, women writers have remained largely invisible and were often dismissed as secondary to male writers. The revolution and its campaign to rid the culture of foreign and Western influence, however, emphasized a "homegrown," native Iranian culture (whether in film, television, or the literary arts), and writers seeking to work within the confines of both explicit and implied rules for cultural production have

Radical History Review

Issue 105 (Fall 2009)   DOI 10.1215/01636545-2009-012

© 2009 by MARHO: The Radical Historians' Organization, Inc.

devised clever ways to document, criticize, and account for the shifts in Iranian society and life after 1979. Women have taken their diminished access to public spaces and have capitalized on the private realm of letters to add their own voices to a literature that has historically excluded them. Another aspect of writing in Iran now is the shift away from poetry, a genre historically tied to the tradition of classical Persian prose, to the genre of fiction. Women lead the way in this new explosion of fiction, and according to Majid Eslami, the editor of the literary and art magazine, *Haft* (*Seven*), women dominate the fiction lists and are, in his words "the avant-garde of Persian literature."[1]

Concomitant with the emergence of women writers has been an increase in female readership, creating a market for women's writing unprecedented before the revolution. While censorship has been a continual force for writers to contend with, both before and after 1979, women authors have commanded an audience for their work despite the prohibition of certain explicit topics and images. Among the most prominent women writers of the new generation who have won acclaim and received notable literary prizes are Zoya Pirzad, Fariba Vafi, and Shiva Arstui. Those authors whose work directly challenges the system or critiques the position of women in the Islamic Republic—such as Shahrnush Parsipur, the author of *Women without Men* (1989)—have had to face formal sanctions or even the banning of their books. Some writers have had to choose exile to continue to write. For some of those writers who left Iran immediately after the revolution, writing has proved a difficult occupation. Finding publishers or translators for their work has proved challenging, and maintaining a connection to their Persian-speaking readers has been at best inconsistent. Those who have been successful have often taken up writing in the language of their host country. These include novelists like Goli Taraghi, who writes in both French and Persian, and American-based novelist Farnoosh Moshiri, who writes almost exclusively in Persian.

Women in the diaspora have also dominated the literary production of the postrevolutionary period in North America and Europe. While a handful of men have written novels and memoirs (the novelist Salar Abdoh most immediately comes to mind), women writers have been largely responsible for making Iran and the postrevolutionary immigrant experience visible in literature. Women writers of the Iranian disapora especially appear to have comfortably left behind any concerns about adhering to the tradition of Iranian letters and have instead made writing one of the most important media for representing their particular experiences of exile, immigration, and identity. Present in much of the writing by women are the tensions between Western and Iranian culture, between Islamic and, say, American culture and values, and the obvious desire to both maintain connections to Iran and Iranian culture and divorce the country from the prevailing view of the Islamic Republic today.

In 1999, when the first anthology of Iranian American writing, *A World*

Between: Poems, Short Stories, and Essays by Iranian-Americans was published, I, a coeditor of the tome, repeatedly had to answer the question why so few men's voices found representation in the collection. I jokingly answered then that I thought it was because men were too busy being doctors and engineers. This is not altogether false. For Iranian women and their Western-born children, the idea of being a writer and narrating something of their experience held more possibilities in the West than in Iran. As long as Iran remained closed to Americans and as long it was held in the static iconography of the revolutionary moment, there was an opportunity for women writers to tell their stories in a fashion that would diverge significantly from the more male didactic and politically discursive style that dominated Iranian letters just prior to the overthrow of the Shah.

Although the period immediately after the revolution found many Iranian immigrant writers and intellectuals unmoored from their reading audiences and with few opportunities to publish their work, the younger generation of Iranian diaspora writers sought opportunities to speak to Western reading audiences. Those writers were largely women who, ironically, suddenly obtained in a Western reading audience the opportunity to speak freely and without fear of judgment about their self-disclosure. Many of these writers were able to move seamlessly between Persian and English or Persian and French, and they have had formative experiences in the West that make it possible for them to connect and relate to the West, while still retaining their "authentic" Iranian sensibilities. These writers include memoirists like Tara Bahrampour (*To See and See Again: A Life in Iran and America*), Marjane Satrapi (*Persepolis* and *Persepolis 2*), and fiction writers like Farnoosh Moshiri (*At the Wall of the Almighty* and *In the Bathhouse*). These writers, whose work appeared in the late 1990s, helped make visible the experiences of living through the Iranian Revolution and its accompanying problems—war, exile, and adjustment to a new culture—but also have found ways to challenge the representation of women both in the Islamic Republic and in the Western media. They are essentially writers whose lives and work operate at the juncture between two cultures.

One of the most obvious phenomena of Iranian diaspora literature has been the explosion of women's memoirs, which have proven particularly popular on the U.S. publishing market. One might argue that the attraction of the memoir as a genre lies in its affording an opportunity for self-revelation and self-representation that might otherwise be difficult in the current literary culture of Iran. The individual experience posited by the memoir seems to align itself nicely with American individualism; the memoir also has been skillfully marketed to suggest that Iranian women are telling their true lives and their secrets to an American reading public who might otherwise not be able to move beyond the occulted, veiled images of Iranian women purveyed in the media. While the memoir is indeed a problematic genre, often privileging the individual life and thus creating a self-other dichotomy or, in the case of the Iranian women's memoirs, suggesting that women's experience serves as the essential symbol for the oppressive forces of Islam or the Islamic Republic of Iran, it has also proved a source of information that Western readers might not otherwise encounter. In Azar Nafisi's *Reading Lolita in Tehran: A Memoir in Books* and Azadeh Moaveni's *Lipstick Jihad: A Memoir of Growing up Iranian in America and American in Iran,* for example, Western readers encounter some of the most problematic ways in which women have had to navigate life in the Islamic Republic. But those images and representations have also faced the harsh criticism from Iranian-born scholars and critics living and working in the West such as Hamid Dabashi, author of *Iran: A People Interrupted* (2007) and Fatemeh Keshavarz, author of *Jasmine and Stars: Reading More than Lolita in Tehran* (2009), who see these memoirs as a kind of collusion with the larger politics of the U.S. government, and particularly in the past eight years, as a reification and cementing of Iran as a kind of static Oriental other. For these critics, the publication of numerous memoirs by women in the period immediately following the 9/11 attacks in the United States only served to underscore an image of Iran that was articulated in George W. Bush's famous "Axis of Evil Speech" of January 2002.

While many of us who work in literature do not dispute the power of self-representation, we also recognize the limits of what the memoir or any other literary representation can and should do. As we reflect on the thirtieth anniversary of the Iranian revolution and mark three decades of literary production that has been largely grounded in the events of the revolution and its impact, one sees a shift in both the literary and political landscape. I am hopeful that a narrative often reading as a "I've lost everything but America has redeemed me" tale, sometimes parroted in the later memoirs, will exhaust itself and lose some of its allure for Western readers, who will move toward a greater curiosity about Iran itself, rather than focusing on lamentations about what Iran once was. I am also hopeful that the literary maturation I have witnessed in the past five years will continue to produce a stylistic and aesthetic shift in the literature of the Iranian diaspora. I am also certain that the urgency of telling one's story (which is a hallmark of the immigrant narrative) eventually will give way to attention on how one tells the narrative, to the idea of *the literary* instead of simple *storytelling.*

More recent novels and memoirs have paid greater attention to language and to the importance of historical accuracy and research, rather than remain obsessed with personal memory, and to the complexities of living between cultures that have long harbored suspicions about one another. These new writers, both women and men, writing either prose or poetry, are looking for ways to draw on their heritage and culture, but they are less inclined to pursue the narrative of revolution as trauma, or to have the idea that Iran and the historical departure from the country should serve as the narrative center of their work. Theirs is a literature that begs the question what it means to move beyond any particular national category, beyond even any particular kind of hyphenated writer, to instead mine the field of cultural, historical, and aesthetic riches that lies at the heart of any cultural transplantation. The perspective of these younger, more culturally syncretic (and maybe more intellectually savvy) writers is less oriented toward the past and more focused on what is yet to be, and perhaps, their work is much more attenuated by the perspective of "neither" and "both." It also remains to be seen if a shift of politics will also necessitate a shift in the literary perspective. As a writer, reader, critic, and educator, and as someone who still believes in the power of literature, I am hoping for both things.

Note

1.   Nazila Fathi, "Women Writing Novels Emerge as Stars in Iran," *New York Times*, June 28, 2005.

Postrevolutionary Trends in Persian Fiction and Film

M. R. Ghanoonparvar

To examine new trends in Persian fiction and Iranian film, a brief look at the old trends seems necessary. If we consider Mohammad Ali Jamalzadeh (1892 – 1997) as the inaugurator of modern Persian fiction and Nima Yushij (1897 – 1960) as the father of modern Persian poetry in the early twentieth century, we should also keep in mind that their work was preceded by the efforts of other fiction writers, poets, and playwrights in the late nineteenth century. A look at *Siyahatnameh-ye Ebrahim Beyg* (*The Travel Memoirs of Ebrahim Beyg*), a bridge between the dominant nineteenth-century prose genre of the *safarnameh* (travel memoirs) and twentieth-century fiction, as well as at the poetry of Mirzadeh Eshqi (and others) and the closet plays of Mirza Aqa Tabrizi before and during the Iranian constitutional revolution (1906 – 11), shows that, in contrast to classical Persian literature, the early modernists veered toward a literature of social and political criticism.[1] Although the political aspect perhaps seems more pronounced in the works of these writers than in the works of Jamalzadeh and Yushij, the latter figures also paid attention to political issues, albeit more obliquely. This also held true for the works of many of the next generation of writers, including Sadeq Hedayat and Bozorg Alavi. But the third generation, which consisted of writers and poets such as Sadeq Chubak, Jalal Al-e Ahmad, Ebrahim Golestan, and Ahmad Shamlu, in many ways followed the trend set by the late nineteenth-century writers, a trend that largely continued until the Iranian Revolution in the works of Forugh Farrokhzad, Gholamhoseyn Sa'edi, Hushang Golshiri, Mahmud Dowlatabadi, and Simin Daneshvar, among others.[2]

Radical History Review
Issue 105 (Fall 2009)   DOI 10.1215/01636545-2009-013
© 2009 by MARHO: The Radical Historians' Organization, Inc.

In regard to Iranian cinema (leaving aside popular entertainment movies), from the 1960s, with the inception of the so-called New Wave, we observe a similar commitment to social and political criticism, although the political undercurrent in these films remained veiled due to the existing strict censorship. Such important films as *Gav* (*The Cow*, 1969) and *Dayereh-ye mina* (*The Cycle*, 1978) by Daryush Mehrju'i, *Khesht-o a'ineh* (*Brick and Mirror*, 1965) and *Asrar-e ganj-e darreh-ye jenni* (*The Secrets of the Treasures of the Haunted Valley*, 1974) by Ebrahim Golestan, *Shazdeh Ehtejab* (*Prince Ehtejab*, 1974) by Bahman Farmanara, *Tangsir* (1973) by Amir Naderi, and *Gavaznha* (*The Deer*, 1976) by Mas'ud Kimia'i offer a few examples of the social and political criticism provided by filmmakers.[3]

The focus here, of course, is on what has been referred to as "intellectual" literature and cinema. But one could find similar political and social engagements in popular fiction and film at the time. With this brief historical introduction, we can begin to consider an investigation of the sort of changes, if any, that have occurred in postrevolutionary fiction and film.

A novel that may be regarded as a transitional work between the prerevolutionary and postrevolutionary trends, mainly in its commitment to social and political issues, is Mahmud Dowlatabadi's monumental epic, *Kelidar*. Although I have described it as an epic and a historical novel elsewhere, *Kelidar* is also a sociopolitical novel. It was published in five volumes, the first of which appeared in 1978, while the last appeared in 1984, a few years after the revolution.[4] While from 1979 to late 1980 much literary output turned overtly political, once the new postrevolutionary Islamic regime had managed to set the machinery of control and censorship in place, the art of subterfuge and allegory returned to literary production: political themes once again became veiled, hidden behind the mask of symbolism, also a dominant feature of prerevolutionary literature. This was true of the works of older writers who continued to be productive, but also in the writing of new writers who entered the scene.

One trend indicative of literary subterfuge is magic realism in fiction. The most important examples of this style can be seen in the works of such writers as Moniru Ravanipur, Shahrnush Parsipur, and Ja'far Modarres-Sadeqi in such works as *Ahl-e ghargh* (*The Drowned*), *Sangha-ye Sheytan* (*Satan's Stones*), *Zanan bedun-e mardan* (*Women without Men*), and *Gavkhuni* (*The Marsh*).[5] But while most of these works may not be regarded as political in the proper sense of the word, they are political in the sense that they mean to challenge the foundations of a political regime based on religion and religious morality. At the same time, with their enigmatic plots and surrealistic characters and events, works of magic realism function as a vehicle of subterfuge for the authors by concealing their intentions from the censors.

Another trend in postrevolutionary literature is so-called escapist literature. The most popular example of this trend is the best-selling novel *Bamdad-e kho-*

mar (*The Morning of Hangover*) by Fataneh Haj Seyed Javadi, which—like its predecessor in the 1950s, *Showhar-e Ahu Khanom* (*Ahu Khanom's Husband*) by Ali Mohammad Afghani, and the popular romance novels of Mohammad Hejazi and Ali Dashti published from the 1930s through the 1950s—belongs to what may be called an Iranian soap opera work, dealing with such themes as arranged marriage, cowives, and so on. In other words, these novels offer up a world in which the reader can take refuge from the harsh realities often imposed by autocracy.

A third trend is autobiographical fiction. Commentators, correctly or incorrectly, have often noted a dearth of autobiographical writing and personal memoirs in Persian literature. Yet postrevolutionary literature manifests a relatively large number of works based on the lives, mostly childhood memories, of their authors. Ravanipur's collections of short stories, *Kanizu* and *Sangha-ye Sheytan*, and her novels, *Ahl-e gharg*, *Del-e fulad* (*Heart of Steel*), and *Kowli dar kenar-e atash* (*Gypsy by the Fire*), are for the most part autobiographical. Similarly, the works of Goli Taraqqi, such as *Neveshtehha-ye parakandeh* (*Scattered Memoirs*), constitute childhood memoirs, and Golshiri's *A'inehha-ye dardar* and *Jennameh* (*The Book of Jinn*) are autobiographies in disguise. Perhaps the most widely read Persian writer in the past couple of decades has been Hushang Moradi-Kermani, whose popular books, *Qessehha-ye Majid* (*The Stories of Majid*) and *Morabba-ye shirin* (*Sweet Jam*), are also based on his childhood experiences. In his recent book, *Shoma keh gharibeh nistid* (*But You Are Not a Stranger*), Moradi-Kermani blurs the line between fiction and autobiography, and even though the book is presented as a novel, it is unabashedly the life story of the author, whose narrator is Hushi or Hushang.

Another new trend that began in the 1980s and continues today is war literature. The Iran-Iraq war had a tremendous effect on all Iranians, whether they were directly engaged in fighting or experienced the bombardment of the cities as civilians. During the war, a series of books consisting mostly of poetry or anecdotes based on war experiences of soldiers were published that fall somewhat short of lasting literary value. In recent years, however, a number of novels have been published that look back at the war with a more sobering eye, reflecting not only on a specific experience of the Iran-Iraq war but also on the human condition in general, such as Ahmad Dehqan's *Safar beh geray-e 270 darajeh* (*Journey to Heading 270 Degrees* which chronicles in detail the experiences of a soldier on the front;[6] Habib Ahmadzadeh's collection of short stories, *Dastanha-ye shahr-e jangi* (*The War-Stricken City Stories*), which chronicles firsthand experiences of the war by young patriotic soldiers; Mohammad Reza Bayrami's *Pol-e mo'allaq* (*The Suspension Bridge*), which is also based on his own experiences as a soldier during the Iran-Iraq war; and Davud Ghaffarzadegan's *Fal-e khun* (*Fortune Told in Blood*), an unusual story told from the perspective of the enemy, an Iraqi officer and an Iraqi soldier.[7]

One of the consequences of the Iranian Revolution and of the establishment of an Islamic Republic was the exodus of a significant number of Iranians, who mostly migrated to Europe and North America. An important development in the past two decades is the publication of many volumes of poetry, fiction, and autobiographical writings by Iranian or hyphenated Iranian writers abroad, both in Persian and in other languages. Regardless of whether such writings should be considered part of the modern Persian literary canon, they represent an important development that will certainly have, and to some extent already has had, an effect on Persian literature (e.g., many stories written and published by writers in Iran today utilize such themes as exile and cultural assimilation, which characterize the works of Iranian writers who have immigrated to other countries). In addition to novels and short stories written by Iranian immigrants and exiles in languages other than Persian, there is also a substantial corpus of literary works by these groups that deal mostly with themes of nostalgia, cultural assimilation, and split identity. Such themes are relatively unprecedented in Iranian literature and must be regarded as a new trend in the postrevolutionary literature.

To these postrevolutionary works in literature, we also should add the large number of novels and short story collections written for children and young adults. Many such volumes are in fact not suitable for these age groups, as they often constitute stories about, and not for, children. Much of the work of such well-known postrevolutionary writers such as Ghaffarzadegan and Bayrami marketed as children's books belong to this category, perhaps in a ploy to evade censorship. This is not dissimilar to the popular trend in Iranian cinema that deals with children and young adults.

One of the most important trends in postrevolutionary Iranian cinema is, in fact, so-called children's films, films about youngsters. Films in this genre by Abbas Kiarostami, Majid Majidi, Amir Naderi, and others have attained international success and need no introduction. This genre did not only emerge after the revolution, however; it was launched by filmmakers affiliated with the Center for the Intellectual Development of Children and Young Adults before the Iranian Revolution.

One can also identify other trends in Iranian cinema, for example, the "humanistic" trend in the films of Kiarostami and others, and also sometimes a mystical trend, which we could to some extent interpret as escapist.[8] Still another trend involves films that deal with women's issues, by both female and male filmmakers. Films such as Rakhshan Banie'temad's *Banu-ye ordibehesht* (*The May Lady*, 1998), Marziyeh Meshkini's *Ruzi keh zan shodam* (*The Day I Became a Woman*, 2001), Daryush Mehrju'i's numerous films about women that carry female names as their titles, Tahmineh Milani's *Do zan* (*Two Women*, 1999), and Bahram Beyza'i's *Shayad vaqti digar* (*Maybe Some Other Time*, 1988) and *Mosaferan* (*Travelers*, 1992) represent this trend. In recent years, with the occasional easing of some state restrictions, a number of films that implicitly challenge the regime have also found their way onto the silver screen. Some of these films—including those dealing with women's issues, such as Milani's *Nimeh-ye penhan* (*The Hidden Half*, 2001)—question traditional religious and social practices, while others, such as Kamal Tabrizi's *Marmulak* (*The Lizard*, 2004), even question the authority of the theocratic regime. Yet the authorities soon banned many such films after their first screening.

The Iran-Iraq war also became an important subject in Iranian cinema after the revolution. A large number of war movies were made during the war, mainly for propaganda purposes, and generally aired on television. The war films also helped to remove the taboo that religious authorities had established and that devout Iranians observed regarding movie theaters and cinema in general; these groups had heretofore considered the cinema a dark place in which debauchery and sinning occurred due to Western cultural influence. With the change in the political system and the start of the Iran-Iraq war, the Islamic regime found cinema a useful tool in the propagation of its ideology, particularly in rallying support and recruiting soldiers. A slogan often shown at the beginning of some films and in movie theaters quoted Ayatollah Ruhollah Khomeini: "We do not oppose the cinema; we oppose debauchery [*fahsha*]." Feature films about war produced by various government organizations depicted battles very realistically in terms of cinematic technique. Thematically, these films emphasized such notions as martyrdom, heroism, camaraderie among Islamic combatants, and self-sacrifice. These films portray Iranian soldiers as "Islamic soldiers," in contrast to Iraqi soldiers, who are represented as "mercenaries," purporting that Iranian soldiers fought for Islam and God, and not for material and worldly gain. While Iranian soldiers are portrayed as compassionate, warm, faithful, and devout Muslims, the Iraqi enemies are generally presented as either bloodthirsty fiends or misguided victims of the machinations of Saddam Hussein and his Western supporters. Examples of these films include *Balami besu-ye sahel* (*Sailing toward the Shore*, 1984) and *Parvaz dar shab* (*Flight at Night*, 1986) by Rasul Mollaqolipur, and *Parchamdar* (*Flag Bearer*, 1985) by Shahriar Bahrani. After the war, films dealing with war distanced themselves from state propaganda and became what one would regard as antiwar films. Well-known examples of these are Beyza'i's *Bashu, gharibeh-ye kuchak* (*Bashu, the Little Stranger*, 1987), Mohsen Makhmalbaf's *'Arusi-ye khuban* (*The Wedding of the Blessed*, 1989), and Ebrahim Hatamikia's *Az Karkheh ta Rayn* (*From the Karkheh to the Rhine*, 1993).

The consequences of the Iranian Revolution and the Iran-Iraq war are also present in the works of Iranian filmmakers who have left their homeland in the past three decades and who focus on the lives of their exiled compatriots. As in the case of literature, outside Iran, some filmmakers have produced films that have been widely, though in Iran clandestinely, viewed, which certainly could have an impact on Iranian cinema. The examples that come to mind include Parviz Sayyad's *Ferestadeh* (*The Mission*, 1984) and Reza Allamehzadeh's *Mehmanan-e Hotel Astoria* (*The Guests of Hotel Astoria*, 1989).

This cursory overview of postrevolutionary Iranian prose fiction and cinema should convey not only the rich and productive artistic developments in these two media but also the scale of diversity and innovation. In addition to the trends mentioned, there is also a continuation of the lyrical and philosophical tradition of classical Persian poetry in the films of major directors. Kiarostami's *Bad mara khahad bord* (*The Wind Will Carry Us*, 1999) and *Ta'm-e gilas* (*Taste of Cherry*, 1997) and Mehrju'i's *Hamun* (1992) embody the philosophical tradition, while Makhmalbaf's *Gabbeh* (1996) continues the lyrical tradition. These traditions are also reflected in stories by well-known veteran writers such as Golshiri's *Jennameh* and Modarres-Sadeqi's *Kaleh-ye asb* (*Horse's Head*) and in the works of younger authors such as Bayrami's *Qessehha-ye Sabalan* (*The Tales of Sabalan*).[9] The prerevolutionary genre of formulaic films geared toward popular entertainment, often referred to as *abgushti*, has survived in different forms. *Abgushti*, literally a "[poor man's] soup," refers to the type of popular entertainment film that dealt with the traditional life of working-class families. The term was first used to describe director Siyamak Yasami's 1965 film, *Ganj-e Qarun* (Croesus's Treasure), the plot and characters of which provided other directors with a formula for subsequent popular movies in this genre. While cabaret scenes and dancing are no longer a part of the recipe, romantic love, intrigues, car-chase scenes, and other formulas still persist and seem to attract similar lower income, uneducated audiences.

Notes

1. For a discussion of twentieth-century Persian prose fiction, see Hassan Kamshad, *Modern Persian Prose Literature* (Cambridge: Cambridge University Press, 1966); and M. R. Ghanoonparvar, *Prophets of Doom: Literature as a Socio-political Phenomenon in Modern Iran* (Lanham, MD: University Press of America, 1984). On the development of modern Persian poetry, see Ahmad Karimi-Hakkak, *Recasting Persian Poetry: Scenarios of Poetic Modernity in Iran* (Salt Lake City: University of Utah Press, 1995). On Iranian drama, see M. R. Ghanoonparvar and John Green, eds., *Iranian Drama: An Anthology* (Costa Mesa, CA: Mazda, 1989). James D. Clark's English translation of *Siyahatnameh-ye Ebrahim Beyg* was published as *The Travel Diary of Ebrahim Beg* (Costa Mesa, CA: Mazda, 2006).

2. Other book-length studies of modern Persian literature in English include, Mohammad Mehdi Khorrami, *Modern Reflections of Classical Traditions in Persian Fiction* (Lewiston, NY: Edwin Mellen, 2003); and Kamran Talattof, *The Politics of Writing in Iran: A History of Modern Persian Literature* (Syracuse, NY: Syracuse University Press, 2000).

3. For a history of Iranian cinema, see Mohammad Ali Issari, *Cinema in Iran, 1900–1979* (Metuchen, NJ: Scarecrow, 1989).

4. M. R. Ghanoonparvar, "Nava-ye naqqal dar *Kelidar*" ("The Voice of the Storyteller in *Kelidar*"), *Fasl-e Ketab* 2 (1991): 96–101.

5. For an English translation of some of these works see Moniru Ravanipur, *Satan's Stones*, ed. M. R. Ghanoonparvar (Austin: University of Texas Press, 1996); Shahrnush Parsipur, *Women without Men: A Novella*, trans. Kamran Talattof (Syracuse, NY: Syracuse University Press, 1998); and Jafar Modarres-Sadeqi, *The Marsh*, trans. Afkham Darbandi (Costa Mesa, CA: Mazda, 1996).

6. Ahmad Dehqan, *Journey to Heading 270 Degrees*, trans. Paul Sprachman (Costa Mesa, CA: Mazda, 2006).

7. Davud Ghaffarzadegan, *Fortune Told in Blood*, trans. M. R. Ghanoonparvar (Austin: University of Texas Press, 2008).

8. With the international popularity of postrevolutionary Iranian cinema, there have been increasing numbers of studies in English, among them, Hamid Dabashi, *Close Up: Iranian Cinema, Past, Present, and Future* (London: Verso, 2001); and Dabashi, *Masters and Masterpieces of Iranian Cinema* (Washington, DC: Mage, 2007); Alberto Elena, *The Cinema of Abbas Kiarostami* (London: Saqi Books, 2005); Michael J. Fischer, *Mute Dreams, Blind Owls, and Dispersed Knowledges: Persian Poesis in the Transnational Circuitry* (Durham, NC: Duke University Press, 2004); Hamid Reza Sadr, *Iranian Cinema: A Political History* (London: I. B. Tauris, 2006); Mehrnaz Saeed-Vafa and Jonathan Rosenbaum, *Abbas Kiarostami* (Urbana: University of Illinois Press, 2003); and Richard Tapper, ed., *The New Iranian Cinema: Politics, Representation, and Identity* (London: I. B. Tauris, 2002).

9. For the English translation of this novel, see Mohammad Reza Bayrami, *The Tales of Sabalan*, trans. M. R. Ghanoonparvar (Costa Mesa, CA: Mazda, 2008).

Islamic Revolution and the Circulation of Visual Culture

Mazyar Lotfalian

In April 2008 a work of the celebrated Iranian artist, Parviz Tanavoli, sold for 2.5 million dollars at Christie's auction in Dubai. The Christie's catalog referenced the piece as *Persopolis*, and the artist himself calls it one of his best. We are finding ourselves in a new moment for the circulation of Iranian art. After almost thirty years of relative isolation for the community of artists in Iran, this sale sent a shock wave through the nervous system of the community, that is, art galleries, art schools, and individual artists. It stirred both concerns and hope: concerns that the work of art would become corrupted by money, and hope for the prospects of Iranian art on the world stage. The generation of modernist artists from the 1960s and 1970s, including those who lived in the diaspora, had felt marginalized after the revolution—although the Tehran Museum of Contemporary Art holds one of the largest collections of modern Western art outside Western Europe and North America—and saw the Christie's auction as a signal of new opportunities.

Christie's constitutes a new venue for Iranian painting and sculpture, though other spaces for the circulation of visual culture have existed since the beginning of the revolution. In fact, much Iranian visual culture has been disseminated in the West through different channels from the beginning of the revolution. If we are to understand the effect of the revolution on the production of visual culture, we have to pay attention to its circulation. This allows us to understand an emerging *sensus communis*, a new possibility for a shared understanding of sense perception that is emanating from various places, different technologies, and emerging forms.

Radical History Review
Issue 105 (Fall 2009)   DOI 10.1215/01636545-2009-014
© 2009 by MARHO: The Radical Historians' Organization, Inc.

It may be instructive to reflect on different media types, institutions, and technologies that have helped disseminate Iranian visual culture since the revolution. Film has a prominent place in Iranian postrevolutionary visual production, as the Islamic Republic both sanctioned and regulated filmmaking. The Islamic Republic's decision to continue sanctioning the cinema as medium of art and entertainment under a new ideology and to fund filmmaking in the early years of the revolution served as a prelude to what is now a flourishing community of Iranian filmmakers. Filmmakers have had to negotiate their production to conform to Islamic codes. They have done so by working through the Ministry of Islamic Guidance, which decides which work can be shown in public. Censorship of this kind has made filmmaking a difficult task, but by no means have films been uniformly ideologically committed to what is deemed Islamic. In fact, a range of filmmakers—avant-garde, committedly Islamist, feminist—have produced equally critical films about postrevolutionary society. Filmmakers such as Abbas Kiarostami and Mohsen Makhmalbaf have shown not only that filmmaking under the Islamic Republic is possible, but that there also exists a place for social critique.

In 1992 the Toronto Film Festival celebrated the international debut of Iranian films as "the new Iranian Cinema." The rest is history. For about a decade Iranian films were on top of everyone's lists as they circulated around the world. The reception of these films was very much driven by curiosity in the West about a newly formed society ruled by an Islamic government. How can one make films under these conditions? How would one encode the rules of modesty or of other religious morality in films? Can film be a source of knowledge about a new society?

The politics of Islam in Iran and anxiety about Islam in the West are major contributing factors that shape the viewing and production of visual culture in Iran and in the diaspora. By the late 1990s, and especially after the tragic events of 9/11, these politics affected the circulation of visual culture, resulting in a shift toward wanting to "account" for Islam, that is, institutions and individual artists began including interpretations of Islam in their agendas. This shift has manifested itself in the works of artists, museum exhibitions, and organized workshops in the post-9/11 period. Shirin Neshat, for example, in her photographic series *Women of Allah*, initiated a wave of works that focused on the use of the politics of Islam in contemporary art. Some critics have been wary of this combination, alleging that it might perpetuate stereotypes about Islam, invoking the politics of representation in Orientalist paintings.

Museums have also experimented with the notion of "contemporary Islamic art" as an organizing theme for exhibitions. Among other examples, in 2006 the Museum of Modern Art in New York City for the first time engaged in such an experiment, creating an exhibition of artists of Islamic background. This exhibition, Without Boundary: Seventeen Ways of Looking, included fifteen Muslim artists, among them Neshat, Mona Hatoum, a Lebanese-born Palestinian installation artist, and Shazia Sikandar, a Pakistani-born painter. The exhibition also included two American artists to show the complexity of identity in the arts. The museum director and curator argued that Islam formed part of these artists' identity, making it relevant to the work of art in the contemporary context.

Islamic art (as it has been known in the field of art history) is not new to art galleries and museums. Under the category of Islam, the works of miniatures, calligraphy, and architecture (as well as Orientalist paintings) have circulated in art galleries and museums. In addition, contemporary Iranian artists, such as Tanavoli, have often used calligraphy or geometrical forms associated with Islamic aesthetics. New are the ways in which, in the works of some contemporary artists, Islam-in-visual-culture becomes the stage for an intermingling of aesthetics and politics. Galleries and museums are, of course, implicated in the process of selecting and promoting arts. For example, the Gladstone Gallery in New York was instrumental in introducing the work of Neshat in the early 1990s. The specific ways that Neshat used Islam in her works attracted their attention. Other works of political art that do not use Islam in the same way as does Neshat, such as those by the Iranian diasporic artists Haleh Niazmand and Gita Hashemi, do not enjoy the same attention and are not circulated with the same impact.

Islam became central to the production of Iranian visual culture in many ways after the revolution. A major thread in the production of Iranian visual culture is the Shi'i commemoration of the martyrdom of Imam Hossein in the seventh century in Karbala. The imaginary surrounding this event constitutes an abstract space that emanates codes of Shi'i Islamic visual culture, hence the formation of the *Karbala paradigm*, denoting the symbolic meaning of everyday events as they relate to the martyrdom of Hossein. After fifty years of alleged decline, various images of martyrdom, trauma, and messianic views of the world began to reoccur with the unfolding of the shift in image-making. These images began to appear in several ways, including through direct representation in films portraying the images of Karbala supported by elegiac sounds (*rowzeh khanii*), narratives coded as battles of good and evil, or the creation of structures of feeling as people face life-changing events.

Broadly speaking there are several different arenas of production in contemporary Iran that implicitly or explicitly draw on the themes of the Karbala paradigm and use the same visual and aural imagery and elements as Ta'ziyeh (the popular theater in which the event of Karbala is enacted) in cinema and television. These arenas include the Iran-Iraq war films in cinema verité style, processions of *ashura* (the street festival during the month of Muharram), and neighborhood organizations (*moludis* and *hayats*) formed around the themes of Karbala. Cinema, particularly during the Iran-Iraq war, employed images of martyrdom and self-sacrifice. This can be seen in the works of filmmakers such as Ebrahim Hatamikia (e.g., *Glass Agency*, 1997) who made war films, and of Alireza Davoodnijad (e.g., *Niaz*, 1991) who made melodramatic films. Similar imagery occurs in the works of avant-garde filmmakers such as Bahram Beizai (e.g., *Travelers*, 1992) and Dariush Mehrjui (e.g., *Leila*, 1996), albeit to critical ends.

As a government-controlled institution, television, with its huge budget, has the liberty to encode Islamic moral codes into its productions. Television productions that relate to Ta'ziyeh have been broadcast frequently since soon after the revolution. Among the TV productions more explicitly referencing Ta'ziyeh is *The Tenth Night* (*Shabe dahom*), a historical miniseries that narrates the banning of Ta'ziyeh in the early Pahlavi era, directed by Hassan Fathi. There is also *The Story of Conquest* (*Ravayat e fath*), a docudrama about the Iran-Iraq war directed by Morteza Avini, broadcast during and after the war. This production is now distributed through the Avini Foundation, which has a well-organized archive and dedicated following.

Streets and other urban spaces have been transformed after the revolution, resulting in the reemergence of traditional rituals. For example, the traditional Shi'i mourning processions that occur during the month of Muharram (the first month in the Islamic calendar) are seen throughout the Islamic world. Since the Iranian Revolution this popular form of cultural production has assumed a more festive and carnivalesque atmosphere than previously seen. This has held particularly true in urban areas, where street processions, previously restricted, have grown in dimension and grandeur and have become popular among youth. In addition, other transformations have occurred: for example, the bloodletting rituals during Muharram have been replaced by people covering their bodies with mud, and women now participate in the public procession.

Social space has also been transformed through technology. For instance, the rituals produced by neighborhood groups (*hayat*) have been recorded and circulated through low- to medium-quality videotapes, video CDs, and DVDs. These include mourning rituals that are also part of Ta'ziyeh, namely, *rowzeh khani* (elegiac songs), and *sineh zani* (self-flagellations and self-beating). Today, the digital camera allows for the quick and easy production and dissemination of these works on the market for local, regional, and international consumption. These productions have received further attention through the visual blogs and YouTube, for example.

The interconnections among these media forms create the condition of possibility for an emergent visual language of Shi'i Islam, with the Karbala paradigm serving as acentral structuring system of meaning in language and culture. Beyond the semiotic level, the interconnection is also about the material circulation and political economy of these cultural productions. The process of circulation of these visual materials constitutes what Walter Benjamin has called "phantasmagoria," the ghost of the market. The emergent visual language has been the result of a collective process of meaning-making, an emergent *sensus communis*, that the Iranian Revolution initiated and from which a new context emerged both locally and globally. The *sensus communis* reflects and emerges out of the abstracted social relationships embedded in the materiality of these forms. For example, as Benjamin suggested, streets, buildings, technologies, and consumer goods become the conduit of ideological and political discourses. The various material forms discussed here, from the postrevolution cinema industry to TV and other media technologies such as YouTube, have become conduits and elements of articulations of the emergent visual language.

Media technology has formed part of the postrevolutionary society from the early days. During the course of the 1978–79 revolution itself, cassettes, for instance, were widely used to disseminate religious sermons inside and outside Iran. The appropriation of cinema and the takeover of television by the postrevolution-ary government added a new dimension to the culture of the revolution. This visual realm set the stage for a new era of visual production in which religion plays a major role. Furthermore, the circulation of these products extended beyond Iran's borders, becoming part of global processes involving both Islam(ism) and avant-garde art. For instance, Ta'ziyeh is both viewed and performed/produced in different parts of the world, and avant-garde art enjoys an active network that cuts across the Islamic world and the West.

Christie's sale of Tanavoli's work offers an example of the circulation of Ira-nian avant-garde art beyond its border. But it has further significance. The Iranian icons of modern art in the 1960s and 1970s who produced critical work must now be understood as important players in the creation of the new *sensus communis*, because after the initial setback following the revolution, they continued trying to articulate a new language for Iranian modern art that could compete in the postrev-olutionary context. The place of Islam in Iranian visual culture after the revolution is a complex one in that materiality, technologies, politics, and new forms of subjectivi-ties interact to negotiate and define new multivocal visual languages.

Intellectual Life after the 1979 Revolution

Radical Hope and Nihilistic Dreams

Ali Mirsepassi

Iranian intellectual life has undergone remarkable developments over the past thirty years since the 1979 revolution introduced a new model of mass movement and political consciousness. Uniquely in the history of modern revolutions, it was a traditional clergy claiming divine right that came to power at the head of a mass uprising rather than a modern social group armed with political parties and secular ideologies. At the general level of modernization theory, the experience called into the question the precept that modernization brings secularization. The 1979 revolution came at the historically precise intersection of the Israeli-Egyptian peace deal and the Soviet invasion of Afghanistan: a constellation that highlighted, first, a perceived weakness and backsliding among Arab nationalist regimes, and second, a perceived "proof" of a direct threat to "Islamic civilization" from the atheistic West. Juxtaposed with these two events, the Iranian Revolution presented a powerful new model — however symbolical — of mass mobilization capable of both overthrowing such compromised secular authoritarian regimes and of meeting the challenge of Western intervention, helping to promote the rise of a popular if loosely conceived new Islamist ideology that has since spread far and wide, often inspiring significant acts of violence, from Paris to Mumbai.

The exaggerated pinnacles of hope and euphoria of the early days following the success of the revolution gave way quickly to tragic experiences of violence and an ensuing sweeping geographical and moral dislocation — for the postrevolutionary Iranian population could scarcely persist in the illusion that an Islamic state could

Radical History Review

Issue 105 (Fall 2009)   DOI 10.1215/01636545-2009-015

provide a solution to modern ills, as remained possible for Muslims still living elsewhere under brutal secular or even liberal states.[1] If the resulting sense of ideological despair bespoke the demise of self-defeating ideas (of returns to a "pure source" in a clean escape from the cash nexus of globalization) and thus spread a mood of nihilism, it also engendered an ongoing endeavor among Iranian intellectuals and the general population to reevaluate old beliefs and certainties, while imagining new ones in light of all that has taken place. We might say, in this context, that Iranian intellectuals today are facing a crisis of value, or even of worldview, and that the road beyond this crisis is still in the process of being paved—with highly uncertain horizons before us.

Throughout the thirty-year period, for all of its mounting complexity and creeping chaos, we may identify one constant theme in the diverse and fragmented intellectual trends dominating Iranian political life: the category of "the West." In the period preceding and immediately following the 1979 revolution, the notion of "Westoxification," or Western cultural and political infection, operated as the principle unifying concept among most intellectuals and intellectual circles. The inflated notion of the West has evolved either through the idea of contagion or through the ideal of a superior, completed form of rational society, but in both cases it has privileged a frozen abstraction over the grassroots cultivation of communicative democratic experience and institutions in contemporary Iran.

Starting with the American hostage crisis in 1979, which initiated the adoption of a more radical and uncompromising anti-Western ideology by the Islamic Republic, secular and later some religious intellectuals reacted by shifting the dominant ideological terrain toward an inversion of the Westoxification discourse. The West has thereby become the principle object of desire among many leading Iranian intellectuals in a mirror ideological construct that may be plausibly identified as "Westphilia." What has remained constant throughout these shifting ideological topographies, however, is the notion of the West as the principal referential category in intellectual debates and reflections—within the context of discussions that have, while aspiring to philosophical sophistication, remained at a level of excessive vagueness.[2] The philosophical inclination to talk in absolutes, or via notions transcending time and historical conditioning, entails a tendency toward nihilism— in which no value is acknowledged as remaining in now extant institutions. Such tendencies, which reject the complexity of moral experience as lived at the everyday level, embrace the destructive yearning for a total beginning while sacrificing inquiry grounded in an interactive and experimental (i.e., reflexive) engagement with communal life. This also undermines mass participation in national and political developments that would foster a democratic public culture. The fostering of such a culture, by contrast, requires a patient, experimental, and context-specific approach focused on the building of the appropriate institutions.

Notions of the West in terms of either contagion or higher rationality, conversely, like the essentialist Western construction of the Orient, have little to do with any actual geographical or cultural entity and instead represent an elusive and slippery concept sustained largely through the imaginative writings of certain influential Iranian intellectuals. The West, in this capacity, may be interpreted negatively as any undesirable ideas, cultural values, and political positions or as anything not deemed "authentically" Islamic as reflected in a narrow understanding of Shi'i Islam envisioned by religious conservatives. These same conservative intellectuals, while touting Islamic authenticity, will then paradoxically attempt to champion their cause by appealing to such Western philosophies as those of Friedrich Nietzsche, Martin Heidegger, and Michel Foucault, as writers framing ostensibly indisputable cases for the historical or ethical decline of the West.[3] At the opposite pole, among the Westphiliacs, the category of the West serves positively as the embodiment of the imagined historical culmination of all rationality and progress to scholars like Aramesh Dustdar and Javad Tabatabai, or as a supreme "world of reason" that Iranians have until now historically misunderstood and failed to appreciate.[4]

These supposedly philosophical tendencies, appealing to an abstract formulation of universal reason, or, conversely, expressing a historico-metaphysical decline, go against the grain of detailed sociological inquiry grounded in the evolving realities of everyday life in contemporary Iran and thus move intellectuals increasingly out of touch with the desires, problems, and aspirations of ordinary Iranians. Yet modern Iran has been distinguished by the public struggle for popular participation in national politics. Iran's history of popular uprising began with the Tobacco Protest (1891–92) and culminated in the constitutional revolution (1905–9), which saw the triumph of a broad popular coalition led by the modern intelligentsia under the ideological banner of nationalist, liberal, and socialist ideals. The constitutional tradition was revived during the democratic interim of 1941–53, during which the intelligentsia in the form of the Tudeh Party and the National Front again effectively organized the masses (particularly urban wage earners and salaried middle classes) on the basis of socialist and secular nationalist political lines. These mass movements in Iran reflect a long historical aspiration for stable economic well-being and for some form of political democracy under the rule of law. The subsequent 1979 revolution, despite coming under the influence of Islamist ideology, was also predominantly social, political, and economic in content. Ruhollah Khomeini's populist and anti-imperialist discourses prior to the revolution promised to extend freedom and social justice to all parties, to redistribute wealth, to bring land, water, electricity, roads, and health clinics, to end wasteful expenditures on arms and corruption in government, and to free the country from foreign domination. It would thus be an error to interpret the support for Khomeini among the modern middle classes as the sudden embrace of a purely religious Islamic utopian vision, rather than as a complex and transient ideological reaction to the economic, social, and political failures of the Shah's modernizing regime, as well as to the perceived weaknesses of secular universal ideologies of political mobilization and national emancipation.

The Prerevolutionary Period

Since the onset of the modernization drive in the nineteenth century, Iranian political culture has been distinguished by a propensity for mass movements of opposition that have frequently mounted successful challenges to the existing order of power. Intellectuals have historically played an important role in the shaping and transformation of political and cultural life—at the level of struggling institutions, frequent mass movements, and changing public sensibilities—in modern Iran. This unique role for intellectuals became particularly visible during the 1960s and 1970s because the Shah's repressive state apparatus systemically undermined and repressed political parties, unions, newspapers, and nearly every other form of independent cultural or political institution—the very rudiments of civil society and secular political organization. With universities (in their relative social isolation) as the only surviving spaces for political opposition in this period, independent intellectuals came to represent the voices of dissent. The second potent force in this period was the Shi'a clergy who, considering themselves rivals to the secular intellectuals, had the support of religious institutions as the only other surviving oppositional space.

The history of Iranian political culture and popular movements prior to the 1960s-70s period had been grounded firmly in the experience of the post–Second World War democratic interval (1941–53), where the public prevalence of secular left and nationalist politics had culminated in Mohammed Mossadeq's 1951–53 Popular Front government—a mass movement dedicated to a secular-democratic and independent national politics. Mossadeq promoted this political line in part by appealing to the values of Iranian religious tradition, while also asserting the supremacy of secular reason over other forms of law. He thus attempted to integrate Enlightenment ideals with Iranian traditions. This political culture was, by its leader's own account, heir to aspects of the 1905–11 constitutional revolution, a mass movement dedicated to a parliamentary constitutional and independent form of government. In the 1960s-70s, this more cosmopolitan and secular-oriented critical political and intellectual tradition began to shift in favor of an alternative vision as cosmopolitan intellectuals started losing ground to intellectuals promoting nativist or Islamist discourses.

This turning became epitomized in the case of Jamal Al-e Ahmad, a radical and cosmopolitan intellectual figure who had belonged to the Tudeh Party and had fought to defend Mossadeq in the buildup to the 1953 coup, but who, following the disillusionment of the coup, came to reject universalism and espoused a highly influential discourse of Iranian Shi'a authenticity as the real key to national independence and emancipation. Al-e Ahmad published his influential *Occidentosis: A Plague from the West* (1962), inspired notably by the Heideggerian philosophy of Ahmad Fardid. Fardid had gained distinction through his teaching, which influenced many major intellectuals in the late 1950s, as an antiuniversalist historicist espousing the ontological primacy of Islamic truth over scientific facts. It was Al-e Ahmad's popularization of Fardid's notion of Westoxication that pushed Iranian intellectual thought more deeply into the obscure terrains of philosophical speculation, forsaking empirical research in favor of metaphysically generalized assertions.

Following in Al-e Ahmad's footsteps, Ali Shariati dominated the intellectual scene among the educated youth of the 1970s. More than anyone else, he proved influential in articulating a radical Islamist intellectual ideology that departed from a cosmopolitan humanist position. While incorporating the most radical messianic content of Marxism stripped of its secular-universal premise, he advanced a politics of religious identity to promote an alternative modernity. Shariati successfully transformed Islam, on the loose philosophical grounds articulated by Al-e Ahmad, into a powerful populist ideology of political mobilization and made the open struggle against the Shah's regime the religious duty of all young Iranian Muslims.

The 1979 Revolution: The New Anti-Imperialism

With the fall of the old regime, the moment appeared ideal for secular intellectuals to boldly articulate their vision of a democratic Iranian future and to abandon any reactionary currents that may have accrued in the interval of the 1960s–70s. However, as it turned out, religiously oriented intellectuals offered support for the new regime and continued to promote anti-Western views. They transferred attacks on the Shah to attacks on his perceived lifeline, the United States, in the name of a new anti-imperialist ideology grounded in religious authenticity. Secular intellectuals were, at this juncture, seemingly confused to see the traditionally conservative and even collusive clergy and religious intellectual factions presenting themselves to the public as radical anti-imperialist militants proposing a new vision of the future under an anti-Western banner that spurned secular universalism itself as a mask for alien designs. After the hostage crisis, the attitude among the secular left and other nonregime intellectuals began to change, first, toward the West and, then, gradually, toward imperialism and even capitalism, as the reactive counterpart to the dominant ideology took shape in the growing discourse of Westphilia.

The context for this curious ideological metamorphosis was the public creation of a dialogic space permitting the confluence of traditional left intellectual sources with emerging Islamist visions, and the appropriation of aspects of the former by the latter. An important event in the early days of the postrevolutionary period was the willingness of Islamist intellectuals, including such leading clerical figures as Ayatollah Mohammad Beheshti, to engage in public debates with secular and particularly Marxist intellectuals and activist leaders. Among those very active in debating secular and Marxist intellectuals were such highly influential figures as Abolhassan Bani-Sadr, Abdolkarim Soroush, and Rezah Davari. While the Marxist intellectuals did their best to talk about social issues and present themselves as legitimately anti-Western, the religious intellectuals persistently challenged them on the ideological and philosophical grounds of following a derivative and alien idea. The general perception among TV viewers was that the secular intellectuals were no match for high-caliber thinkers such as Soroush, and debates were remembered as a victory for the religious intellectuals. The problem, to be sure, was that it was very difficult for the Marxists to openly criticize the Islamic Republic and its ideology. Moreover, because the Marxists viewed liberalism as a more dangerous force than Islamism, they did not defend a democratic or secular politics.

Nevertheless, because radical and Marxist ideas and groups remained popular and influential on university campuses, the government decided to abruptly end their dominance in this realm. A cultural revolution (1980–83) was declared, and the universities were shut down with the aim of "cleansing" the system of higher education. University professors who were considered undesirable were expelled, and a committee was appointed to design and change the curriculum in a process of the Islamization of higher learning in Iran.

Post–Cultural Revolution

After the short-lived period of relative intellectual freedom, the new Islamist government more aggressively asserted the ideological and political supremacy of its position. Hope for reconciliation with Islamist forces therefore disintegrated as former revolutionary allies in secular intellectuals were now targeted in earnest by the regime. This resulted in a process of mass migration among intellectuals and professionals, whether coerced or in the form of self-exile. It also produced a condition of alienation from the new state among secular intellectuals, as well as a sense of alienation from the general society in its support of the Islamic state. The literary intellectuals who had dominated the Iranian intellectual scene almost since late in the nineteenth century—of which the talented short story writer Al-e Ahmad had been an outstanding example—lost their influence and their prominent voice.

Significantly, a new process took shape in which philosophers, or intellectuals with philosophical inclinations, began to dominate the Iranian intellectual environment with the merging of the modern universities with traditional religious forms of education. This development had a great impact on secular intellectuals, pushing them away from an applied and context-specific sociological approach toward increasingly abstract plateaus of reflection. Religious intellectuals continued their traditional philosophical direction, this time by appropriating Western icons of the "master thinker" in German philosophy and French poststructuralist thought.

Elaborate philosophical terms therefore came increasingly to dominate and define the Iranian intellectual sensibility, and debates centered on such intangible issues as the "Iranian mind," the nature of universal "rationality," the essence of "Islam" or "Muslims," and so fourth, always with tacit reference to the core category of the "West" in its good or bad interpretation. Notable thinkers who came to dominate the Westphiliac genre were Aramesh Dustdar and later Javad Tabatabai. These two leading intellectuals have much in common, both being philosophers who studied in Germany and were much influenced by Orientalist literature on Islam and Iran. Both argue that a radical break from Islamic thought is the precondition for a true understanding of modernity and for overcoming the current cultural crisis in Iran. Dustdar, after studying in Germany, spent the 1970s in Iran before returning to Germany in the early 1980s, where he currently remains. Tabatabai, after studying in Germany and France, returned to Iran and now divides his time between Iran, the United States, and France. He is particularly influenced by the Hegelian philosophy of history and is almost obsessed by the theory of cultural decline. During the post-Khatami years, he has influenced certain intellectual circles with members who had earlier belonged to Islamist groups.

Dustdar has articulated a historical discourse in which Iran emerges as the victim of a culturally engrained "fear of thinking," a condition conceived metaphysically as rooted in the Islamic religious worldview. Religious thinking, by his analysis, entails the so-called art of "non-thinking," in which most important questions we might feel inclined to ask are stifled in advance by ready answers provided by inherited religious dogma. Habitual cultural behavior in Iran, Dustdar argues, is marred by this condition, explaining the difficult situation in which the nation finds itself in the modern world. Ventured in the form of an argument making sweeping philosophical claims about a purported Islamic essence, Dustdar thus proposes an "epistemic revolution" as the only way out of Iran's contemporary impasse. It is necessary for Iranians to completely overhaul their existing manner of thinking and begin anew, in the imaginary of the eighteenth-century French Enlightenment and revolution, on fresh foundations in "universal Reason." Following the same line, Tabatabai argues that "unthinking" is the core political problem in modern Iran, and that it is necessary to introduce modern philosophical reason in an absolute overcoming of the Islamic tradition. It is notable that neither of these influential thinkers addresses Iran's contemporary problems at the institutional level in terms of democracy or the rule of law. Rather, the problem appears altogether a matter of effecting some profound transformation in the manner of thinking among Iranians through the power of philosophy. The end result of the trend initiated by such thinkers is a kind of Islamophobia and an uncritical attitude toward what is defined, inevitably vaguely, as rational and modern thinking.

There have also been important developments among Islamist intellectuals in the postrevolutionary period. The leading intellectual Soroush, who came to acclaim during the cultural revolution and later championed a notion of religiously based democracy, now lives outside Iran and has become more interested in nonpolitical or "spiritual and theological" matters.[5]

We might say that Iranian religious intellectuals in general have gone through three important phases: First, following the revolution they experienced a relative unity in their common concern with effectively combating the prevalence of Marxism and other secular intellectual tendencies. Second, after the cultural revolution brutally cemented this victory, Soroush and others around him became very active and articulated a more liberal doctrine of a "religiously based democratic state." As a part of this campaign they introduced British analytical philosophy and ideas from British moral philosophy to interested religious leaning Iranians. The monthly journal *Kyan* and some cultural institutes and publishing houses also helped spread their ideas. Third, in the 1990s, an important group emerged, influenced by Shariati and to some extent Soroush, turning away from purely theological and philosophical ideas and emphasizing theories of civil society, political development, and the social sciences. This group helped Mohammad Khatami's presidential election (1997–2001) and was instrumental in opening up the intellectual space inside Iran for an important period of time.

However, with the closing of the Khatami presidency in 2005 and renewed political and intellectual difficulties at the national and international levels, this important group of religiously minded intellectuals could not effectively respond to rising challenges and did not produce much in the way of new ideas. With the rise of Mahmoud Ahmadinejad to power, many of the religious intellectuals turned once more to the level of more abstract and theological issues including revelation, the divine nature of the Qur'an, the historical and factual basis of belief in the Hidden Imam, and similar subjects, all of which are discussed intrepidly by thinkers such as Soroush, Mojtahid Shabastari, and Mohsen Kadivar. Yet it now seems, nevertheless, that at least some leading members of the Islamist intellectuals are coming closer to forms of secular thinking, and they believe increasingly in the need to challenge what they refer to as the "sacred basis" of political power in today's Iran.

Conclusion

The Iranian Revolution was a dream realized within the lifetime of many of the radical intellectuals. They embraced the revolution and all that it could bring about. Since the time of the revolution, however, many of them have struggled to understand its meaning and consequences. In the interim, they have found themselves at an increasing distance from the revolution, and increasingly less relevant to their own society as intellectuals. Nowadays, to an ever greater degree, many Iranian intellectuals experience a deeply felt sense of bitterness on this account. They feel bitterness both at what has happened in Iran and at themselves, and many of them seem ready to exchange hope for nihilism.

Intellectuals often find themselves at home in articulations of nihilism, or in calls for the total destruction of existing ideas and institutions. The underside of celebrations of nihilism as a destructive ideal, however, is the despair of disconnection from the existing world of practical reality. Such totalizing outlooks have their opposite in hope, which encourages the creative, imaginative, and philosophical, while always staying in contact with the practical realities of the world as it exists. This hope is also what links people across difference, and it is the flame giving reality to democratic political experiments of all kinds.

Notes

Tadd Fernee, my research assistant, helped me a great deal with this essay. As always, I am grateful for his assistance and his contribution to writing this piece.

1. Soon after, the revolution began a process of emigration (forced and voluntary), and now many of the prominent dissident intellectual figures are based in Western Europe and North America.

2. The most conspicuous evidence of West-centric ideas appear in the writings of Aramesh Dustdar, *Derakhshesh hay-e tire* (*Dark Sparkles*) (Berlin: Negah, 1993); and Javad Tabatabai, *Zaval-e andisheh-ye siasi dar Iran* (*Decline of Political Thought in Iran*) (Tehran: Tarh-e No, 2000).

3. This ironic use of Western ideas as sources of the Islamic discourse of authenticity is prevalent among more "radical" conservative intellectuals such as Fardid (in the 1960s and 1970s) and Reza Davari (in the postrevolutionary period). Fardid argued in the early 1970s that all Islamic countries had lost possession of their own historical trust in the wake of the eighteenth-century Western Enlightenment's rise to the status of dominant world paradigm, along Heideggerian historicist lines.

4. Masha'allah Ajodani, *Mashru'iyat-e Irani va pishzamineh-haye nazariyeh-ye velāyat-e faqih* (*Iranian Constitutionality and the Precedence in the Idea of the Guardianship of the Jurist*) (London: Fasle Ketab, 1997).

5. For some of his writings in English, see Abdolkarim Soroush, *Reason, Freedom, and Democracy in Islam*, trans. Mahmoud Sadri and Ahmad Sadri (New York: Oxford University Press, 2002).

Contested Narratives of the Present

Postrevolutionary Culture and Media in Iran

Niki Akhavan

Mehdi Semati, ed., *Media, Culture, and Society in Iran: Living with Globalization and the Islamic State*. New York: Routledge, 2008.

Nasrin Alavi, *We Are Iran: The Persian Blogs*. Brooklyn: Soft Skull Press, 2005.

Both Mehdi Semati's *Media, Culture, and Society in Iran: Living with Globalization and the Islamic State* and Nasrin Alavi's *We Are Iran: The Persian Blogs* reflect the continuing draw of the media, particularly Internet-based media, as sites for examining Iranian politics and political culture. With the exception of one article in Semati's diverse anthology, which shares with Alavi affinities in approach and conclusions, the overall similarities between the two works do not go beyond their mutual attention to the significance of media in shaping and understanding contemporary Iranian society. While Alavi reinforces familiar frameworks for assessing the intersections of Iranian society, politics, and media, Semati takes on the task of interrogating and moving beyond these models to capture the nuances and contradictions of Iran.

Semati's edited volume is organized in three sections. Part 1 covers an impressive array of media in Iran including the printed press, the Internet, rock music, satellite television, video technology, advertising, poetry, and local and diaspora cin-

Radical History Review

Issue 105 (Fall 2009) DOI 10.1215/01636545-2009-016

© 2009 by MARHO: The Radical Historians' Organization, Inc.

emas. Part 2 consists of three chapters that address issues related to state, culture, and religion in Iran through respectively examining the discourses of veiling, the local and global role of religious intellectuals, and the relationship between state-sponsored religiosity and the rise of secularization. Part 3 of the volume consists of an epilogue by Majid Tehranian that casts a long glance at Iranian history with a view toward forecasting possible scenarios for Iran in the near future.

All three sections of the volume are preceded by Semati's introductory article, "Living with Globalization and the Islamic State," which provides a lucid assessment of the shortcomings of discourses on Iran. Semati begins with a brief review of the global and regional developments that lend a particular urgency to the study of Iran and the Middle East, noting that despite the army of "experts" that have arisen in response, the narratives produced about Iran remain surprisingly shallow. For example, Iran is often described in terms of a "theocratic state," "theocratic society," or a "rogue nation." Semati maintains that none of these descriptions capture the dynamism and contradictions of political and cultural developments in Iran. Hence he claims that the volume mainly aims to challenge such reductive accounts. Given the state of discourses on Iran as accurately described by Semati, the straightforward diagnosis and intention to intervene by themselves make an important contribution to expanding and enriching the field. Moreover, Semati's emphasis on culture, including pop culture and media, as important sites for analysis and intervention distinguishes his edited volume from most accounts of contemporary Iranian politics, which either offer a cursory treatment of culture or completely ignore it. Whether the volume delivers on providing a more nuanced analysis of Iran while foregrounding culture is an issue that I will discuss below.

Considered as a whole, the chapters in part 1, "New and Old Media in Iran," come closest to meeting the volume's aims. Gholam Khiabany's "The Iranian Press, State, and Civil Society" stands among the strongest chapters both in considering the sociopolitical implications of the Iranian press and in interrogating the concepts at the center of his analysis. Khiabany's piece is also significant for moving beyond celebratory assessments of the potentials of the Iranian press and civil society to expose the neoliberal logic that propels them. While both popular and scholarly accounts of Iran take the term *civil society* for granted, often lauding its potentials for challenging the repressive maneuvers of the state, Khiabany indicates the various conceptualizations and shortcomings of the notion, suggesting that the tendency to set rigid boundaries between public and private and between the state and civil society is indicative of the same paradigm that "reduces everything into the state/non-state binary of free market ideology" (19). Noting that the press in Iran has increasingly been celebrated as a "fourth estate," Khiabany also questions the liberal theory that he argues places the Iranian press outside and opposed to a repressive state. Through an analysis of the Iranian press, factional politics, and the complex political structure to which they are linked, Khiabany shows how civil society, the so-called fourth estate, and the state are variously intertwined. Khiabany convincingly argues that to consider the press as part of an independent and oppositional civil society not only misses the links between these spheres and a complex and contradictory state but also does not "offer a critique of liberalization, nor a substantive analysis of class relations and disparity in access to communication resources in the country" (33).

Hamid Naficy's "Iranian Émigré Cinema as Component of Iranian National Cinema" also stands out in moving beyond familiar frameworks for understanding contemporary Iranian society. In the most theoretically grounded article in the volume, Naficy argues that the films of exilic and diasporic Iranian filmmakers—works that form a part of a "global cinema of displacement" that he terms "accented cinema" (159–60)—should be considered as part of Iran's national cinema. The article is densely packed with empirical data and analysis about trends in the production, distribution, and reception of this cinema. Naficy's most significant contribution in terms of the stated aims of the volume is his transnational framing of Iranian cultural production in ways that consider the nuances and ambiguities of playing off of host-country and home-country politics. The reciprocal interplay of the local and diasporic constitutes an increasingly important axis of inquiry that should be incorporated into other analyses of Iran; Naficy provides a helpful model for how this may be done.

Also taking up film, Zohreh T. Sullivan's "Iranian Cinema and the Critique of Absolutism" considers contemporary Iranian art cinema with a focus on Mohsen Makhmalbaf and Abbas Kiarostami to argue that these films are modernist in the sense of resisting what she calls "mass appeal," "traditional pieties (like prayer, nation, and poetry)," and resolution (200). As such, Sullivan contends that the films do the important cultural work of encouraging audiences to move beyond familiar ideological trappings for seeing film and the world. While students of Iranian film may seek to supplement Sullivan's work with analyses that also address the directors' cinematic style and language, the article makes concrete contributions in assessing the complexities of Iranian cultural products and the society to which they are linked.

One of the most cited statistics about Iran is that 70 percent of its population is below the age of thirty. Although speculations about this youthful demographic are at the center of many assessments of the possibilities for change in Iran, there are few in-depth studies about this population. Two of the chapters in this volume, Laudan Nooshin's "The Language of Rock: Iranian Youth, Popular Music, and National Identity" and Kavous Seyed-Emami's "Youth, Politics, and Media Habits in Iran," refresh in carrying out much needed research that directly engages segments of this population. Nooshin considers the role that rock music has played for Iranian youth in negotiating notions of place and national belonging and identity. Clarifying that in the Iranian context rock refers to largely unauthorized and nonmainstream music,

Nooshin highlights the ambiguities of producing and consuming rock music in Iran. On the one hand, the rejection by the official establishment garners musicians a particular kind of credibility, as well as control over their music. Yet the price they pay, Nooshin points out, often proves fatal for bands who cannot sustain themselves for very long within the shadow networks and economies that have formed around producing, distributing, and performing this music. Nooshin also highlights how this music has diverged from the conventions of popular Iranian music both in its musical language and the text. In terms of the latter, Nooshin relies on interviews with musicians to explain the increasing use of English lyrics. The main reasons musicians cite for singing in English are the incompatibility of the Persian language with rock rhythms and the desire to reach and be a part of broader music communities. Although Nooshin puts forth a convincing case for the ways in which rock music is allowing Iranian youth to be innovative and to imagine themselves as part of transnational communities of rock musicians and fans, her claims that they are also challenging and creating Iranian national identity require further development.

In his research on the young segment of the population, Seyed-Emami presents the results of empirical studies on university students' preferred source of news. Seyed-Emami claims that while the subjects of the surveys are all university students in Tehran, they hail from cities and villages around the country and thus represent populations beyond the capital city. Comparing results of 2005 surveys with those conducted in 2000, Seyed-Emami notes that while Iranian national television programs still constitute the primary source for students, they are increasingly diversifying their news sources, with the Internet in particular serving as a new site for alternative information. Seyed-Emami also surveyed students about their trust in various media, with the Internet again gaining in this regard. Expecting to find less political engagement among those who primarily rely on television over those who read newspapers, Seyed-Emami notes that his data did not reflect this correlation but that further studies are needed.

Mahmoud Shahabi's "The Iranian Panic Over Video: A Brief History and a Political Analysis," is an exciting article insofar as it takes up a little-studied but widespread phenomenon of 1980s Iran, namely, the shadow economy of outlaw private video clubs and the government's eventual acceptance of authorized and regulated video stores in the early 1990s. Shahabi uses the notion of "moral panic" as the theoretical backdrop for making sense of the Iranian government's official discourse on videos. In tracing the trajectory of official responses to video, Shahabi's article not only reveals the contestations inside the government but also shows the entrepreneurship of those who found opportunities despite (or perhaps because of) official restrictions.

Like the government's reactions to video, the advent of satellite television in Iran in the early 1990s fostered intense debates among officials. In "the Politics of Satellite Television," Fardin Alikhah's fairly detailed overview of developments in official discussions and legislation regarding satellite dishes will serve as a useful starting point for scholars interested in further investigating the social and political impact of satellite technology.

The remaining articles in part 1 cover the three very different topics of advertising, poetry, and the Internet in Iran. In "Sociolinguistic Aspects of Persian Advertising in Post-revolutionary Iran," Mohamad Amouzadeh and Manoochehr Tavangar focus on a number of brand-name ads of the "reform" period (1997–2005) to note and analyze a number of fascinating changes. To begin, they observe the increasing use of both foreign texts (English) and non-Persian Iranian languages. They attribute the former to the symbolic capital of the English language in conveying international status and product superiority, while they explain the latter as providing products with an air of authenticity and local flavor. In addition, Amouzadeh and Tavangar point out new trends such as ads claiming an environmental ethic or featuring movie stars. Finally, the authors note gradual movements from suggestions of femininity and womanhood in early ads to the explicit appearance of women in advertisements. Amouzadeh's and Tavangar's readings of the visual and textual elements of the advertisements, as well as their explanations for what these trends indicate, show not only the subtleties of the ads themselves but also that of the society in which they appear. Finally, the authors have included photographs of some of the ads, allowing the reader to also closely consider the visual and textual components of the advertisements.

Unlike other areas of inquiry noted earlier, Persian poetry has been the subject of a rich and varied body of literature intended for scholarly, literary, or general audiences. Alireza Anushiravani's and Kavoos Hassanali's "Trends in Contemporary Persian Poetry" contributes to this body of work by providing an overview of new forms of poetry from the prerevolution years through the 1990s.

The Internet continues to be an area of inquiry not only for scholars of Iran but also for general audiences, governmental or quasi-governmental think tanks, policy makers, and activists, all of whom are to various extents interested in assessing the social and political implications of the Internet and its concomitant technologies. Babak Rahimi's "The Politics of the Internet in Iran" makes for one such example. Rahimi touches on much ground: for example, he addresses developments in Internet technology in Iran, various forms of online activity and dissent, as well as governmental reactions and restrictions. While his overview of such developments is generally straightforward, his terminology is at times puzzling. For example, he refers to the Islamic Republic of Iran variously as the "Islamist Republic" or the "Islamist state" as though his use of the term *Islamist* in this context were self-evident or conventional. While this chapter may serve as a useful introduction to those interested in an overview of the Internet in Iran, it makes for an odd choice for inclusion in this volume as it repeats many of the generalities about the Iranian state and society that the collection as a whole aims to challenge. In other words, Rahimi's chapter reflects often repeated accounts regarding the Iranian state, society, and Internet use, a narrative also evident in Alavi's *We Are Iran*, considered below.

Before moving on to an analysis of this second work, however, it is necessary to say a few words about the articles in part 2 of Semati's collection. In his introduction to the volume, Semati indicates that the three articles in part 2 were included given religion's importance to Iranian society and how little understood it is among many, particularly among mainstream commentators and media pundits. After the rich collection of articles covering a range of media and cultural productions, the shift to analyses that do not directly engage either appears somewhat awkward. If the articles in part 2 were broader in scope, they may have served well as a background section preceding the articles in part 1. Yet although the two sections do not appear to work well together side by side, the articles do meet Semati's goal of providing detailed information about various aspects of religion in Iranian society.

The first article in part 2, Fatemeh Sadeghi's "Hijab in Contemporary Iran," makes a distinction between what the author calls "traditional Shi'ite Islam" and "fundamentalist Shi'ite Islam" to argue that the two differ in their interpretations of Islam, specifically as it relates to their ideas about the role of women and *hijab*. The article may prove quite useful for scholars following the debates and contestations surrounding women in Iran.

Abbas Variji Kazemi's "Religious Intellectualism, Globalization, and Transformation in Iran" lauds religious intellectuals for their part in globalizing their role, as well as in "indigeniz[ing] modern principles and [for] inject[ing] universal, modern, and broad principles to the structures of traditional society" (235). The article appears to be overreaching in its optimistic conclusion that "it is difficult to overestimate the importance of the religious intellectuals to the future of Iranian society" (236). Whether or not the reader is convinced by the article's claims about the importance or success of the religious intellectuals' projects, however, the piece provides a solid account of the work of these intellectuals in the 1990s.

A joint essay by Yousef Ali Abazari, Abbas Varij Kazemi, and Mehdi Faraji, "Secularization in Iranian Society," constitutes the third and last article in part 2. Arguing for the specificity of the notion of secularization in Iranian society, the article claims that it does not mean the elimination or irrelevance of religion but rather concludes that it is to be achieved through processes such as "rationalization" and "specialization," as well as through various other related forms of bureaucratization. The emphasis on the particularities of Iran and on the role of the mosque offers a welcome and much needed approach, but many of the article's claims, including its core arguments about secularization on the level of the society and the individual in Iran, would benefit from further clarification.

Overall, Semati's collection makes a much needed contribution to intervening in mainstream accounts of Iran, accounts such as those exemplified in Alavi's

We Are Iran. The book consists of Alavi's claims about contemporary Iran interdispersed with excerpts from blogs, as well as various cartoons and photographs of Iran and Iranians, including some bloggers. On a positive note, the author has translated excerpts of many Persian blogs, thus making them available to English-speaking audiences who may otherwise have no access to this material. She also provides the links to the blogs she cites, allowing Persian speakers to examine the Web sites themselves.

Yet Alavi very rarely provides the reader with any information about the specific blogs she cites. There is no information about Alavi's methodology, nor is there an introduction or a preface that might explain the author's selection process. Any data about the bloggers themselves, including their locations, is similarly hard to come by. For the most part, blog excerpts simply appear after Alavi's statements, ostensibly in confirmation of her various claims, and the reader rarely has a way of ascertaining any substantive information about the blog or the blogger based on Alavi's text alone.

To take just one example, one can refer to chapter 7, "Spreading the News," where Alavi mentions bloggers organizing thank-you notes to international aid workers who had helped Iran during the Bam earthquake of 2003. The first blogger she cites, Pedram Moallemian, has been based in North America for over twenty years, during which he visited Iran twice, the last time in 1996. Furthermore, with the exception of one post written in Persian, all Moallemian's blog posts, including the post cited in this chapter, were written in English. Yet Alavi does not mention any of these details. Unless the reader has some prior knowledge about the blogs and the bloggers cited in this work, he or she will be in the dark about potentially significant details about them.

The physical location of the blogger or the language of blogging need not determine whether a blog counts as part of the Iranian blogosphere, but it is important for the readers to have some sense of Alavi's thinking on the matter. Similar to Naficy's argument about émigré cinema noted above, Alavi could have made a convincing case for why the Iranian blogosphere should not be delineated according to the borders of the nation-states in which individual bloggers reside. Yet she does not appeal to this or any other framework for explaining her choice of selections.

Even if theorizing the issue went beyond what Alavi was willing or capable of carrying out, it would have been helpful for the readers to consistently have some minimal indication about what the blogs are about, who and where these bloggers are, and why the author chose to include them in her book. After all, this is a work that asserts the complete representation of Iran in its title. As such, it should carry some burden in justifying the interlinked claims that the blogosphere represents Iran and that the version of the blogosphere presented in this book in fact offers an accurate reflection of the myriad extant blogs. Otherwise, the audience, particularly those readers who do not speak Persian and/or are not familiar with the blogosphere, has few options other than to accept the author's assertions at face value. The fact that we know almost nothing about the pseudonymous writer (the cover says she studied and taught engineering in the United Kingdom and is living between Tehran and London), makes it even more difficult to simply accept the book's claims without further clarification about its approaches to the subject.

In addition to the issues pertaining to research methods and the presentation of the blog excerpts, the book reads like a haphazardly compiled collection of random historical facts paired with sound bites and generalizations about contemporary Iran. A series of one or two paragraphs musings (followed by excerpts from blogs) on everything from elections to Valentine's Day to drug use in prisons is used to assert the plight of a society "controlled and ruled by radical clerics" (89). The overall picture Alavi presents about Iran is the very image that Semati identifies as problematic and reductive: making no room for the contradictions and interconnectivities of the Iranian state and society, Alavi presents a rigid binary between an Iranian society and blogosphere that is almost exclusively oppositional to a monolithic, theocratic state.

As such, pairing Alavi's *We Are Iran* with Semati's *Media, Culture, and Society in Iran* proves a useful exercise. One can begin with Alavi to get a sense of the dominant accounts about contemporary Iran and Iranian culture and media spheres and follow up with Semati to understand why such narratives are thoroughly inadequate.

Ervand Abrahamian teaches Middle East history at Baruch College and the Graduate Center of the City University of New York. He is the author of *Iran between Two Revolutions* (1982), *Khomeinism: Essays on the Islamic Republic* (1993), *Tortured Confessions: Prisons and Public Recantations in Modern Iran* (1999), and, most recently, *A History of Modern Iran* (2008).

Mahdi Ahouie received a PhD in international relations from the Graduate Institute of International and Development Studies (IHEID) at the University of Geneva, Switzerland. He also has a master's degree (DEA) from the University of Geneva specializing in international history and politics. He previously studied at the School of International Relations in Tehran. Having worked at several research institutions in Iran and in Switzerland, Ahouie is currently a visiting lecturer at Imam Sadiq University (ISU), Tehran.

Niki Akhavan received her PhD from the University of California, Santa Cruz, in 2007. Her research is focused on the relationship between new media and transnational Iranian political and cultural production. She is currently a visiting assistant professor of media studies at the Catholic University of America.

Saïd Amir Arjomand is Distinguished Service Professor of Sociology at the State University of New York, Stony Brook. He is the founder and has served as president of the Association for the Study of Persianate Societies and serves as the editor of the *Journal of Persianate Studies*. He is the author of *The Turban for the Crown: The Islamic Revolution in Iran* (1988). His most recent (edited) book is *Constitutionalism and Political Reconstruction* (2008), and his *After Khomeini: Iran under His Successors* is scheduled for publication in October 2009.

Mansour Bonakdarian (University of Toronto, Mississauga) is an editorial associate member of the *RHR* collective. He is the author of *Britain and the Iranian Constitutional Revolution of 1906–1911: Foreign Policy, Imperialism, and Dissent* (2006). His current projects include a monograph on the contentious confluences of nationalism, internationalism, and transnationalism in India, Iran, and Ireland (1905–21) in the framework of global networks of "anti-imperialist" nationalist solidarities, and a monograph on empathy and cross-cultural/cross-racial epistemology in the "Age of Empire."

Behrooz Ghamari-Tabrizi is an associate professor of history and sociology at the University of Illinois, Urbana-Champaign. He is the author of *Islam and Dissent in Postrevolutionary Iran: Abdolkarim Soroush, Religious Politics, and Democratic Reform* (2008). He has written widely on Islamic movements and Muslim intellectuals. His current project deals with the conception of trauma and the memory of war among Iranian veterans of the Iran-Iraq war (1980–88).

M. R. Ghanoonparvar is a professor of Persian and comparative literature and of Persian language at the University of Texas, Austin. He has published widely on Persian literature and culture in both English and Persian. His books include *Prophets of Doom: Literature as a Sociopolitical Phenomenon in Modern Iran* (1984), *In a Persian Mirror: Images of the West and Westerners in Iranian Fiction* (1993), *Translating the Garden* (2001), and *Reading Chubak* (2005). His forthcoming books are on Iranian film and fiction and literary diseases in Persian literature.

Hanan Hammad is an assistant professor of history at Texas Christian University in Fort Worth. She earned her PhD in history at the University of Texas at Austin in 2009. Her dissertation is entitled "Mechanizing People, Localizing Modernity: Industrialization and Social Transformation in Modern Egypt, al-Mahalla al-Kubra, 1910–1958."

Taraneh Hemami's multidisciplinary works explore the complex cultural politics of exile through personal and community projects and installations. Hemami has participated in many international exhibitions, including the 2007 Siggraph, the 2006 Inter-Society of Electronic Arts (ISEA), and the 2003 Sharjah Biennial, and has received many awards and residencies, including a 2008 residency at The LAB, a 2007 Kala Fellowship award, and a 2004 Visions from the New California Award. She is an adjunct professor at the California College of the Arts. For more information on the project and the interviewee, see theoryofsurvival .com/taranehhemami.info.

Persis M. Karim is an associate professor of English and comparative literature at San José State University. She is the editor and a contributing author to *Let Me Tell You Where I've Been: New Writing by Women of the Iranian Diaspora* (2006) and the coeditor of *A World Between: Poems, Short Stories, and Essays by Iranian-Americans* (1999). She has written numerous articles on literature and the emergence of Iranian American identity and coedited the summer 2008 special issue of *MELUS* (*Multi-ethnic Literatures of the United States*) on Iranian American literature. She lives in Berkeley and can be reached at persiskarim.com.

Mazyar Lotfalian is a cultural anthropologist who conducts research and writes on science, technology, and visual culture in the Islamic world. He has taught at several institutions including Yale University and the University of Pittsburgh, and he has had fellowships at Harvard University, the Massachusetts Institute of Technology, New York University, and the University of California, Santa Cruz.

Ali Mirsepassi is a professor of Middle Eastern studies and sociology at Gallatin School, New York University. He is currently a Carnegie Scholar (2007–9) working on a book project on the Western influence on political Islam. He has published in such journals as *Contemporary Sociology*, *Radical History Review*, *Social Text*, and *Nepantla*. He is the author of *Islam and Democracy* (forthcoming), *Intellectual Discourses and Politics of Modernization: Negotiating Modernity in Iran* (2000) and *Truth or Democracy* (2001). He is also the coeditor of *Localizing Knowledge in a Globalizing World* (2002); and was the guest editor of a special issue of *Comparative Studies of South Asia, Africa, and the Middle East* entitled "Beyond the Boundaries of the Old Geographies: Natives, Citizens, Exiles, and Cosmopolitans" (2005).

Minoo Moallem is a professor and the chair of the Department of Gender and Women's Studies at the University of California, Berkeley. She is the author of *Between Warrior Brother and Veiled Sister: Islamic Fundamentalism and the Cultural Politics of Patriarchy in Iran* (2005). She is also the coeditor (with Caren Kaplan and Norma Alarcon) of *Between Woman and Nation: Nationalisms, Transnational Feminisms, and the State* (1999), and the guest editor of a special issue of *Comparative Studies of South Asia, Africa, and the Middle East* titled "Iranian Immigrants, Exiles, and Refugees." Moallem has recently ventured into digital media. Her online project, "Nation-on-the-Move" (design by Eric Loyer), was recently published in *Vectors: Journal of Culture and Technology in a Dynamic Vernacular* (2007). She is currently working on a book manuscript on the commodification of the nation through consumptive production and the circulation of such commodities as the Persian carpet, as well as devoting time to a research project on gender, media, and religion, and another on Iran-Iraq war movies and masculinity.

Nima Naghibi is associate professor of English at Ryerson University in Toronto. She is the author of *Rethinking Global Sisterhood: Western Feminism and Iran* (2007) and is currently working on trauma, cultural memory, and nostalgia in diasporic Iranian women's autobiographical writings and documentary films.

Nasrin Rahimieh is Maseeh Chair and Director of the Dr. Samuel M. Jordan Center for Persian Studies and Culture at the University of California, Irvine, where she also holds an appointment as a professor of comparative literature. Her teaching and research are focused on modern Persian literature, Iranian diaspora literature, Iranian women's writing, and contemporary Iranian cinema.

Ahmad Sadri is a professor of sociology and the James P. Gorter Chair of Islamic World Studies at Lake Forest College. He is the author of *Max Weber's Sociology of Intellectuals* (1992) and of three books in Persian. He has translated books from Persian and Arabic into English and has served as a columnist for the *Daily Star* of Lebanon and *Etemade melli* of Iran.

Djavad Salehi-Isfahani is currently a professor of economics at Virginia Polytechnic Institute and State University and a nonresident guest scholar at the Brookings Institution. He has served on the Board of Trustees of the Economic Research Forum (2001–6), a network of Middle East economists based in Cairo, and on the board of the Middle East Economic Association. His research has been in demographic economics, energy economics, and the economics of the Middle East. He has coauthored, with Jacques Cremer, *The World Oil Market* (1991), and edited two volumes: *Labor and Human Capital in the Middle East* (2001) and, with Douglas Eckel and Joseph C. Pitt, *The Production and Diffusion of Public Choice Political Economy: Reflections on the VPI Center* (2004).

Kamran Talattof is a professor of Persian language and literature and Iranian culture at the University of Arizona, Tucson. He has taught Iranian studies for over fifteen years. He is the author, coauthor, or coeditor of *The Politics of Writing in Iran: A History of Modern Persian Literature* (2000); *Modern Persian: Spoken and Written* (with D. Stilo and J. Clinton, 2005); *Essays on Nima Yushij: Animating Modernism in Persian Poetry* (with A. Karimi-Hakkak, 2004); *The Poetry of Nizami Ganjavi: Knowledge, Love, and Rhetoric* (with J. Clinton, 2000); and *Contemporary Debates in Islam: An Anthology of Modernist and Fundamentalist Thought* (with M. Moaddel, 2000). He has also translated several works from Persian, and many of his articles focus on issues of gender, ideology, culture, and language pedagogy. His forthcoming projects include a monograph on sexuality, modernity, and the popular arts in 1970s Iran.

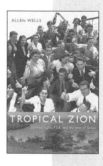

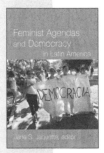